European Gastronomy

The story of man's food and eating customs

W.K.H. Bode M.Phil. Dip.Ed. MHCIMA
Lecturer in Food Studies
Department of Management Studies for Tourism and Hotel Industries
University of Surrey

Hodder & Stoughton

A MEMBER OF THE HODDER HEADLINE GROUP

Cataloguing in Publication Data is available from the British Library

ISBN 0 340 58734 2

First published 1994

Impression number	10 9 8 7 6 5 4 3 2 1
Year	1999 1998 1997 1996 1995 1994

Typeset by Wearset, Boldon, Tyne and Wear.
Printed in Great Britain for Hodder & Stoughton Educational, a division of Hodder Headline Plc, 338 Euston Road, London NW1 3BH by St Edmundsbury Press Ltd.

Contents

This book is dedicated to my sons

Michael and Magnus

'In the hope that they never lose the respect for their food and always have the grace to share it.'

Acknowledgements

My grateful thanks and acknowledgements must go to all those who made me aware and taught me the subject of gastronomy. Particularly my old Maître de Cuisine, the late Count Wilhelm von Divald of Gebhards Hotel in the University town of Göttingen, West Germany, and the late M. Robert Cherrier, Principal Lecturer in Food Studies at Bournemouth College of Technology – the first was my teacher, the second was my friend and mentor when I first started to teach food preparation and gastronomy some thirty or so years ago.

Both gentlemen, with their so very different backgrounds, have always impressed me by their considerable knowledge of food and food preparation, the care they took in the execution of their work, as well as their integrity and professionalism. This, in no small measure, laid the foundation of my interest in and love for this subject, which I have subsequently studied and practised for more than fifty years.

I am especially grateful to Professor B.H. Archer who suggested that I might undertake to write the Master of Philosophy thesis on which this book is based, and Dr J. Thomson for his supervision during the writing of my thesis, his help, encouragement, advice, as well as ironing out difficulties of layout and grammatical presentation, in a language which is not my first.

Much thanks must also go to many thousands of my students, who over the years always wanted to know *how* good food is prepared, but who challenged me again and again with the question 'But *why* do we do it this way, what are the reasons?' As to the 'how', I have always found it relatively easy to show how it was done or to give the answers, as to the 'why' less so. Their questions gave me the motivation for continuing reading and research throughout my teaching life.

Introduction

Much has been written about the subject of food, and some considerable research is now being undertaken into various aspects of food and eating. However, the references are almost all in respect of such disciplines as archaeology, anthropology, biology, economics, history, zoology, food science and nutrition, and on the psychological aspects of eating.

Little or nothing has been written or researched on purely the history of food and eating – the joys of preparing, presenting, eating and enjoying food and drink for its own sake.

The tools of food and drink, its gathering, growing, preparation, presentation in all its various forms and times, may have given framework, milestones and even proof to many of the above-named disciplines.

The history of gastronomy itself, writing which may wholly or in parts identify the factors which make up this subject, which may have aided or stifled its evolution to the height of food eating towards the end of the nineteenth and beginning of the twentieth centuries, are most certainly lacking.

This is true, of course, only if we exclude the thousands of cookery books and other articles on food which have been published over the years. But cookery books only identify and aid one component of gastronomy – the practical preparation and presentation of food. The subject of gastronomy has many components which lead to the enjoyment of food. Besides the practical facet of gastronomy, we have to consider the historic, social, cultural, aesthetic, as well as the delightful, pleasurable features of eating.

This book aims to attempt to correct this lack of structured writing in respect of gastronomy. It will try to identify these various component parts in a chronological order, and show how, over time, they came together and made their contribution to the understanding of the subject.

Man spends between six and seven years of his life eating – from the first suck on his mother's breast, to his very last day, man normally enjoys three meals a day. However simple or elaborate his meals, man eats most of them with pleasure. There is no other activity of man so basic, so important and so continuously enjoyable, than man's three meals a day.

No poem will be transcribed,
No symphony composed,
No masterwork of literature written,
No philosophical thoughts contemplated;
Until this basic need is appeased,
A hungry man will simply not be able
To think of the higher, more human things of life.

To no other need and activity has man given, and continues to give, so much thought, effort, work, development of skills, care and love, than to the most basic of his needs – his food and drink.

At its best it is an art.

CHAPTER 1

The Basic Quest

The World is nothing without life
And all that lives takes nourishment.
There is a difference, though,
All animals feed
Only man eats,
And only man of intellect, thought and care,
Knows how to eat.(1.1)

Prehistoric Man and his Food

Without food there would be no history of man at all. Very little has been written about early man's need and supply of food, how he found it, identified it as safe and developed the various preparation methods so obviously a considerable part of his basic need for existence and survival. Where references to man's early need for food are made, they are usually almost all in respect of other disciplines, such as anthropology, archaeology, biology, ecology, economics, early technology and zoology.

For the purpose of this book, such material is diffuse, and, in many cases, contradictory or mere conjecture.

Although there is comparatively little real evidence to be found about the world of our ancestors before 10,000 BC, archaeologists have discovered tools and other artefacts in various parts of the world, and dug up food residues which, with modern methods, make it possible to guess the diet of prehistoric man. No-one knows when man first appeared. Some scientists say it was about four million years ago.(1.2) Other scientists believe it was as much as thirty million years ago.

1.1 Brillat-Savarin, J.A., *The Philosopher in the Kitchen or the Psychology of Taste*, translated by Ann Drayton, Penguin Books, London, 1970.

1.2 Wilson, A.C. and Sarick, V.M., *Proceedings of the Academy of Science of the United States*, vol. LX, 1968, p. 5.

It is generally accepted that for more than 90 per cent of his history, man's ape-like ancestors lived in vast tree forests on the mostly vegetarian diet of fruit, nuts, roots and birds' eggs. He was forced out of his tree habitat when his traditional diet became scarce. On the ground and on the open grassland he found new foods, such as lizards, porcupines, tortoises, squirrels, moles and some of the larger insects and grubs, changing from a vegetarian diet to a mixture of vegetarian and flesh diet. He devoured the animals with such enthusiasm that he wiped out a number of the species completely.(1.3)

In the next three million years or so, man developed new skills. Having found a liking for the taste of flesh, he learned to kill the larger animals by hurling rocks at them and he learned to hunt in packs – in sometimes quite large groups. He had to compete for his food with other, often faster, carnivores such as lions, hyenas, large cats and wolves. He had to be able to run and to be fast to catch his prey, and so evolved slowly from walking on four legs to walking on three legs (still to be observed in some apes) and later on two legs. So it was his need for food and speed which led to the development of *Homo erectus*, the beginning of modern man.(1.4)

His teeth, no longer necessary to his vegetarian diet and fighting, changed shape, and a simple grunting speech-signal developed, so vital for hunting within a pack. Gradually this refined into speech itself – man's speech may even be a development from his need to hunt for food in groups. His forefeet gradually changed to two hands, which eventually proved capable of making simple tools and weapons.

Peking man, an early type of man, was more ape than man, with a broad nose and high cheek-bones. Peking man's enduring fame is in the fact that he is considered to be the first man to make use of fire. This does not mean that he could make it or control it, but he used it where he naturally found it.(1.5)

Prehistoric Man and Fire

Early man's use of fire was most certainly for warmth and comfort. It was much later, and most certainly more by accident than design, that man used fire to cook his food. It was almost as if by divine hand that man had learned the benefit of fire, for we had then the onset of several cold spells or early ice ages.

1.3 Tannahill, R., *Food in History*, Palladin, London, 1973, p. 6.

1.4 Olson, A., *Om Allmogens Kosthall* (Everyday Food Needs), Lund, Sweden, 1958, p. 8.

1.5 Brothwell, D. and P., *Food and Antiquity: A Survey of Diet of Early People*, Thames & Hudson, London, 1969, p. 8.

Figure 1.1 'Avez-vous une table pour deux?'
Source: Nestlé Pro Gastronomia Foundation, © 1993

With fire as his ally, man did not have to retreat before the ice altogether, but could stay or live closer to the fringes of the ice. He adapted his diet, living much more off meat than ever before. With improved hunting techniques he was able to kill woolly mammoths and large deer.(1.6)

In this now colder climate, man was in need of continuous fire. It had become a basic necessity of life and he found ways of controlling it and using it in various ways. Those who were too young or feeble to join in the hunt were given the task of tending the fire – a task which was to assume great importance.

In the case of the first nomadic tribes, fire was carried in a hollow stone secured with simple ropes on two poles slung between two men. The men tended the fire while they travelled, and reassembled it on the ground at the end of the day's journey.(1.7)

Fire changed the state of all manner of things around the fire, from cold to hot and from wet to dry, and, in the case of food, from raw to cooked. Women, in particular, observed and gradually used this in developing the early methods of dry cooking.

1.6 Tannahill, R., *Food in History*, Palladin, London, 1973, p. 16.

1.7 Ejdestam, J., *De Fattigas Sverige* (The Sweden of the Poor), Bonnier, Stockholm, 1969, p. 9.

Food left by accident on a hot stone of the fireplace was cooked and changed character and taste. Meat hung overnight near the heat of the fire became partly roasted. One can recognise clearly here the very early development of dry methods of cooking we now call roasting, grilling, baking, but not yet really understood or in common use.

Around 75,000 BC, the clumsy figure of *Homo sapiens* appeared on the prehistoric scene. This large-brained successor to *Homo erectus* is known today as Neanderthal man. Some consider this stocky but more intelligent man a physiological adaption to the new climate; others have seen signs that he suffered a vitamin deficiency, possibly vitamin D, which resulted in rickets.(1.8)

Man had by now become a very skilled hunter. He had begun to speak a simple language, evolved some simple rules for rites and rituals, perfected some simple medical techniques and showed some care and concern for the sick, the young and the old. The young represented the future and an assurance for old age; with no written language, the old were looked after for their experience, knowledge and wisdom. Yet with all this concern for others in the group, Neanderthal man still regarded his fellow man (from another tribe) as acceptable food when meat was scarce.(1.9)

As the climate became milder and the ice shrank towards the north, man returned to eating more vegetables. A more advanced breed of man then evolved and in about 30,000 BC, he was able to refine his tools and weapons, resulting in simple fishing hooks, the use of horns and shells, and some simple stoneware. Under the influence of the warmer climate and warm winds, great fields of various types of wild grain appeared in several areas of the Middle East.(1.10)

With a much more varied plant life in a now considerably warmer climate, a new type of man appeared, who still hunted, but who now also gathered and, eventually, grew his food.

Prehistoric Man, the Gatherer of His Food

As we have seen, earliest man was more ape than man, living on the food the tree-tops provided. Even when man left the trees and turned to a diet of nearly

1.8 Ivenhoe, F., in *Nature*, August 1970.

1.9 Tannahill, R., *Food in History*, Palladin, London, 1973, p. 166.

1.10 Flannery, K.V., in Ucko, P.J. and Dimbleby, G.W. (eds), *The Domestication of Plants and Animals*, Series of papers, Gerald Dunckworth & Co., London, 1969, p. 79.

all meat, he still ate plants and fruits. While the men and older boys went out hunting and fishing, the elders in the tribe occupied themselves with domestic tasks, such as making and repairing tools, building or repairing shelters, brewing early medicinal potions and guarding and instructing children.

The women and older girls of the tribe had the daily task of gathering edible roots, nuts, acorns, berries of various types and small plants. Experience had shown them which types of vegetation were pleasant and safe to eat and which were not. They would also watch herbivores to give them a clue as to which plants were safe to eat.

Root vegetables, protected from the ravage of the weather, must always have been important to early man's diet, particularly when the hunt was not successful. Onions, swedes, turnips and a large type of radish almost certainly date back to prehistoric times in Europe.

Root vegetables of several types may have saved many of the early inhabitants of the Americas from starvation. Man did not spread over the Americas until about 20,000 BC, some say nearer to 10,000 BC.(1.11) The retreat of the glaciers opened up a north–south corridor over the country, which exposed lands to a searching wind direct from the Arctic. In the prairie provinces, the horse, camel, giant bison and mastodon fell victim to the sudden drop in temperature.(1.12) With only a limited access to meat, man had to rely on the gathering of vegetables, particularly roots, for a substitute. Vegetables, such as yams, potatoes and sweet varieties of manioc, were readily eaten and the diet, for a time anyway, became almost vegetarian again.

Vegetables growing above the ground have a long history of use in both Asia and Europe. This includes the various members of the cabbage family, birch shoots, nettles, ferns and various water weeds. Moist and shady places almost certainly provided mushrooms and fungi of many types. From Tierra del Fuego, Charles Darwin reported that the natives ate, with the exception of some types of berries, 'no vegetables other than fungus'.(1.13)

As most vegetable foods leave no archaeological traces, there is, nevertheless, some evidence that vegetable seeds, such as beans, lentils and chick-peas in various forms, were favoured in the Near-East, Central America and parts of Europe; that seeds of a number of grass-like plants were gathered for seasonings; and that ground squash can, with certainty, be dated back to prehistory.(1.14)

1.11 Willey, G.E., 'Introduction to American Archaeology in *Archaeology*', vol. 1, New York 1960, p. 14.

1.12 Zeuner, F.E., A *History of Domesticated Animals*, Harper, London and New York, 1964, p. 18.

1.13 Charles Darwin in Brothwell, D. and P., *Food and Antiquity: A Survey of Diet of Early People*, Thames & Hudson, London, 1969, p. 87.

1.14 Tannahill, R., *Food in History*, Palladin, London, 1973, p. 287.

When man was successful in his hunt, he may have turned a blind eye to such delicacies as snails, river crab, fresh-water mussels and small turtles. But if the hunt was unsuccessful, the gathering of all types of vegetables and fruits by women, as well as small molluscs, may have been the salvation of an otherwise disappointing meal and, although not yet realised, provided a more balanced and healthier diet to prehistoric man.

Prehistoric Man and Agriculture

For many thousands of years, man had eaten fruits, plants, nuts and roots before observing the young shoots sprouting from the discarded seed or leftovers. This led to the embryonic beginning of prehistoric agriculture, and generally the date for this is given at about 10,000 BC.

However, Tudge argues that the beginning of agriculture given at about 10,000 BC is too much of an '*idée fixe*', and although unwilling to give a more precise date, he speaks of a span of development of 100,000 years or more.(1.15) He says that in matters of prehistoric timing, we should speak of spans of time which made any such developments possible, and not fixed dates, even when prefixed by 'about'.

For example, no one will ever be really sure when the Neolithic revolution, the change from a primarily hunting/fishing/gathering existence to one which made man a settled farmer and stock-breeder, took place. What is certain, however, is that it took place at different times in different places. The generally accepted view – that the development had two clearly defined regions (one to the west and south-west of the Caspian Sea and the other in Central America) – was seriously challenged in 1970 by the findings of the University of Hawaii expedition to the 'Spirit Caves' near the Burmese border of Thailand. This clearly showed that the seeds of peas, beans, cucumbers and water-chestnuts must have been cultivated by man at roughly 9,750 BC, almost two thousand years before true agriculture can be proven to have begun in the Near East or in Central America.(1.16)

The theory that man gave up his life in the widely scattered cave communities only after finding that the tilling of the land and herding of flocks needed a

---

1.15 Tudge, C., 'Who were the First Farmers?', *New Scientist*, 6 September 1979.

1.16 Reported in *The Times*, 16 April 1970.

sizeable labour force, and that this was the reason that led clans to converge into large groups and found villages, was again challenged in 1970.

Now it seems more likely that in the Near East, archaeologically the world's best documented region, villages sprang up long before either farming or stock-breeding began.(1.17) It was not the fields of cultivated grain, but the new and abundant fields of wild grain which gave rise to the foundation of early settlements and villages.

The climate of the Near East resulted in conditions which favoured fast-growing plants, particularly grassy plants, which would grow, mature and seed themselves before they would be affected by the dry heat of the summers. Thus rippling fields of wild wheat and barley soon appeared on all suitable land in the now climatically favourable conditions.(1.18)

Wild grain as dense as that which has been cultivated can be found even today in various parts of the world, often twice as rich in protein as cultivated varieties. It was possible for an early man, with a family of six or eight, to reap enough wild wheat to provide them with a pound or so of grain per head per day throughout the year.(1.19) To reap such a harvest of free food, early man had to be on the spot at the right time, and so settlements grew up around the grain fields in readiness for the short-lived periods of harvesting.

By about 9,000 BC, villages were to be found in Mallaka in northern Israel, which relied on a combination of hunting and very intensive gathering/farming of wild grain.

'In imperceptible stages over considerable spans of time, here and in other places, the early gatherings of wild grain developed into cultivation of the same.'(1.20)

For, however plentiful the harvest of wild grain, the new villagers discovered that, if they harvested too efficiently, the following year's harvest would be reduced, but leaving some of the ears on the stalks would improve the next year's harvest. Exactly when they took the logical step of distributing the seed evenly by hand on to the land, ceasing to be merely gatherers and becoming farmers, must remain conjecture.

1.17 Campbell, H. and Braidwood, R., 'An Early Farming Village in Turkey', *Scientific American*, vol. CCXXII, 1970, p. 56.

1.18 Flannery, K.V. in Ucko, P.J. and Dimbleby, G.W. (eds), *The Domestication of Plants and Animals*, Series of papers, Gerald Dunckworth and Co., London, 1969, p. 79.

1.19 Harland, J.R., 'A wild wheat harvest in Turkey', *Archaeology*, March 1967, pp. 197–201.

1.20 Tudge, C., 'The Pleasure of the flesh', *New Scientist*, 6 September 1979.

Prehistoric Man: Hunting and Animal Domestication

Prehistoric men became very skilful hunters. They could send a wooden or stone-tipped spear straight through an animal's eye into its brain, or home a stone missile on the lethal spot on its skull, or cripple the animal by slashing the heel tendon with a flint knife as it ran past them.(1.21)

A study into seventeen sites of the Zagros mountains of Iran, which covered a period of more than thirty thousand years beginning at 50,000 BC, has produced six thousand identifiable animal bones, mainly from goats and deer as well as from hare, fox, leopard and wild cattle. The number of bones may at first seem scanty over such a long period of time, but when we consider that we have but one person to every 31 square miles, it must imply consistently good hunting.(1.22)

Killing his prey may have been much less of a problem to the hunter than was carrying it home and preserving it. The musk-ox and bison found during the colder spells of the Pleistocene era were extremely large. With many four-legged predators in the vicinity only too eager to join in the feast, the dead animal would be cut up and carried to safety.

When an animal had been killed, the group would gorge themselves on the meat for days. The meat had to be eaten quickly, for in the warmer climate it would not keep for long, and it cannot have taken man long to associate upset stomachs with spoiled meat.

In his basic task to secure his juicy meat by hunting, man had learnt that his prey was more easily hunted and killed when driven into rock enclosures or small ravines which could be blocked off. It was then only a small step – a short span of time of a thousand years or so – before man realised that he could preserve his hunted animals by keeping them alive in the blocked off rock enclosures or ravines. That way he need only kill the animals when there was a need for fresh meat. In many cases, a man was placed in front of the blocked off enclosures, and we have here the first herdsman or shepherd of early history. This task was made very much easier when in the Near East twelve thousand years or so ago, fields of various types of wild grain sprang up. For the wild grain was fed to the herded animals – wild sheep and goats – long before early man took interest in the grain for feeding himself.

1.21 Tannahill, R., *Food in History*, Palladin, London, 1973, p. 19.

1.22 Hole, F. and Flannery, K.V., 'Proceedings of a pre-historic society', *Society*, February 1968.

From the first herdsman or shepherd guarding the blocked off enclosures, to the eventual domestication of suitable animals needed again but a short span of time. By 8,920 BC in the case of sheep, domestication had taken place at Zawi Chemi Shanidar in Iraq (1.23), and at Dobrudja in Romania (1.24).

We have to wait until about 7,000 BC for the pig to be domesticated. The reason for this is quite simple: as the pig is unable to digest straw, grass, leaves and twigs like the ruminant animals, such as goats, sheep, cattle and deer, man had to delay domestication of this animal until he was prepared to invest some of his own food, such as nuts, acorns, meat scraps and, later, cooked grain and roots, in its upbringing.(1.25)

The last major food animal to be domesticated was the cow, which is understandable when one thinks of its size and stubbornness. Archaeologists seem unable to agree but, by about 6,000 to 5,000 BC, this larger animal was well in the domesticated fold in the Catal Hijirk in Turkey or Nicomedia in Macedonia.(1.26,1.27)

These domesticated animals provided not only meat for food, but also other benefits to man. The glossy waterproof skin of the goat made excellent water containers; and the sheep provided wool and substantial amounts of fat useful not only in cooking, but also as an ingredient in the dressing of wounds and as tallow for the earliest rush light and simple lamps.

Later, the pig's bristle became a valuable commodity in the prehistoric household, as did the pig's lard and skin; and cow hide became useful for building shelters and making clothing. Cow dung proved to be an excellent fuel for the domestic fire and is still used today in many parts of the world.

Prehistoric Man and Fishing

To the supply of food discussed above must be added that of fish and shellfish. Early man used clubs and spears to catch large fish, such as pike and eel, or trapped smaller migratory fish by damming their streams with stones or upright

---

1.23 Coon, C.S., *The History of Man: From the First Human to Primitive Culture and Beyond*, Jonathan Cape, New York, 1954, London, 1955, p. 10.

1.24 Coles, J.M. and Higgs, E.S., *The Archaeology of Early Man*, Faber & Faber, London, 1969, p. 273.

1.25 Tannahill, R., Food in History, Palladin, London, 1973, p. 40.

1.26 Daumas, M., *Histoire Grenerale des Techniques*, 3 vols, Presses Universitaire, Paris, 1962–9, p. 43.

1.27 Singer, C. with Holmyard, Hall and Williams, *A History of Technology*, 5 vols, Clarendon Press, Oxford, 1954–8, p. 452.

stakes or laced branches – the early pattern of a fishing net. The hunting techniques of laying bait to attract animal quarry on land may have led to the idea of bait on a line. By 25,000 BC, man in the Dordogne region had developed the fish gorge.(1.28)

Thorns were used as hooks, perhaps with bait attached, simply to block the fish's mouth for an easy catch. By 12,000 BC, harpoons had been added to the fisherman's armoury, and not much later the bow and arrow gave fishermen and hunters a useful new weapon.(1.29)

Dug-out canoes and early reed-rafts of prehistoric times were of no use to man in deep water until, during the Neolithic era, he began to use oars. Fishing nets made from twisted fibres, hair or thongs, were used from about 8,000 BC, and these led to considerable inshore fishing in some places.(1.30)

The various shells of shellfish became prized containers, which, as will be seen, may have helped the vital development of liquid cooking in vessels; fish bones became needles for early sewing; and fish skins were used in the making of decorations and ornaments.

Prehistoric Man and Cooking: The Vessel

For thousands of years, prehistoric man ate his food raw. But between about 500,000 BC and the appearance of Neanderthal man at about 75,000 BC, some simple cooking of, or more correctly, the application of heat to, food, particularly meats, was discovered and used. As we saw earlier, prehistoric man used fire in the first place for warmth and comfort, and it was by accident rather than by design that food became cooked. But we can recognise the gradual development of methods of dry cooking familiar to us today.

At first, man just threw the meat into the fire, but it was eaten more burned than cooked. In time, man learned to raise his meat above the fire by various means and from this came the method of cooking we know today as spit-roasting. Meat placed on the hot stones surrounding the fire, or in the embers of a dying fire, developed into the method of cooking we now recognise as grilling. Food placed on or into hollow stones surrounding the fire must have developed into the method of cooking we know as baking. Much later came the method of

1.28 Coles, J.M. and Higgs, E.S., *The Archaeology of Early Man*, Faber & Faber, London, 1970, p. 273.

1.29 Raglan, A., in The *Sunday Times*, 16 April 1972.

1.30 Singer, C., with Holmyard, Hall and Williams, A *History of Technology*, 5 vols, Oxford University Press, Oxford, 1954–8, p. 452.

Figure 1.2 'Sans titre'
Source: Nestlé Pro Gastronomia Foundation, © 1993

cooking we know as boiling. But this would need a waterproof and fireproof container to put on the fire, to separate food from the flames.

If archaeologists are to be believed, no progress was made in respect of a vessel or containers until about 6,000 BC, when true pottery had evolved and was clearly used for, among other things, cooking food with water. Some recent discussions consider the possibility that pottery might well have been a development of early dry cooking methods. Prehistoric man dragged his kill home over a muddy path, carelessly laying it down in a clay-muddied corner. Then, placing it on or near the fire, he must have observed that the meat, cooked in its own clay and mud-covered 'container', produced a more succulent piece of meat than a piece of meat which was cooked 'clean'.

Until as late as 1928, the gypsies of Eastern Europe covered their freshly killed hedgehogs with a thick, wet layer of clay and then placed the balls of clay and meat in their open and simple camp fires. The hard-baked clay shell, inclusive of the inedible spines, was removed in one action and the juicy meat eaten.(1.31)

1.31 Ejdestam, J., *Samking Kring Bordet* (Congregating Around the Table), Roben and Sjögren, Stockholm, 1975, p. 141.

But this is not the only way food in prehistory was cooked protected from the open flame. In pit cooking, stony pits were filled with water and the meat to be cooked. The water was brought to the boil and kept boiling by continually adding red hot pebbles and removing the cooler ones.

Food may also have been cooked by wrapping it in leaves or in wet seaweed, and placing it in natural rock-pits, then covering it with more large leaves or seaweed and building a fire above it. The food would emerge some hours later, moist and savoury, more steamed than boiled, and with a tasty, soupy, nutritious liquid found in the base of the pit as an added benefit. This is a cooking technique which survives in many parts of the world to this day, in particular it is employed on a large scale in the cooking of North American clambakes.

In several parts of the world, large mollusc or reptile shells were used to boil food before the advent of pottery. This form of container is still used today and was used in the early nineteenth century when the naturalist Henry Walter Bates was served a dish of turtle made into a delicious soup-stew called Sarapatel when he visited the Amazon. This dish was obviously cooked and served in the concave upper shell of the dead animal.(1.32)

Around 7,000 BC, in the Tehuacan Valley of Central America near the south-west corner of the Gulf of Mexico, people lived in rock shelters. Their basic diet was wild maize and, to make it more palatable, it seems that they used simple stone cooking pots. These pots were sited in the centre of the hearth and left there permanently. As the pots were extremely heavy, they would have been suitable only when a community was settled in its cave abode, or willing to fashion a new stone pot when the community moved to another cave.(1.33)

In various parts of Asia, that productive tree, the bamboo, was probably used in the boiling of food. A hollow section was filled with meat, fish and water, and the ends blocked with stone and clay before being laid on or near the fire. This method of cooking is used in Indonesia today.

At least one type of container that was waterproof and heatproof up to the point of being hung over (if not in) the fire was an animal stomach, and there is evidence that this was widely used for boiling before the advent of pottery or bronze. Like twentieth-century Eskimos, prehistoric man may well have regarded the hot and only partially-digested stomach contents of his kill as a special treat of hot boiled food.(1.34)

In his liking for hot boiled food, it would be a logical development for man to cook the contents of one of the stomach bags and use the container again for

1.32 Bates, H.W., 'The River Amazon', *The Naturalist*, London, vol. 2, 1863.

1.33 Willey, G.E., 'Introduction to American Archaeology in *Archaeology*', vol. 1, New York, 1960.

1.34 de Vries, A., *Primitive Man and His Food*, Chandler Books, Chicago, 1962, p. 28.

other dishes. The result would not have been far removed in its finished effect from the modern casserole.

As late as the fifth century BC, the nomad Scythians placed all the meat they could find into an animal's stomach (the rumen of a twentieth century cow has a capacity of 30 to 40 gallons), mixing it with water, roots and herbs and slowly cooking it over a fire. In this way, an ox, or any other sacrificial beast, is ingeniously made to boil itself.(1.35)

As late as the eighteenth century, the American explorer, Samuel Heard, noted a dish cooked in a stomach bag called 'beata', 'tasty and handy to make'. He described a 'kind of haggis made with blood, water, fat and some of the tenderest of the flesh, as well as heart and lungs of the animal' cooked in this way. A most delicious morsel, even without pepper, salt and other seasoning. It was important that the stomach should not be over-filled as its content would expand and could easily burst during cooking, an observation which would have been made over time.(1.36)

Sausages, salamis and other charcuterie preparations may well have had their origin in the search of prehistoric man to cook or, more precisely, to boil his food in a container.

In prehistoric times, life was short. During the Neanderthal period, for example, less than half the population reached the age of twenty, and nine out of every ten of the remaining adults died before the age of forty. Vitamin deficiencies, seasonal malnutrition, plant poisoning and all types of contaminated foods and lack of hygiene took their toll. The discovery of cooking, particularly boiling, was an important contribution to the survival of mankind. It helped make a number of formerly indigestible foods edible, it increased the nutritive value of many other foods in breaking down fibres and releasing protein and carbohydrates. More importantly, the discovery of boiling gave prehistoric infants a nutritive liquid broth, in many ways more valuable than mother's milk.

As the distinguished American anthropologist Carlston Coon put it:

> *'The introduction of cooking may well have secured early man's survival, and been the decisive factor which led man from a primarily animal existence into one that was more fully human.'(1.37)*

1.35 Herodotus, *The History* 446 BC, vol. IV, p. 60, translated by Aibrey de Selincourt, Penguin, London, 1954.

1.36 Galton, F., *The Art of Travel*, London, 1860, p. 4.

1.37 Coon, C.S., *The History of Man: From the First Human to Primitive Culture and Beyond*, Jonathan Cape, London, 1955, p. 63.

Prehistoric Man: Early Social and Cultural Evolution

'Man is a singular creature, he has a set of gifts, which make him unique among the animals; so that unlike them he is not a figure in the landscape, he is the shaper of the landscape, the ubiquitous animal who did not find, but made, his home in every continent.'(1.38)

Zoology gives us many examples of beautiful and exact adaptations by which animals fit into their given environment, and only this given environment will support their existence. When this environment changes gradually, the creatures will adapt with the changes. But when the change is sudden and too drastic, they may become extinct.

'But nature, that is to say biological evolution, has not fitted man for any given existence, or locked man into any environment.
'On the contrary, by comparison with most animals, man's survival kit is rather crude, and yet it is in this that lies the paradox of human condition, it is one which fits man into all conditions and locks him into no environment.'(1.39)

'Whereas many animals are locked into their limiting environment, man, by his reason, imagination, power of observation, toughness and foresight, which we may call the spirit of man, is free from all environmental straight-jackets.
By his developing gifts, early man has made a series of important observations, acquired a series of important basic skills, leading to a series of important inventions, which made it possible for man through the ages not to accept but to remake his environment. We may call this evolution, but in respect of man it was not only a biological evolution as observed in animals, but also the important social and cultural evolution which raises him above them.
More remarkably, much of present human behaviour and condition may be traced back to prehistoric man's basic quest for survival in an ever-changing environment.
'I believe that the above sections have given a very basic but, nevertheless, important account of the evolution of the spirit of man, in his fight for his most basic early need, his food. In this lies the basis of much of the behaviour of present man. It is very tempting to believe that the most original and important

1.38 Bronowski, J., *The Ascent of Man*, 4th edn, Futura, London, 1981, p. 13.
1.39 *Ibid.*, p. 14.

of man's achievements in the arts and sciences are the most recent, and we have indeed cause to be proud of much of modern work. But, in retrospect, we must not forget and give due attention and respect to the fundamental achievements of our earliest ancestor, prehistoric man. Indeed, in his fight for survival, prehistoric man's very simplest of achievements may well be considered the very foundation of today's achievements.'

'Every human action goes back in some parts to our animal and/or prehistoric origin, we should be cold and lonely creatures if we were cut off from that blood stream of life.'(1.40)

The previous sections have given an account of some of prehistoric man's achievements. His other achievements, particularly in behaviour, must be considered, as they determine much of man's behaviour today.

The first important achievement must be the gradual change – both in place and time – of early man's diet from vegetarian to omnivorous. The consumption of small grubs, insects and small animals at first, and some larger animals later, had considerable consequences. It secured a more valuable diet for the development of man, and meant that he could spend less time looking for food.

'This became possible about two-million years ago, when man made his first important invention. By a simple blow of his rudimentary stone tool, he put an edge on a pebble. By this simple act of skill and foresight, a symbolic act of discovery, as important as and equal to the 'splitting of the atom', man had released the brake which the environment imposes on all creatures. The subsequent use of this simple tool for more than a million years shows the strength of this simple invention, clearly a meat-eater's tool, to strike out with, to kill and to cut.'(1.41)

'From this, the gradual change in man's dietary existence became really possible. Prehistoric man gained more time which he could spend in the development of better tools still, as well as the development of more indirect ways of securing food, not just being the consequence of hungry brute force alone. With a more concentrated and omnivorous food supply thus more readily secured, it helped in due course to promote by natural selection the tendency of all primates to interpose an internal delay in the brain between stimulus and response, gradually developing into the more fully human ability to postpone the

1.40 *Ibid*, p. 20.
1.41 *Ibid*., p. 20.

gratification of desires for food, and later, other basic needs.
'One may consider this the second big step in the behaviour change of man; early civilisation had now begun. The hunt by the individual almost stopped; the realisation of the need for help by others to secure the kill of now larger and faster animals, had a considerable effect on social awareness. Because of this, we see the development of the family and tribe unit out on the hunt, the caring for and sharing of the skill. In short, the more marked interdependence of the hunting group.
'The hunting in larger groups, for larger and quicker animals, obviously showed a need for communication, to secure the kill. This need for communication during the hunt is by some considered to be the basis of the development of human speech.'(1.42)

A slow creature like man can stalk, pursue and corner a larger animal that is very much faster and well adapted to flight only by co-operation with others on several levels.

Hunting requires conscious planning and organisation by means of social arrangements, by means of communication with a developing language, as well as new weapons and skills.

'Language indeed, as still used, has something of a character of a hunting plan, in that unlike the animals, we instruct one another in sentences. They are put together from movable units. The hunt is much more than the kill, it is a communal undertaking on several levels, of which the climax, but only the climax, is the kill.'(1.43)

A further development of human behavioural characteristics is also considered as having its base in the need for new developing group hunting methods. This is the pair-bonding characteristic of the human race which, in its way, is unique and which developed into various forms of marriages, still considered the basis of all civilised life today.

'To find the reason for this we have to look back again at his origins. What happened?
'First, he had to hunt if he was to survive. Second, he had to have a better brain to make up for his poor hunting body. Third, he had to have a longer childhood to grow the bigger brain and to educate it. Fourth, the females had to stay put and mind the babies while the males went hunting. Fifth, the males had

---

1.42 Levander, L., *Mat Ock Miljö* (Food and Environment), Lund University Press, Sweden, 1940, p. 114.

1.43 Bronowski, J., *The Ascent of Man*, 4th edn, Futura, London, 1981, p. 28.

to co-operate with one another on the hunt. Sixth, they had to stand up straight and use weapons for the hunt to succeed.

'The writer is not implying that these changes happened in that order; on the contrary, they undoubtedly all developed gradually at the same time, each modification helping the others along. I am simply enumerating the six basic, major changes that took place as the hunting ape evolved. Inherent in these changes there are, I believe, all the ingredients necessary to make up our present behavioural complexity.

'To begin with, the males had to be sure that their females were going to be faithful to them when they left them alone to go hunting. So the females had to develop a pairing tendency. Also, if the weaker males were going to be expected to co-operate in the hunt, they had to be given more sexual rights. The females would have to be more shared out, the sexual organisation more democratic, less tyrannical.

'Each male, too, would need a strong pairing tendency. Furthermore, the males were now armed with deadly weapons and sexual rivalries would be much more dangerous: again, a good reason for each male being satisfied with one female. On top of that there were the much heavier parental demands being made by the slow-growing infants. Paternal behaviour would have to be developed and the parental duties shared between the mother and the father – another good reason for a strong pair-bond.

'Given this situation as a starting point, we can now see how other things grew from it. The naked ape had to develop the capacity for falling in love, for becoming sexually imprinted on a single partner, for evolving a pair-bond. Whichever way you put it, it comes to the same thing. How did he manage to do this? What were the factors that helped him in this trend? As a primate, he will already have had a tendency to form brief mate-ships lasting a few hours, or perhaps even a few days, but these now had to be intensified and extended. One thing that will have come to his aid is his own prolonged childhood. During the long growing years, he will have had the chance to develop a deep personal relationship with his parents, a relationship much more powerful and lasting than anything a young monkey could experience. The loss of this parental bond with maturation and independence would create a 'relationship void' – a gap that had to be filled. He would, therefore, already be primed for the development of a new, equally powerful bond to replace it.

'Even if this was enough to intensify his need for forming a new pair-bond, there would still have to be additional assistance to maintain it. It would have to last long enough for the lengthy process of rearing a family. Having fallen in love, he would have to stay in love.

'By developing a prolonged and exciting courtship phase he could ensure the former, but something more would be needed after that. The simplest and most

direct method of doing this was to make the shared activities of the pair more complicated and more rewarding.'(1.44)

Another writer makes the same point, but more in respect of the prehistoric orphan, and his need for social care and education rather than pair-bonding. One realises, of course, that the two are very much interrelated, and very much complement one another.

'The other invention is social, and we infer it by more subtle arithmetic. Skulls and skeletons of Australopithecus that have now been found in largish numbers show that most of them died before the age of twenty. That means that there must have been many orphans. For Australopithecus surely had a long childhood, as all the primates do; at the age of ten, say, the survivors were still children. Therefore there must have been a social organization in which children were looked after and, as it were adopted, were made part of the community, and so in some general sense were educated. That is a great step towards cultural evolution.'(1.45)

Thus, it can be clearly seen that the strategy to enhance the basic food supply very much fostered new social interaction and communication. Another important symbol for early man was the developing use of fire. First to give warmth and comfort, and eventually to cook some of early man's food. His early home was the cave, and this was replaced by simple shelters which in turn grew into settlements and, with the advent of agriculture, early villages. Many writers believe that the settlement of early man for whatever reason was the beginning of civilisation. For now, because of the hearth, because of emerging agriculture, it became necessary for man to settle.

The best anthropological record for this is the Bible, the Old Testament, which records in some considerable detail the struggle of a people to make the decision to stop the nomadic life and to settle. One of the most respected scientists of recent years states: 'I believe that civilisation rests on the decision to settle.'(1.46)

Those people who did not settle contributed little to the emerging civilisation. Nomadic tribes today still journey from one grazing ground to another. For example, every year the Bakhtiaris of Persia must cross six mountain ranges in the search for new pastures. They march their animals through snow

---

1.44 Morris, D., *The Naked Ape*, Corgi Books, London, 1968, pp. 56–8.

1.45 Bronowski, J., *The Ascent of Man*, 4th edn, Futura, London 1981, p. 28.

1.46 *Ibid.*, p. 37.

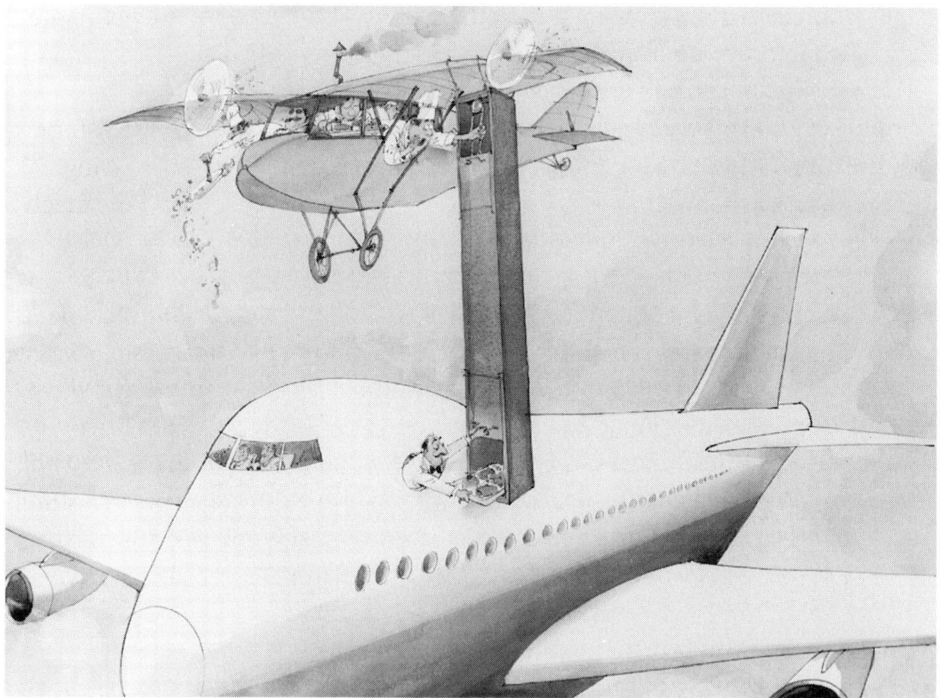

Figure 1.3 'Catering aérien'
Source: Nestlé Pro Gastronomia Foundation, © 1993

and spring flood water on a journey that never ends and not much is new or very real. They know only the simplest of technology and accept only that which can be carried on their daily journey from place to place. At best, if something is found useful, it is bartered for. This simplicity is not romantic, it is a matter of survival: everything movable must be light and portable. Little is, therefore, new, little advancement is observed and everything in nomad life seems immemorial.

Why should man want to eat his food hot? There are several alternative explanations, one of which is that man cooked his food to simulate 'prey temperature'. Although we no longer consume warm, freshly killed meat, we nevertheless consume it at much the same temperature as other carnivore species do.

Their food is hot because it has not yet cooled down; ours is hot because we have cooked or reheated it. Another interpretation is that we now have such weak teeth that we are forced to 'tenderise' the meat by cooking. But this does not explain why we should want to eat it while it is still hot, nor that we should heat or cook so many foods that obviously do not require 'tenderising'. The last explanation is that, by increasing the temperature of the food by cooking, we very much improve the flavour.

Compositional cookery does indeed add to many foods and dishes a complicated range of tasty subsidiaries or aromates which take this process still further.

> *'This relates back, not to our adopted carnivore, but to our more ancient primate past. The foods of typical primates have a much wider variety of flavours than those of carnivores. When a carnivore has gone through its complex sequence of hunting, and killing its food, it behaves much more simply and crudely at the actual crunch. It gobbles; it bolts its food down. Monkeys and apes, on the other hand, are extremely sensitive to the subtleties of varying tastiness in their food morsels. They relish them and keep on moving from one flavour to another. Perhaps, when we heat and spice our meals, we are harking back to this earlier primate fastidiousness. Perhaps this is one way in which we resisted the move towards full-blooded carnivore.'(1.47)*

Maybe it is in this fact that we must see the development over time of compositional cookery in general and gastronomy in particular.

The Story of Genesis

I am well aware that this chapter has taken a very evolutionary stance. But, in a Christian European context, there is another story to be told: the story of Genesis. This story tells of the creation of man, not by evolution, but by the hand of 'God, the Father'. This story, from the first book of Moses, tells the ancient story of creation, and places this happening into a golden age and a beautiful legendary landscape called the Garden of Eden.

As scientists have not really been able to prove an acceptable link between apes and prehistoric man, it is not surprising that the story of Genesis remains so important a story, and is believed by many all over the world. Yet it is almost certain now that man first existed, or was created, in Africa, near the equator. Typical of the place where the creation of man may have taken place is the savannah country that stretches across northern Kenya and south-western Ethiopia near Lake Rudolph.

The lake lies in a long ribbon along the great Rift Valley. Much of the water of

1.47 Morris, D., *The Naked Ape*, Corgi Books, London, 1968.

the lake comes from the winding, sluggish Oma River. The remains of creatures like man can be found here, along with the remains of animals that lived at the same time. The remains of animals are a surprise because one can see that animals have changed so very little. But when one looks at the fossil of the creature which has become man, one is struck by the difference between his skeleton and ours.

Why have animals remained virtually unchanged for over two million years while man changed so dramatically?

Evolution alone cannot be the answer, for one would suppose that animals would develop at the same rate as man developed. What, or who, changed or made man into this unique creature, the shaper of his own environment, the creature with insight, thought, in short, spirit, not found in any other creature?

We do not have a scientific or religious explanation. To many the gradual evolutionary progress by man, with a yet-to-be-found missing link, seems the only answer. To millions, the touch of a higher being, the bestowing of grace on to the human race, or simply the creation by God the Almighty, or whatever we wish to call Him, is the explanation why man ascended so far higher than the animals. Maybe the answer lies somewhere between the scientific evolutionary stance and that of the creation of man by a higher being. Maybe creation as told in the story of Genesis was not so much an actual physical happening, but more of a natural, gentle directing, a presentation of opportunities to man, which, with his inherent insight, he recognised and used.

Bronowski divides the history of man into two distinct parts. First, man's biological evolution – the steps that separate us from our ape-ancestors, which occupied millions of years. Second, man's natural cultural evolution – the long swell of civilisation that separates us from a few surviving hunting tribes of Africa, or from the few remaining food-gatherers of Australia. The first took millions of years; the latter was crowded into a few thousand years, going back something more than ten thousand years, but much less than twenty thousand years, and containing the whole ascent of man.

What happenings, what giving of direction, what presentation of opportunities will account for the concentrated cultural development of man in this short span of time? The change of man's diet from vegetarian to omnivorous, as we have seen, may be one. The use of fire, the application of heat to this new diet, and derived benefits, may be another.

The decision to settle into caves, or to make small hamlets or villages near the fields of wild grain, must be considered an important decision.

The obvious socialising influences of the above decisions are not yet fully realised, or accepted, but they must have given prehistoric man considerable benefits over time, thus considerably aiding his progress. But what, to quote Bronowski again:

'. . . accelerated the ratio between man's biological evolution and his cultural evolution by one hundred to one, once it took off, only some ten thousand years or so ago?'(1.48)

There must have been some extraordinary explosion, an explosion which was the end of the ice age: it accelerated and aided man's extraordinary progress in a comparatively short space of time. Man had gone through some considerable hardships in his short prehistoric life. Suddenly he found himself in a much warmer climate, in a landscape flowering in abundance, and he moved into a new, newly created, kind of life.

The kind of wild wheat that the earliest inhabitants in the fertile crescent of the Middle East harvested, at first in fistfuls, no longer survives. But grasses that still grow there today must have looked somewhat like the wheat grass they found and gathered, and later cultivated. One of the many wild wheat grasses that grew and spread through many parts of the world, within the burst of vegetation in a new, very much warmer climate, must have made a decisive contribution to man's sudden and accelerated progress.

Or, as in the story of Genesis, was blessed or created for man, for some such wild-grass crossed, by a genetic accident, with wild goat-grass and formed a fertile hybrid called Emmer.

In terms of the genetic machinery which directs plant growth, it combined the fourteen chromosomes of wheat-grass with the fourteen chromosomes of goat-grass, producing a new wheat with twenty-eight chromosomes, very much plumper and richer.(1.49)

This hybrid was still able to spread naturally like its two predecessors because its seeds were attached to the husk in such a way that they could be easily carried and seeded by the wind. For such a hybrid to be fertile is rare, but not unique among plant life.

Some time later, in the burst of new plant life which followed the end of the ice age, we have the second, much more surprising, 'genetic accident'. This second 'divine accident' crossed the now widely cultivated Emmer wheat with another goat-grass which produced an even larger hybrid with forty-two chromosomes, which became bread wheat. As plant life goes this is improbable enough in itself, and experts now know that it would not have been fertile but for one specific genetic mutation on one chromosome only. Two accidents may be possible in plant life, but something even stranger now happened. The new

---

1.48 Bronowski, J., *The Ascent of Man*, 4th edn, Futura, London, 1981, p. 164.

1.49 Kimber, G., and Athwal, R., 'A re-assessment of the course of evolution of wheat', *Proceedings of the National Academy of Sciences No 4*, April 1972, pp. 912–15.

plump and richer ear of wheat was too tight to be broken up, and too heavy to be carried by the wind.

It grew where it fell – it had lost the ability of wind dispersal.

Now man had the wheat to live on, but the wheat needed man to scatter and harvest it, for only in this way could it be propagated. Thus the life of man and the life of the plant from which he will eventually get his bread are for ever dependent one upon the other.(1.50)

Man had arrived on the threshold of the land of milk and honey, of civilisation?
A likely story of genetic progression?
Or a happening, a giving of direction,
A presenting of opportunity,
A blessing from a Higher Being,
A divine intervention?
To give man the 'Bread' by which he lives, and from which all life, all civilised life, flows.

The Christian religion, at least, has no doubt about the latter. In its greatest prayer, immediately after the acknowledgement of the Higher Being, in:

'Our Father who art in Heaven, hallowed be Thy name.
Thy Kingdom come.
Thy will be done on earth as it is in Heaven . . .'

it continues with:

. . . '*Give us this day our daily bread.*'

1.50 Piggot, S., *From the Beginning of Agriculture to Classical Antiquity: A Survey*, Edinburgh University Press, Edinburgh, 1965.

CHAPTER 2

Gastro-geography

Introduction

The word gastro-geography has two very distinctive meanings. First, the generally accepted understanding of the word implying:

'. . . *the availability of various foods and dishes, and subsequent eating habits relating to climate, in a given part or region of the world* . . .'

and, secondly, and more importantly for this publication, that of the historic development of:

'*the subsequent cultivation, husbandry, preservation, storage, preparation, available technology, cooking and composition of dishes, as well as the various ways of presenting food for human consumption*'.

Allied to this development one can observe certain food- and eating-connected customs, habits and attitudes which are at times surprising. This is of particular interest when a naturally available food is prepared and eaten so very differently in one part of the world from another. Sometimes the various preparation and presentation methods employed will make a given food a highly regarded delicacy in one place, whereas elsewhere no preparation and presentation method employed could make the same food acceptable.

Connected to these differing conceptions of what is and what is not considered acceptable food, one can often observe very strange food-related and eating-related ceremonies, customs, habits and attitudes, the origins of which are often shrouded in mystery.

This chapter will concern itself only with the two above-stated gastro-geographical definitions, and attempt to trace stages of development. Food-related attitudes, customs, rites and taboos, as well as the subjects of food-related art and food technology, are considered in Chapter 7.

Neolithic Revolution

Before I attempt to identify the gastro-geographical factors involved in the advancement of food supply and development, I must look back at the Neolithic revolution. The change of man from a hunting, fishing, gathering existence to one which made him a settled farmer and stock-breeder, took place at different times in different parts of the world, and at varying pace.

Some see the earliest development in Africa, others place it in China. What is known, though, is that developments in the Americas evolved later and at a much more leisurely rate. In the Near East and on the shores of the Mediterranean generally, Neolithic man showed a considerable flair for advancement. Food-related discoveries, inventions and technological developments took place maybe as long as 10,000 years ago with purposeful speed. Settlements grew into villages, villages into towns, and towns into the early cities. The most striking developments accompanying the more controlled 'filling of bellies' were the maturing early societies and civilisations, in particular, those of Sumaria and Egypt.

'Here developing disciplines and organisations mostly if not all akin to the supply of food, became agents for many other civilising developments.'(2.1)

This included the embryonic development of early specialisms and professions, as well as traders, closely followed by trade and commerce. Having mastered the supply of grain and with it ensured a continuous, if somewhat monotonous, diet, man applied the knowledge and skills gained in the growing of wheat to the cultivation of other food plants. Besides wheat and barley, beans, chick-peas, cucumbers, garlic, leeks, onions, turnips and a kind of lettuce and watercress filled the stomachs of the Sumerians. 'Even a type of mushroom/truffle had been discovered and was gathered and sent as a delicacy in basketfuls to the King.'(2.2)

Years of established farming had proved that a specific acreage of land given to growing wheat filled more hungry mouths than the same land given to raising livestock – an argument not unknown and recommended today.

For early civilised man, grain and other vegetables and fruits had supplemented meat as the mainstay of the daily diet. Meals consisted of barley-paste or early barley or wheat, unleavened bread, onions, a handful of beans and

2.1 Tannahill, R., *Food in History*, Palladin, London, 1973, p. 54.

2.2 Saggs, H.W.F., *Everyday Life in Babylonia and Assyria*, Batsford, Putman, London and New York, 1965, p. 61.

some fruit or berries. The food was washed down by water or an early beer-type beverage.

Meats and fowl were reserved for special days and feasts, but fish was more common and contributed at times considerably to the daily intake of protein. 'Almost fifty types of fish swarmed in the rivers of Mesopotamia.'(2.3)

The network of irrigation canals dug in southern Mesopotamia provided ideal conditions for growing palms. They were cultivated along the canal banks, leaving the open land on either side for the growing of old and newer crops. The date fruit would be eaten fresh or dried. The juices could be added to puddings and sweet breads – a valuable alternative to honey, the only other known sweetener at the time. Chopped up dates were added to simple barley bread or paste to satisfy those with an early sweet tooth who could not afford the honey. Xenophane remarked on the size and succulence of the dates he ate during the Persian expedition, saying that:

'Their colour was just like Amber, the way the villagers had dried them with care, eating them like sweets.'(2.4)

'Even the date palm shoots, sprouting from the older trees, contributed to the diet, when boiled and eaten like a sort of cabbage.'(2.5)

The fig was another much prized fruit with a high sugar content. It was cultivated in the Near East and other warm parts around the Mediterranean where palms would not grow. In Greece it became a much valued fruit 'and addition to the diet for rich and poor Greeks alike, mostly in dried form'.(2.6)

'Rich Sumerians and Egyptians at least must have lived quite well, with the developing early agriculture and experimentation with new and old foods in their diets. Among the relics excavated from a tomb dated as early as the third millennium BC*, such delicacies as barley-porridge, cooked quail, kidneys, pigeon stew, dried figs and fresh fruit, as well as beef-ribs, wheat bread, cheese, ale and wine were found, to help the Nobu man on his way to the other world.'(2.7)*

2.3 Kramer, S.N., *The Sumerians: Their History, Culture and Character*, Chicago University Press, Chicago, 1964, p. 110.

2.4 Warner, R., *Antiquitates Culivariae*, R. Blamire, London, 1791, p. 17.

2.5 *Ibid.*, p. 34.

2.6 Tannahill, R., *Food in History*, Palladin, London, 1973, p. 65.

2.7 Emery, W.B., *Archaic Egypt*, Penguin, London, 1961, p. 24.

The Sumerians and Egyptians experimented with their livestock, though not always successfully.

'Besides the already quite advanced domestication of goats, sheep and cattle for both milk and meat production, attempts were made to domesticate other animals, including most probably the antelope, gazelle, ibex, and oryx. When this did not prove rewarding man turned his attention to the many waterfowl found in various large areas of marshland, developing and preserving these areas for hunting and fishing and the gathering of wild fruits, berries and vegetables. Wild celery, papyrus-shoots and lotus-shoots, both raw and cooked, became part of the diet.'(2.8)

The small birds of the marshes became most popular and were prepared and served in many ways, even salted for consumption out of season. Hipparchus is said to have turned a jaundiced eye on the place where, he said, they were forever plucking quail and slimy magpies'.(2.9)

Availability Factors

Chapter 1 identified the premier factor in the development of gastronomy, namely, man's basic need for nourishment and his fundamental quest to secure this nourishment by whatever means available to him. This chapter aims to identify the next important factor, which is that man could only select and develop foods which the local flora and fauna provided. This availability and provision would rely on the following:

Geography

The ecosystem, the functioning and interacting systems of flora and fauna, climate and soil, has had an important part to play in the development of man's diet.(2.10)

2.8 Hagsdahl, C.E., *Kokkonst sone Vetenskap ock Konst* (Cooking as a Science and Art), Bonnier, Stockholm, 1879, p. 74.

2.9 Singer, C., *et al.*, A *History of Technology*, 5 vols, Clarendon Press, Oxford, 1954–8.

2.10 Hurst, M.E., A *Geography of Economic Behaviour*, Duxbury Press, Massachusetts, 1972, p. 72.

Climate

The climate sets limits to the available plant and animal life suitable for food. Each has an optional and marginal area of growth and development, which is imposed by prevailing and changing temperature, rainfall and frost-free requirements for both flora and fauna life.

Soil

The prevailing climate determines the soil conditions and growing potential. Thus the stiff boulder clay of the wetter parts of the earth make it ideal pasture and grazing land, while fine loam or silty soil is very fertile and ideally suited for the growing of grain crops of many types. The light, rich soil found near estuaries and rivers is suitable for growing vegetables and fruit.

Season

The season denotes a time when, in the circle of life and growth, a plant or animal may or may not be available for consumption, either because the climate does not bring it forth in the case of plants, or because animals, as a result of their own changing food needs, have migrated. In the case of domesticated animals, it could be the wrong time for slaughter – just before the new generation of animals is born.

Today the term 'in season' is considered by many to be out of date, as modern technology, in the form of fridges and freezers and other preservation methods, has made most foods available to man at almost any time.

From the gastronomical point of view, the term 'in season' has a different connotation; it means that not only is a certain food available, but that the food is available fresh, at its best, at the right stage of ripeness or age and at the best stage of yield. Combinations of the above will always be, and always remain, gastronomically important.

Most of us prefer fresh cauliflower to frozen, and appreciate the taste of a ripe to an under-ripe apple or pear. A plaice, however freshly caught, but caught out of season and heavy with roe, will yield smaller portions from the same weight as from one caught in season. The flesh of a plaice in season is more succulent, less oily, and much better-tasting.

Choosing the correct season does not necessarily mean having to deny ourselves fish, for nature has wisely arranged that different fish are in or out of season at different times.

Thus the four points of geography, climate, soil and season have, since time began, determined the availability of nourishment to man and limited or enhanced his choice according to time and place. The following two examples make this point very clearly: Eskimos exist almost entirely on a fish/meat diet, as fruits and vegetables are not readily available to them in the polar regions where they live. A similar diet is known to keep Caucasians and others in relatively good health for what is often a long life, without such diseases as rickets and scurvy normally associated with such a narrow diet. In contrast, the inhabitants of the tropical regions of the earth live well on a diet of mostly vegetables and fruit, with only a scant addition of protein in the form of flesh – fish or fowl – on special occasions.

It is not because the inhabitants of these contrasting parts of the world have different physiological needs one from another, for these needs are the same for every man, everywhere, but their more carnivorous- or more vegetarian-based diets are a result of the limits set on the availability of foods by the locally prevalent gastro-geography.

Selection

Thus from the locally available flora and fauna early man made his selection of suitable food. At first this was often a matter of trial and error. In lean times man would eat almost anything which he thought would give him nourishment, discovering in the process new foods not previously considered, including some not at all suitable, which often made him ill or even killed him.

When uncertain, particularly in new surroundings, man would observe animals and take the lead from them as to what might or might not be 'edible and agreeable diet for himself. In most cases, if not in all, did this observation serve him well.'(2.11)

When the season changed early man followed the animals as they migrated, and for some this led to the beginnings of a nomadic lifestyle. In his changing environment, besides learning from animals what was suitable for food, he also encountered people from other tribes, observing and, if allowed, partaking in their meals, thus discovering and tasting new foods, encountering new methods of preparation, and gradually incorporating these into his diet.

2.11 Hagsdahl, C.E., *Kokkonst sone Vetenskap ock Konst* (Cooking as a Science and Art), Bonnier, Stockholm, 1879, p. 37.

In times of plenty or in a particularly good season, man could be much more selective and eat only the foods he knew from experience that he liked, and which, besides satisfying his hunger, he would enjoy. Hagsdahl saw in this the first selection of food for man. Some factor of preference must also, particularly in times of plenty, have been exercised over the type of food man would select. It was not only the ones he liked best, but those which were easily available to him, from the nearest or lowest tree or bush to be had without too much hard work or exertion, conveniently available by just reaching out. Convenience food, in this respect at least, is really not all that new.

Yet, most of the time early man lived a life on the edge of mere existence and starvation. A good season might give him weeks of easy and plentiful supply but, for the rest of the year, it was hard work searching for food of all types, and trying new things and new ways to prepare it.

This selection of suitable foods for man has continued to this day. However, the selection of modern man has become one of contraction rather than one which would widen the scope of choice and variety. Maybe this contraction represents a conscious decision of modern man to eat only what he likes and prefers, others consider it more a lack of both nutritional and gastronomic imagination, particularly when we find that:

'One-fifth of the human race today lives almost solely on a rice-based diet, another fifth again lives almost solely on a grain diet. From the wealth of available plants, only 60 or so contribute to the Western world's vegetable/fruit consumption today. In contrast to this, the contemporary hunter-gatherer in the Gold Coast of Africa has been reported to consume 114 species of fruit, 46 kinds of leguminous seeds and 47 types of green vegetables. Of the thousands of edible species of wild animals, only about 50 have been successfully domesticated in various parts of the world.

'The Western world have taken their selection so far as to depend on only three (four), namely the ox, pig and sheep (fowl).'(2.12)

Selection has played a considerable part in what is acceptable to man as food, and what he is prepared to develop and bring to his table. In the Western world, this selection has narrowed to the same, few basic vegetables, fruits, fish and meats. Western civilisation seems to compensate the lack of variety of their contemporaries of the Gold Coast of Africa, by varying their few foods with highly developed methods of preparation. One can see clearly in this the development of cookery, *haute cuisine* and gastronomy.

2.12 Ebling, F., 'Man the Consumer: Attitudes to Food from the Stone Age to the Present', Edith Clark Lecture, University of Surrey, 1984.

Cultivation

Prior to the Neolithic revolution, man contributed nothing to the land – he merely had to look for food, reach for it and eat it. With the Neolithic revolution came a price to be paid: man's dependence on grain and the land on which it grew. In Genesis, Chapter 3, verse 9, we read:

'In the sweat of thy face shall thou eat thy bread, till thou returnest upon the ground.'

This now became the rule and has remained to this day. Man does not nowadays necessarily till the soil, but he must work in some form or other to pay for his nourishment. Yet, for the price to be paid, he gained considerable benefits. The early millennia of the Neolithic era became the years of discovery, development and expansion, nowhere more so than in respect of cultivation. Man was required to become involved in the provision of his daily bread and rose to the challenge.

Once the interdependence with plant and soil had been understood man gained the benefit of a more controlled harvest. Man quickly learned that his new-found wheat and other crops would grow best in the warm, fertile lowland regions and that in higher altitudes it would not fare so well.

In highland regions, two weeds were later developed as rye and oats, and were eventually to become the more suitable staple grain diet of the middle and northern European regions. In the Americas, the wild tomato, a then weed-pest accompanying the growth of, and thriving in the field of both maize and beans, was to become in this same way an extremely valuable supplement crop to what was and still is a mainly vegetarian diet in this part of the world.

Both in a nutritional and a gastronomical sense, the success of this one-time humble weed is not unique in the development by man who would now consider a salad not to be a salad without tomatoes; its almost universal acceptance should surprise no-one. One must not be surprised that in some parts of France at least, the people call this bright red, succulent and refreshing fruit (or is it a vegetable?) *le pomme d'amour*.

The development continued: man soon gave equal consideration to the important need for sun and water to grow his crops with more and more success:

'The farmers who strung out their farms and settlements by removing shrubs and trees, along the streams and rivers of the regions now known as "Khuzistan" at the head of the Persian Gulf, would break the banks of streams

and rivers to water their crops for better results. The water then flowed out in tiny canals for up to three or four miles, from either side of its sources, in what was to become the first of a primitive irrigation system known to exist at around 5,000 BC.*'(2.13)*

Gradually the farmers learned to improve and expand these irrigation systems and techniques, resulting in more and richer crops, and leading to what was to become a very sophisticated food administration system, which made no small contribution to the development and birth of Sumaria and, later, Egypt.

In pre-preparation, man prepared his ground, his soil, assisting nature to provide his nourishment in many different ways. By his thought, discoveries and endeavour, he gained a better life for himself and his family, and established what we know today as agriculture. The newly learned skills and knowledge gained from the cultivation of one crop were applied in the development and growing of other crops. This is particularly true in respect of vegetables which man had found wild, and made part of his daily diet.

Soon he brought even these under cultivation, securing a varied diet. Yet all was not well. Great fields of sprouting grain encouraged the multiplication of insect pests; and the storage of dried grain in the silos stimulated a population explosion among the smaller rodents.

Agriculture at this stage was concerned only with taking from the land as much as possible and as quickly as possible, often by two growing seasons a year, and giving nothing back to the soil. In three to four years the soil was exhausted. Man left the infertile patch and moved on to the next fertile patch, repeating the same mistake. He did not know why the crops failed and did not understand the need for crop rotation.

In the heartland of the Neolithic civilisation, the land which had been cleared of shrubs and trees, then overworked or overgrazed, often turned into deserts. Irrigation, thought to be the answer to bigger and better crops, ceased to give the early good results.

Neolithic man did not know or understand that unless he had good drainage, it leached out of the earth the nutrients essential for plant growth. The basic crop, wheat, began to fail. Added to this the Neolithic era experienced a population explosion. The children of this population explosion moved, settled and then, in turn, sent out new waves of people to even more distant lands. There they had to adapt to new gastro-geographic conditions in respect of both the seeds and the livestock which they took with them.

2.13 Flannery, K.V., in Ucko, P.J. and Dimbleby, G.W. (eds), *The Domestication of Plants and Animals*, Gerald Dunckworth & Co., London, 1969, p. 88.

Animal Husbandry

The lessons learned from the cultivation of Neolithic man's crops were gradually applied to the domestication of animals. The principles applied in giving crops the right ground and conditions to grow made sense in respect of getting the best out of what were to become the modern farm animals. For several reasons Neolithic man had to give some urgent thought and attention to the husbandry of wild animals. The fields of wild, and later cultivated, grain which appeared about twelve thousand years ago did more than feed mankind. They attracted a number of small animals also, which had begun to thrive and multiply in the open glades around the edges of forests and marshes. When man began to remove the shrubs and trees to cultivate his land, the sprouting crops of wheat must have been a considerable attraction to wild goats and sheep and, in many cases, these were a serious threat to the settlers' future food supplies.

Man could defend his newly cultivated fields: he could try to exterminate the animals or he could bring the animals under control, which had the double advantage of saving the crops and ensuring a meat supply to supplement the grain supply. The domestication of the first two animals, the goat and sheep, must have been a relatively easy task, for both are gregarious beasts, eating almost anything put before them, and where one is led, the rest will follow.

'Man may have helped in the more easy adaptation of these animals by adopting a baby-orphan, reared it by hand and the so-tamed ewe was allowed to mate with a wild sire. Thus in the course of a few years man would have quite easily established a village flock.'(2.14)

As to which was the first of these two animals to be domesticated, history favours the much maligned goat, closely followed by the sheep. The first stage of the domestication of the sheep is thought to have begun as early as 8,000 BC.(2.15)

The possibility does exist that both animals may have been instrumental in clearing the land for early cultivation. The goat's talent for devouring almost anything is well known. Likewise, the sheep's need for more than one hundredweight of greenery in a week might have made both animals the first agricultural labourers in history – they helped to clear the land for cultivation.

2.14 Reed, C.A., in Ucko and Dimbleby, *ibid.*, p. 361.

2.15 Higgs, E., and White, J., 'Autumn killing', *Antiquity*, no. 37, 1963.

The reason for the pig's late arrival on the domestic scene was that: 'The submerging agriculture and its surplus aided its late but very successful progress.'(2.16)

The prolific pig was an ideal food animal. It did not need to be herded, it could be kept in or close to the house or in a pen, and it was satisfied with a feed of roots and greens with the cooked wild grain and food debris of the household.

Cattle were the very last major food animal to be domesticated:

> *'The task may have been postponed, simply because of the very size of the animal. Though the ancestral type of early domestication cattle breed had died out in the seventeenth century, if the fierce and agile smaller modern version is anything to go by, Neolithic man must have really had his hands full to bring the ancient larger cattle under control. Once caught and secured, it was probably controlled by poor feeding, closepenning, hobbling and castration in the case of the bull.'(2.17)*

The ox, in particular, was soon to become a welcome labour animal for the land, and transport animal for emerging trade and commerce. Until now man had either eaten what nature provided or what he may or may not have liked. With the advent of the establishment of cultivation, man assisted nature or the local gastro-geography.

The Preparation Factor

The Neolithic revolution, at least in its latter moments, was responsible for the first stage of the development of gastronomy. Indeed, one could argue that it provided the basis, the first step, in gastronomical development as we understand the term today. I like to call this next important step the 'preparation factor'.

Early Grain Cooking

Man's sudden dependence on grain, whether from wild or cultivated fields, raises some interesting questions. What did the people of the early Neolithic period do

2.16 Perkins, D., 'Food and Science', *Science*, no. 11, 1969.
2.17 Tannahill, R., *Food in History*, Palladin, London, 1973, p. 40.

with all the grain? How did they prepare it for eating with little or no technology?

An ear of grain is made up of many layers, and only the very middle (the 'germ') gives any nutritional value to man. This germ, surrounded by starch and bran, forms the part known as the seed, the whole of which is contained in a harsh shell, the chaff.

Various methods were used for separating the seed from the chaff. These included roasting ears of corn before attempting to separate the two by themselves, and rubbing the grain in very early pestle and mortars.

Given that grain is notoriously indigestible however, the next step was to develop a good method of cooking it. In these very early times, before pottery was in use, that was not as simple as it might have been. The method highlighted by most historians is a continuation of the roasting method mentioned above. The threshing floor of a barn would be heated by fire to a high enough temperature to cook the grain, as well as making the chaff brittle enough to splinter off. To make the resulting dry grain the least bit appetising, water would be added until the resulting mixture formed the grain-paste that was a standard feature of classical diets.

This grain-paste was a remarkable nutritional breakthrough for pre-historic man. The fact that food could now be prepared in advance and taken on journeys opened up realms of opportunity. It is even more remarkable to think that almost exactly the same food is a staple of diets around the world today, differing only in the basic grain used. It was improved gradually with a little fat, and by being exposed to heat, firstly on hot stoves, later on flat metal sheeting. The result became today's Greek maza, Indian chappati, Mexican tortilla, Scots oat cake and Scandinavian knakebrot – all examples of the first type of unleavened bread.

Although the paste improved when cooked however, there was the disadvantage that the final product was distinctly worse when a few days old. Uncooked grain-paste therefore remained the norm for neolithic man.

The Discovery and Making of Beer

In Sumer several types of beer seem to have been made, some from barley, some from wheat, and others from a mixture of grains. The Goddess of Ninkasi was said to be guiding and overlording the making of beer and it was she who 'baked and shovelled with lofty shovels the sprouted barley'.(2.18)

2.18 Kramer, S.N., *The Sumerians: Their History, Culture and Character*, Chicago University Press, Chicago, 1964, p. 10.

'A Greek saga tells of the god Dionysus fleeing from Mesopotamia in disgust because the people were so addicted to beer, or, more correctly, to ale, as hops and other bitter herbs necessary to make beer were not discovered and used until the end of the Middle Ages.'(2.19)

Beer making may most most certainly have first evolved from methods of making early breads. The Neolithic housewife had learned how to make more digestible bread by leaving it to sprout, for she had discovered that sprouted grain which was then allowed to dry and pounded would make better bread and keep longer than bread made from conventionally available grain flour.

'It is almost certain that the early Egyptians made beer not from grain but from bread, which was made from sprouted barley or wheat. These specially made bread loaves were broken up in pieces and soaked in water and were allowed to ferment for 2–3 days. After this simple fermentation the resulting liquor was drained and the earliest simple ale was ready to drink.'(2.20)

Egyptian brewers made a considerable variety of spiced and flavoured beer breads and their customers had a correspondingly wide range of brews to choose from.(2.21)

The brewers were in most cases women, who sold their beers from their houses to the neighbourhood. For a very long time the making of beer was a hit or miss affair, for the presence of the micro-organism which cause fermentation, even in the hot climate of Egypt, was a fortuitous matter. But brewers gradually observed that the old beer-making jar, full of chips and cracks ideal for bacteria, would make a better beer than the shiny new ones.

But until yeast came along and allowed the more controlled production of ale, most drinkers must have looked forward to each new brew with some anticipation if not trepidation as to what it would be like. *Haz* was the commonly used name for beer drunk in early Egypt. By all accounts it was a relatively mild brew but occasionally some beer would have an alcohol content of as much as 10 to 12 per cent if conditions were right. Not surprisingly we find in the Code of Hammurabi, written about 1750 BC, the familiar condemnation of 'the evils of ale houses and their under-strength and over-priced beers'.(2.22)

2.19 Singer, C., *et al.*, *A History of Technology*, 5 vols, Clarendon Press, Oxford, 1954–8, p. 279.

2.20 Wiedeman, A., *Das Alte Aegypten* (Old Egypt), Heidelberg, 1920, p. 299.

2.21 Singer, C., *et al.*, *A History of Technology*, 5 vols, Clarendon Press, Oxford, 1954–8, p. 279.

2.22 Saggs, H.W.F., *Everyday Life in Babylonia and Assyria*, Batsford, London and Putman, New York, 1965, p. 137.

Advice given on an Egyptian papyrus dated about 1,400 BC remains good to this day:

'Do not get drunk in the taverns in which they sell and drink beer for fear that people repeat words which have gone out of our mouth without our being aware of having uttered them.'(2.23)

Ale remained the favoured drink along the Nile, but as irrigation spoiled the soil and excessive farming made the soil infertile, grains became more difficult to grow. There very soon was no grain to spare for making beer, and so the Sumerians and Egyptians changed to drinking wine made from dates and, later, to wine imported from Greece and made from grapes. The making of wine would again be a worthy example of man's developing preparation, thought and skill.

Raised Bread

The thought and skill that went into the development of raised bread is a particularly good example of the preparation factor applied by early man. Egypt is reputedly the place where leavened bread is thought to have been discovered, although the evidence is very elusive, and the probable date even more so. The prerequisite for leavened bread was a particular kind of wheat – other grains and early wheat were unsuitable for leavening because of their chemical composition.

Conditions in Egypt in early historical times favoured the development of such special wheat – in Sumaria, wheat had already become scarce. This new wheat contained gluten-forming proteins in its starchy endosperm. Yeast, under favourable conditions, produces carbon dioxide gas. Mix the flour of the new wheat and yeast with water and the result is a spongy mass containing gas bubbles in an elastic framework. The subsequent application of heat will force the gas bubbles to the surface but, trapped in a tight gluten coat, they will, in rising, raise the bread. Heat will make the bread crusty and leave it almost permanently in its raised shape. But if the crucial gluten protein had been subjected to heat before being brought into contact with yeast, as was the custom with the early toasted and sprouted grain, the elasticity was lost and the loaves became hard and would not rise in the baking process.

As in most early discoveries, the observations made in respect of more elastic and raised bread were accidental. Favourable micro-organisms must have drifted

2.23 Quoted by Myer, J., *The Oldest Book in the World*, Kegan Paul Ltd., London, 1900, p. 132.

into the bread-dough of the new wheat type, and inquiring minds must have set about to reproduce the likeable accident.

Observation showed that fermentation was in some way involved, which man had learned in the making of his early ale, for various fermenting agents were introduced to the dough deliberately to make raised bread. Pliny commented 'that some natural sourness would make the dough ferment'.(2.24)

The leaven used for the raising of bread came from various sources, for example, the skimming of the froth of fermenting beer and the sour milk of goats and sheep. In Greece and Italy, where no beer was made and where the people did not drink beer, the bread-dough was dipped in grape-juice or wine until it had the required sourness for fermentation. But the recommended method evolving was to keep a piece of sour-dough from one day's bake as the starter for the next day's bake.

This sour-dough starter was used most successfully by my grandmother in her twice-weekly family bake as late as 1938. In many parts of Europe today, it is still preferred to the commercially produced and readily available block-yeast, especially in the making of various types of rye bread.

The new wheat had not only the described gluten-protein properties, it also parted more readily from its chaff than the earlier types, and needed no roasting before being made into the new flour. However, the production of yeast-leavened bread was time-consuming and expensive, and in early Egypt it was produced mostly for the household of the king and other wealthy people. The average Egyptian went on to chew the old, flat, hard bread, as the worn teeth of surviving Egyptian skulls of that period clearly show.(2.25)

The fact that the bread could be made only with a particular type of wheat, not yet widely grown, allied to the demanding nature of the flour-making process and then the making of the bread itself, restricted the production of raised bread for several thousands of years to come. Even as late as the Middle Ages, leavened wheat bread was uncommon in most parts of Europe.

These examples of the eventual making of raised bread serve well to explain what the writer means by the 'preparation factor'. Not only did early man have to solve each important and distinct task to reach raised bread, but the tasks had to be solved in the correct order to give the final result of 'our daily raised bread'. Namely:

- preparation of grain;
- preparation and making of unleavened bread (leading to beer breads);

2.24 Tannahill, R., *Food in History*, Palladin, London, 1973.

2.25 Ruffer, M.A., *Abnormalities of Ancient Teeth: Studies in Palaeopathology of Egypt*, Chicago University Press, Chicago, 1921, p. 288.

* preparation of new grain using fermentation (to produce raised bread).

All of these, by whatever means, show purely human acts guided by accident, observation, thought and learned skills.

Storage Factor

The next important factor to be considered must be those thoughts and developing skills man gave to the storage and subsequent preservation of his food: to carry what was still a very scarce commodity from times of plenty to times of lean.

Again, the development of storage is a very human act. Although there are animals which store or hoard some of their food, the way in which man stored and preserved his food is unique. It very much reflects the gradually developing human ability to postpone stimulus and response, or availability and continuous eating, as well as the very human act of foresight that one may wish to eat tomorrow as well. In many respects, the storage and gradual development of the preservation of food is a natural follow-up to the preparation factor considered above. In the natural sequence of events, storage is the first factor we should consider. With a more controlled and continuous food supply available, food had to be protected from wind and weather as well as from the emerging pests, for example, rodents, after the harvest.

We see here a new factor which influenced the rapid development of new storage containers, giving man the much discussed early and important pottery storage jar of early Egypt. How and when pottery was discovered and developed was discussed above. Later findings seem to confirm the speculation.

> *'An oven was found containing more than 2,000 fire-baked pieces of clay, in the form of tiny models of animals, their heads, bodies and feet dating from about 25,000* BC *during excavation at Dolni Vestonice in Moravia.'(2.26)*

This finding at least seems to suggest that the principles of the making of pottery were understood long before the time pottery was thought to have been invented. Whenever it was invented, it is almost certain that pottery making was a most welcome and necessary invention to early man.

The making and large-scale production of pottery jars received a new and

2.26 Coles, J.M. and Higgs, E.S., *The Archaeology of Early Man*, Faber & Faber, London, 1969, p. 296.

important impetus around 6,000 to 5,000 BC. Easily breakable, but equally easily replaceable, pottery jars became available in large numbers, in various sizes, and for varying uses. Ideally suitable for the storage of dry goods, such as grain, grain-flour and pulses, pottery jars were also used for the carrying and storage of liquids, especially water and milk, and also fresh and dried berries, fruits and vegetables.

Fermentation Factor

To store dry grain and other dried pulses in large pottery jars is one thing, to apply this method of storage to liquids, such as milk or fruit juices, or fruit and berries quite another. Yet this led to the making of beer, raised bread, wine, vinegar and, later, cheese from sour or curdled milk. The storage of 'soft' items of foods in pottery jars was to add a whole new dimension to the preparation factor, as well as new variety to man's diet.

Preservation Factor

Preservation was a more gradual act of man, combining his thoughts with a long-term observation of nature. There is no way of knowing now when the various preservation methods were discovered, understood and generally used.

Freezing

Conditions during the glacial ice periods in mid- and southern Europe must have been favourable for early man's gradual understanding of the preserving effects of ice and extreme cold on his food. For example, when man had killed a large animal and could carry only parts of it back to his village, on his return to collect the remaining part of the carcass he would find, in pre-Neolithic times, that it would be frozen, or at least well-chilled.

Whether he ever made the connection between frozen and chilled meat and better preserved meat is not recorded. However, when the ice age receded to the more northern parts of Europe, we find the deliberate preservation of food by freezing and chilling recorded as late as the Middle Ages.(2.27)

2.27 Nylen, A.M., *Hemslöjd* (Cottage Industries), Hapstan Solna, Sweden, 1969, p. 117.

Drying

The understanding of the process of drying and preserving food must have been aided by the natural drying of vegetables, such as beans and peas, in their pods and on the bush. The flaying winds which swept the northern hemisphere in the period between 20,000 and 15,000 BC must have helped this process and its understanding. In many countries of northern and south-eastern Europe today, beans, peas and other crops are dried in this way by small farmers: bushels of peas and beans, still in their pods, hang upside-down from the eaves of houses. Cold and flaying winds may have also aided the development of drying of pieces of meat and fish.

Smoking

The full understanding of the preserving properties of smoke must have come only when man used fire for warmth and cooking as a matter of fact in everyday life, allowing all types of meat, fish and fowl to be, if at first by accident, exposed to fire and smoke.

The process has continued to this day and in the last twenty years or so has even been applied to the smoking of cheese. With today's preservation methods, modern man does not really have to preserve his food by smoking any more as better and simpler methods are available. The important point to make here is that the smoked food attained a particular and distinct flavour to which man became accustomed and which, today, he would not wish to miss.

Salting

Almost since the beginning of time, and certainly since the beginning of recorded history, salt has been a vital ingredient in man's diet and important in the economy of some nations. As Cassiodorus is thought to have said: 'It may be that some seek no gold, but there lives not a man who does not need and seek salt.'(2.28)

The salting of fish and meat has a long and chequered history, the origin of which remains obscure. But we find a definite link in early Egypt: salt was used for the embalming of the bodies of the dead, so why not for the preserving of food for the living?(2.29)

2.28 Quoted by Molmenti, P.G., *Venice, Its Growth to the Fall of the Republic*, vol. II, John Murray, London, 1906–8, pp. 14–17.

2.29 Forbes, R.J., *Studies in Ancient Technology*, vol. II, E.G. Brill, Leiden, 1955–8, p. 174.

Salt-mines are well documented in the Old Testament, and salt was mined from land lakes and obtained from the sea. The quality of salting and brining varied from place to place and without, as yet, a reliable system of weights and measures, the preserving of various foods by salt remained for a long time a hit or miss affair. Instead of preserving his food, early man could, more often than not, spoil it by over-salting. On the other hand, too little salt would not have the desired preserving effect, and the meat would go rancid. However, the early Egyptians got the balance right and began to run a thriving trade in salted and dried fish. In the first century BC, Strabo reported that the fish salting industries in Spain were 'not unimportant'.(2.30)

Christianity did much for the salting industry. Lent, the forty-day fast which preceded Easter, made fish an essential commodity. It was easily obtainable near the sea, but inland fresh fish was not readily available and salted fish took its place. So strict were the rules of Lent that even as late as the mid-sixteenth century, it was still possible for an Englishman to be hanged for eating meat on a Friday.(2.31)

So it is not surprising that salting became a big and profitable industry, in respect of fish at least, to secure a good supply for Lent and for Fridays. In Medieval times, salting and brining became important when farms and smaller households could not feed their livestock through the winter and so slaughtered it and salted it down. Salt, however, was very expensive and could add as much as 40 per cent to the cost of the meat to be salted. For this reason only the best animals and the choicest cuts were salted. It is not surprising that comparatively little lamb or mutton seems to have been preserved by salt for the winter, its tough, fatty meat was 'not worth its salt'.

The storage and subsequent preservation factor was to have considerable and important influences on the gastronomical developments of diets throughout the ages in nearly all parts of the world, but particularly in Europe.

Gastro-geographical Belts

In consideration of climate, soil and season, the early gastronomic world was partitioned into three different belts, each with a different flora and fauna from which man made his selection for his nourishment. In their very basic model, the three gastro-gastronomical belts may be considered as follows:

2.30 *Ibid.*, p. 180.

2.31 Hibbert, C., *The Roots of Evil: A Social History of Crime and Punishment*, Penguin, London, 1966, p. 37.

Figure 2.1 Basic gastro-geographical belts
Source: Drawn by James Llewellyn-Smith to instruction of the author

Northern Belt

This gives us the grain, root, fish, game, pig and cattle belt and its subsequent bread, vegetable, fish, meat diet. The original beverages of this belt were all grain based, such as the whisky of Scotland and ales of England, the beers and Schnapps of Scandinavia and Germany, as well as the vodkas of the Russo-Polish regions.

Middle Belt

This is the rice, fruit wine and cheese belt. Again, climate, season and soil are the basic relevant factors. Its many pastoral and mountain regions with goats, sheep and, later, cattle, make it the natural birthplace of one of the oldest of man-made foods – cheese.

The rice-based diet of this belt almost circles the world and is represented in basic dishes such as the *paellas* of Spain, the *risottos* of Italy and the *pilaffs* of the Balkan and the Middle East countries. A basic rice diet can be seen in some form or other in India, China, Indonesia and Japan.

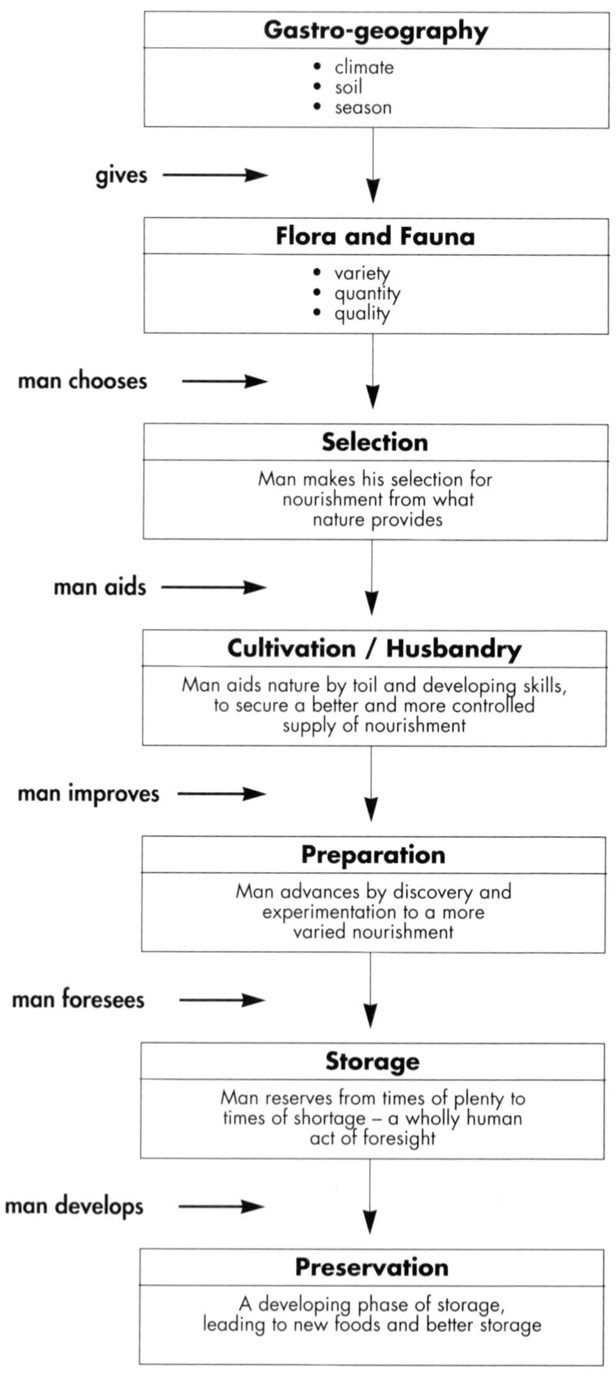

Figure 2.2 Availability factors
Source: Drawn by James Llewellyn-Smith to instruction of the author

The grain-based drinks of the north are here replaced by fruit- and rice-based beverages, represented by the red and white wines of Spain in the west, to Italy, and the Balkan and south Russian regions in the east. The stronger spirits are also fruit- or wine-based, such as the *brandies* from wine, *calvados* from apples, *slibovitz* based on plums, or *Kirsch* from cherries, as well as numerous liquors based on herbs or fruits.

The basic drink pattern is interrupted by climatic as well as strictly religious reasons in the Near and Middle East, but it reappears as an important part of the diet and eating further east in the form of rice wine and stronger rice-based spirits. These regions have also given the world man's oldest non-alcoholic drinks – tea and coffee.

Southern Belt

Represented by parts of Africa, South America and other Southern regions, this belt is less clearly defined in its basic diets because of the dietary influence and customs of early European immigrants. But it is true to say that we could call it the herb and spice belt, with a vegetable-based, almost vegetarian-based, diet. Only in parts was its diet influenced by the fish and meat, and milk and cheese dishes, of Europeans. The diet has made a considerable contribution to the world's gastronomy in the form of such products as peppers, potatoes, tomatoes, cocoa, tea and coffee.

Gastro-geography	**Flora and Fauna**	**Selection**	**Cultivation/ Husbandry**	**Preparation**	**Storage**	**Preservation**
• climate • soil • season	• variety • quantity • quality	Man makes his selection for nourishment from what nature provides	Man aids nature by toil and development, to secure a controlled supply	Advancement by skill, discovery and experimentation to a more varied nourishment. Application of heat cookery	Man reserves from times of plenty to times of shortage – a wholly human act of foresight	A developing phase of storage, producing more foods and new composition of foods and flavours

Figure 2.3 Gastronomic and cultural step-by-step ascent
Source: Drawn by James Llewellyn-Smith to instruction of the author

The drinks of the southern belt are not clearly defined and, where they originally existed, were of the simpler fermentation process. Later European influence coloured their production and names

Changing Patterns?

The South American tomato may now grow in an English garden, Arabian coffee in Columbia, the maize of Mexico now thrives in Spain and in the American mid-West now graze European cattle. Many species of southern flora, such as herbs and spices, have been successfully transplanted to other more northerly belts, when others have stubbornly refused to accept new climate soil and different seasons.

Yet allowing for this expansion of the world of foods, it is remarkable how much of the base diets of people within these belts has stayed within the limitations provided by climate, soil and season.

Figure 2.4 takes account of the possible gastronomical limitations and advances a little further by suggesting, via the expansion of the world of food in

Continental Limit	**Expansion of the World**	**National Character**	**Regional Character**	**Cultural Character**	**Social status**	**Personal attitudes**
Food limited to continent, prevailing technology and experience	World expansion brings gastronomic exposure, new foods, new methods of preparation, new attitudes, and import and export of food	Prevailing supply and methods develop national preference, character and attitudes to food and eating	Living in regional parts of nation – familiar with common foods but lack of wider opportunity. Compare experience of man in London, Devon or Paris	Gastronomic opportunity determined by: • family • education • religion • friends • peer group • work type	Gastronomic opportunity affected by social status: • social class • economic band • male • female • child • labourer • sedentary worker	Experience affected by individual interest in food, and personal likes and dislikes. Individual may be a traditionalist, adopter, adapter, innovator or technologist with regard to food and eating

Figure 2.4 Continental, national, regional, religious, social, cultural, personal development of attitudes to food
Source: Drawn by James Llewellyn-Smith to instruction of the author

the widest sense, a developing national, regional, cultural, social and individual, as well as religious, character and attitude to food and eating. This evolution will be further considered in subsequent chapters.

Application of Heat

Most of early man's discoveries, particularly in respect of food, were made by observing nature and accidents which occurred within the 'preparation factor' in their daily lives and toil. This most certainly applies to the application of heat to food and the subsequent gradual discovery of early cooking methods. This would have happened only as part of the 'availability factor', making fire available as an everyday occurrence.

In Chapter 1, man's earliest contact with fire and application of heat to foods was considered. It was, however, very important, regardless of whenever or wherever it happened, that it should not be called 'cooking'. Prehistoric man may have made some of his food more digestible, nutritious and palatable by applying heat, but cooking and cookery as we understand it today means so very much more than the mere application of heat.

We are not sure when and where the common and intentional application of heat really happened. What we do know is that Peking man was the first likely candidate to use fire, and that he may have applied heat to some of his food. We also know that during the Neolithic revolution, fire was used intentionally for warmth and, possibly, for preparing some foods.

For this reason we must begin a new line of sequential development in respect of cooking and cookery. This, in my opinion, should start somewhere just before, or possibly at the position of, 'selection' showing a parallel and important line with a very obvious effect or effects one upon the other (Figure 2.5).

The application of heat may give some recognition to the beginnings of cookery and does, in some cases, identify early and simple cooking methods still recognisable today, but cannot be called cookery as yet.

Cookery

It is probable that the advancement of cooking and cookery really developed from the point where man found a vessel to separate the food to be cooked from

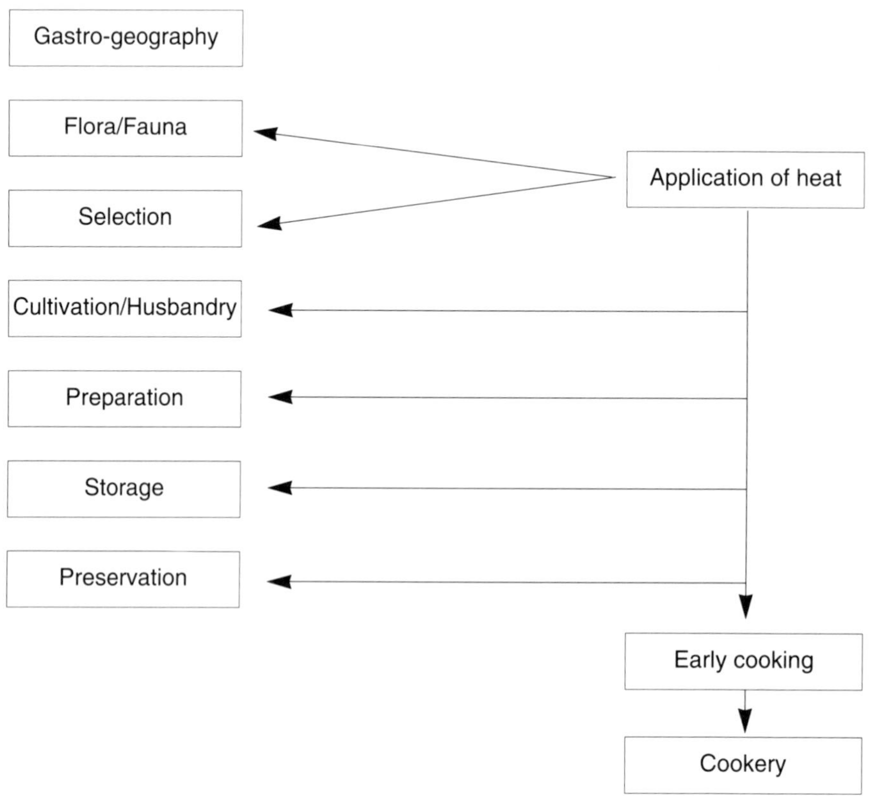

Figure 2.5 Likely development of cookery according to time and place
Source: Drawn by James Llewellyn-Smith to instruction of the author

the as yet uncontrollable flames of the open fire. That stage of development came with the manufacture of pottery containers.

We may argue whether pottery was made firstly for cooking, and then adapted for storage, or vice versa. Be this as it may, what is important is that the vessel had arrived, and was commonly available.

Cookery is much more than the mere application of heat. In my opinion, as well as that of many other professionals in the field, cookery is considered to combine three different aspects, namely:

* preparation;
* cooking (application of heat);
* presentation.

Preparation

This is the first stage in the understanding of modern cooking, and an aspect of the 'preparation factor' which early man would recognise as part of their largely vegetarian diet. In the case of modern cookery, it means the preparation of various foods for consumption which may, but not necessarily, need the application of heat, or the need for cooking, for example:

- a compound salad, made from various vegetables and fruits and flavoured with a simple dressing;
- a fruit fool made from a purée of fresh fruit and whipped cream;
- a roll of savoury butter.

But the term preparation or, better still, pre-preparation for cooking or *mise-en-place*, is also an important part of foods and dishes where the application of heat is necessary, for example:

- choosing the right meat, fish, fowl for a given dish;
- choosing the right part, joint or cut for a given dish;
- choosing the right size, shape or form for a given dish;
- choosing the right coating, for example, flour, crumb and batter for a given method of preparation and cooking.

Cooking

In the first place consideration should be given to the right, or maybe preferred, method of cooking, which may be chosen from the following modern classifications.

Table 1: Modern classifications of cooking

WET METHODS	DRY METHODS	FAT-ASSISTED METHODS
boiling	roasting	deep frying
poaching	baking	shallow frying
steaming	grilling	some types of grilling
stewing	*en papilotte* (bag)	griddling
braising		
pot-roasting		

Then the right vessel must be selected – the pot or pan best suited for the commodity and method of cooking to be employed. The best source of heat and or energy comes next.

While heat is being applied other and often more important parts of cooking and cookery have to be considered:

- joints have to be turned;
- roasts basted;
- shapes tossed;
- liquids stirred;
- dough proven;
- portions tested;
- something removed;
- something added.

In short, while heat is applied to various foods, the food is nursed by various and continuous consideration to both nutritional and gastronomical perfection. This is particularly important with the more advanced compositional cookery, where several different commodities are combined and cooked in the same vessel. More often than not, flavouring a given dish is achieved by the cooking method employed and the compositional additions made at the beginning of cooking, during cooking, or after the end of the cooking process, quite apart from the addition of seasonings, herbs and spices.

Presentation

Presentation is the last, but not the least, of the three distinct stages of modern cookery. The most nutritious and tasty of foods will not be acceptable nor fully appreciated when brought to the table heaped willy nilly on to the plate or platter. How food will look at the point of consumption must always be of prime concern. It is not, however, a matter of presentation alone; what early stages have not considered, presentation will not put right. Good, modern cookery gives thought to all three stages – preparation, cooking and presentation.

As we shall see, much consideration has been given throughout the ages to the presentation of our food. The development of pottery made it first possible, and it has continued with earthenware, chinaware, glassware, crystalware and silverware. The use of cutlery of whatever metal, a linen tablecloth and napkins are all to be considered when presenting our daily bread at its best. Indeed, the very table itself is part of this development of the presentation of food, which has played a not inconsiderable part in raising man's food and man himself from the ground.

CHAPTER 3

The European Tale

Daily Life in Ancient Greece

Precise facts about Ancient Greece are scarce. However, the life of the people can be assessed and understood with the help of the writings of philosophers, historians and poets, and from plays and dramas. Some conclusions can also be drawn from archaeological sites and from drawings and paintings on Greek vases and other artefacts, as well as wall-reliefs.

The streets of Athens around the fourth century BC were narrow, winding and dirty, full of refuse and filth. Street cleaning and lighting were unknown. Houses in classical Greece were relatively small and only occasionally of the two-storey type. Built from air-dried bricks, they were of square design, with an inner yard from which one had sheltered access to all rooms, which also gave added light by small windows and doors. Windows to the street were not common, and existed only when the building was of two storeys.

The size and design of dwelling did not vary much between rich and poor. The richer inhabitants of Athens, however, had the whole house for living and entertaining, whereas the poorer working people had to give some of the space in the house to their workshops or offices, and also to any beast of burden they may have used. The accommodation of the men and women was strictly separate. When the dwelling was of two storeys, the women and younger children, and all the slaves, occupied the upper floor.

The rooms were seldom large, but they were square and varied from about 15 to 50 square yards. The men's hall, however, was somewhat larger and essential to almost every home. This would also be the most elegantly furnished room. Yet furnishing was very spartan, almost simple, consisting of wooden boxes for both storage and seating, low tables and simple bed-couches. The latter were called klines, and were the most important pieces of furnishing in any home.

Built on an oblong wooden frame and feet, which in exceptional cases might be made of ivory, the frame of the kline was covered with a mattress filled with either hay or straw or, in richer houses, with sheep's wool. A colourful wool blanket covered the mattress.

Figure 3.1 Greek-Roman dining-room (triclinum) with eating sofas (klines)
Source: Hellenic and Roman Culture, Stehle J Nordhausen, 1891

The kline served as a bed for sleeping, but also it was an essential item of furnishing in the men's hall upon which the Greeks lay to eat and drink, think and discuss, and philosophise. Even though the Hellenes loved things of beauty, colour and form, they had at the same time strong taboos against the excesses of life, including their house furnishings. When as late as the fifth century BC, Alcibiades, a friend of Socrates, had the walls of his house decorated with paintings and murals by a famous stage designer and artist, he gained more reproaches than praise.

The male citizen of Athens did not consider his house as important a space or possession as the modern European does. He lived most of his life outside his house in the places of philosophy, of politics or commerce, of arts and sports. The life of the ladies, however, was almost solely limited to the house and family. Second wives or mistresses were common. No lady had any of the much-discussed freedoms and rights. She was just like a slave, unacceptable for simple purchases or contracts of sale – all this was the sole right of the master of the household. The master of the house would, after a bath assisted by a slave, leave the house in the morning accompanied by another slave. He would go to the market to make purchases for the daily requirements of the household. As he had left the house on an empty stomach, he would seek sustenance in the form of a snack or simple meal from the many professional food-sellers on the streets or in the marketplace. Here he would make the necessary purchases for the daily needs of the household as far as food was concerned. The accompanying slave would be sent home with the urgently needed fresh food items, while the bulkier purchases would be delivered by the traders to the house.

On his arrival home, the slave would deliver the foods to the lady of the house, who would delegate to the individual slaves the various tasks in the preparation of the only real meal of the day – the all-important evening meal. Such mealtimes as breakfast, lunch and dinner were not yet known, and until the big evening meal, the members of the household would be content with eating fruits, nuts, figs, and drinking wine mixed with water, or sometimes milk to refresh themselves during the day.

But things were changing, particularly in the lower, hard-working classes in Athens. In their toil these folk needed a more ordered and more regular supply of food two or three times a day, and some of these new eating habits moved upwards to the upper classes of the Hellenic nation. Hippocrates expressed great surprise and some concern when he became aware of these new eating customs, remarking that 'in these good times some had begun and could eat three full meals a day and like it once they got used to it'.(3.1)

After the purchase of the fresh food in the markets, the master of the household, the free citizen of Athens, gave his time to the more leisurely pursuits and interests of a gentleman of Greece. He gave his time to state political interest, or just to meet his friends to discuss the latest issues of political interest, including gossip of a social nature.

He might also visit places of learning, give time to the management of his estates, or simply visit his mistress. During this time the ladies of the household looked after the house and the children. This applied especially to the girls or young ladies in the family who, until the age of fifteen or sixteen, were instructed in the various tasks and duties of the household, so that one day soon they would be able to run a home of their own. By the age of sixteen or so, they were considered ready for what was often an arranged marriage.

At about the same age a boy or young man would be handed over to padagogos, pedagogues or literary slaves to be educated for the more serious responsibilities of adult life as a gentleman of Athens. The pedagogues were sometimes elderly male relatives, but mostly they were educated slaves whose duties were not only to impart knowledge and etiquette to their young charges, but also to protect them from both female and male lovers who were only too

3.1 Pullar, P., *Consuming Passion*, Sphere Books, London, 1970.

eager to introduce them to the delights of love and sex within the new era of freedom, love and beauty.

Sometimes, the youth would be taken by his father to the market to be introduced to the commercial life and duties of the household, and to make him familiar with the purchasing or selling of, or bargaining for, goods. When a little older, the boy might be taken by his father to a political meeting or discussion in the Forum, or be exposed to, or even partake in, the delights of athletic festivals and competitions.

Food and Drink of Ancient Greece

The markets of Athens and other large towns in Greece were the larder supplies of food for the nation. To judge by modern standards, the variety of basic foods, fresh, partly, or wholly prepared, was considerable. Bakeries sold numerous types of breads, of rye, barley, wheat, in varying shapes and sizes and with various additions such as sesame or poppy seeds or enriched with olives, figs, raisins or dates. Assorted sweet cakes were also available sweetened with honey, whitened with milk, and again varying in size and shape, and which could be flavoured with raisins, dates, figs or herbs of different types. Butchers offered all kinds of meat, such as antelope, beef, pork, kid, goat and lamb; and meat preparations, such as joints, crowns, offal, hams, trotters, potted meats, pâtés, and sausages of various types and flavours. Poulterers sold chicken, duck, fowl, fox-goose, goose and ham; and game, such as grouse, partridge, peacock, pheasant, pigeon, quail, swallow, swan and thrush for the table of the Ancient Greek.(3.2)

The vegetable market made available to them beets, beans, green beans, cabbages, cauliflowers, celery, cucumbers, cress, endives, fennel, greens, leeks, lettuce, marrow, mushrooms, nettles, olives, onions, palm shoots, papyrus shoots, peas, peppers, radishes, turnips, truffles and tubers of many types as well as pulse of beans, lentils and chick peas.(3.3)

The table would be enriched with such fruit as apples, figs (fresh or dried), grapes (white, green or red), melons, mulberries, peaches, pears, plums, pomegranates, pumpkins and quinces, which might be eaten in combination with almonds, pine nuts, pistachio nuts, hazelnuts, walnuts and raisins.

Greek fishmongers would have given the fishmonger of today some considerable competition with their offerings of freshwater and salt-water fish,

3.2 Gulick, C.B., *Athenaeus*, *The Deipnosophis*, vols 1–7, Heinemann, London, 1927.

3.3 *Ibid*.

such as boar-fish, bass, carp, cod, dogfish, eel, grey-fish, herring, lamprey, mackerel, octopus, perch, pigfish, plaice, sardines, sprats, sturgeon, trout, turtle, tuna and turbot. Available shellfish included crab, crayfish, crawfish, lobster, prawns and shrimps, as well as cockles, oysters, mussels, snails and periwinkles. Besides such fresh fish named above, fish when out of season would be available pickled, salted or smoked, including some fish preparation of various pickles and fish pastes. The Greeks liked their dishes to be spiced and flavoured, and besides olive oil used for salads and cooking, giving a particular flavour to food, salt was the main seasoning.

To give variety of flavour, herbs and spices were added, such as anise, basil, bay-leaves, cummin, caraway, dill, marjoram, mint, mustard, oregano, poppy-seed, rapeseed, sage, savory and thyme, both wild and cultivated. The imported and much more expensive flavourings, such as coriander from Persia and pepper from India, were less commonly used even in the finer houses.

The greatest gastronomic contribution of Greece, however, must be the development of wine-making on a large and controlled scale, thus adding sister wine to brother food. The development was a gradual one, producing many different wines, mostly red, strong and sweet, but also some of the first white wines ever produced by man based on grapes cultivated on Caucasian vines, brought to Greece for this purpose. It is true that many consider wine-making to be an Egyptian invention – they are thought to have made wine 2,000 years BC, but this wine was made from dates not from grapes, and was used almost entirely for temple rituals.(3.4)

It was, however, not until Greek influence began to be felt in Egypt in the first millennium BC that (grape) vineyards were established along the Nile and elsewhere around the Mediterranean and wine became the common popular drink.

It is very possible that the Greek wine-makers and wine-shippers exported to secular Egypt the knowledge that they had once, maybe unconsciously, imported from priestly Egypt. That the above-mentioned foods and wines were available and eaten or drunk is now a well-accepted fact. As to how these foods and wines were prepared, cooked and presented, we are less sure. We know much more about how they were regarded, eaten and enjoyed than prepared, cooked and presented – a common shortcoming in early gastronomical knowledge.

The remains of Greek household and kitchen utensils which have been found, although not common, do help us to understand the methods used by the Ancient Greeks to prepare and cook their food. Most household goods were made of pottery, as were containers for jewellery, ornaments and cosmetics, decorative vases, oil lamps and the ever-present water jug.

The kitchen was strewn with pottery of all types, large storage jars of all

---

3.4 Tannahill, R., *Food in History*, Palladin, London, 1973, p. 78.

Figure 3.2 The pressing of grapes in Egypt
Source: Emanuel Ranke, Mohr. JEB Tübingen, 1924

shapes and sizes containing water, wine, oil, grain, grain-flours, and pulses such as beans and peas, nuts, herbs and spices. On shelves or tables one would find earthenware pots, casseroles, bowls, sieves, saucers and platters, dishes for mixing and blending, as well as plates and platters for presentation.

In the hall between the kitchen and dining hall one would find wine-mixing jugs, wine jugs, wine cups and beakers, wine clarifiers (decanters), wine coolers and, in very good houses in late Ancient Greece, maybe the first wine glasses. Utensils in the kitchen or dining hall would, according to the excellence of the finish, their form, shape and decoration, be considered items of luxury. Glass was introduced into culinary use and, less often, one would find utensils of metal silver or gold.(3.5)

That we know much more about the availability and eating of food in Ancient Greece, and very little about the preparation and cooking of food, is not really that surprising, for two reasons:

First, nearly all foods were prepared and cooked by illiterate slaves trained to prepare certain foods in a certain repetitive way. They were usually under the supervision of an older kitchen-slave, the lady of the house, or, in the case of more humble abodes, the housewife, all of whom were uneducated. Thus, recipes and modes of preparation were never or seldom written down, but handed down from one generation to the next by mouth. Improvements and advances that did

3.5 Gulick, C.B., *Athenaeus*, *The Deipnosophis*, vols 1–7, Heinemann, London and New York, 1927.

Figure 3.3 The mixing of wine in Egypt
Source: Emanuel Ranke, Mohr. JEB Tübingen, 1924

take place reflected more often than not the gradually emerging technology in the kitchen, or came about by accident. In this way many advances were imposed rather than developed.

Slaves had no time or inclination to think, improve or develop things associated with the preparation of food. The daily menus, even at the best of houses, were by our standards modest affairs. The staple diet consisted of a dark and firm unleavened bread, usually made of barley flour. For various special occasions and dinners, this bread might be made with wheat or with a mixture of barley and wheat-flour, given various shapes, and enriched with oil, milk, raisins, dates or sweetened with honey. Pearl barley also played an important role in the composition of dishes and as bulk, not unlike the use of potatoes and rice in various parts of the world today. Wheat and wheat flour were seldom used because wheat had to be imported from Egypt and was expensive.

In the hot climate of Greece, much food was eaten raw, particularly fruit and vegetables in the form of salads. Such cooking as did take place was reserved for some vegetables and confined to the boiling, stewing or braising of meats, fish or fowl.

Figure 3.4 The presentation table sideboard
Source: Emanuel Ranke, Mohr. JEB Tübingen, 1924

The cooking was executed on a simple brick-built stove, often free-standing in the middle of the room to let the smoke escape through a hole in the ceiling or nearby windows. Cooking in earthenware pots and pans had its problems, as prolonged close contact with the flames would break the vessel. For this reason, pots and pans had to be raised on stone tripods to keep them away from the fire. The fuel used was, in most cases, wood, brushwood or a type of early charcoal for those who could afford it.

Radiant heat cooking was restricted to spit-roasting, often whole or part carcasses, with a slave tending the roast for the four to six hours it would take to cook, turning and basting it continuously. The baking oven was much in use for the baking of bread, and was a part of the stone-built stove structure. This oven

Figure 3.5 Kitchen equipment from Pompeji. Drawing by Overbeck Pompeji
Source: Emanuel Ranke, Mohr. JEB Tübingen, 1924

was gradually used to bake – roast – smaller joints of meats once the bread had been removed, an approach which led to the modern methods of pot-roasting and oven roasting still used today. The last method of cooking, what we call today grilling, applied mostly to fish and some smaller cuts of meat. The grilling would be done on hot stones, as metal sheeting or metal grills were not yet widely available.

How far the Greeks advanced in compositional cookery is not very well recorded. But judging by the wide use of herbs in Greek kitchens in ancient times, some early compositional cookery was in existence, if only by adding to the pearl barley one herb today and another tomorrow, or one type of vegetable or fruit today and another tomorrow to give it a new flavour or a new appearance. This must be considered the beginning of compositional cookery as far as Europe is concerned.

The presentation of food was, by modern standards, relatively simple. Yet with some ten or, on special occasions up to twenty, hot and cold dishes, as well as salads, breads, nuts and many fruits, brought to the table in beautifully decorated

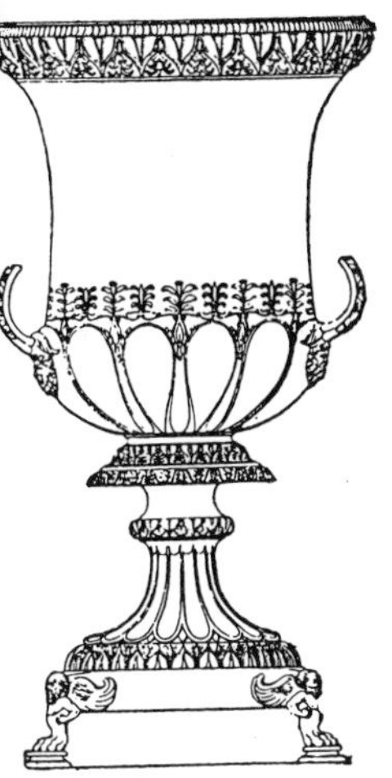

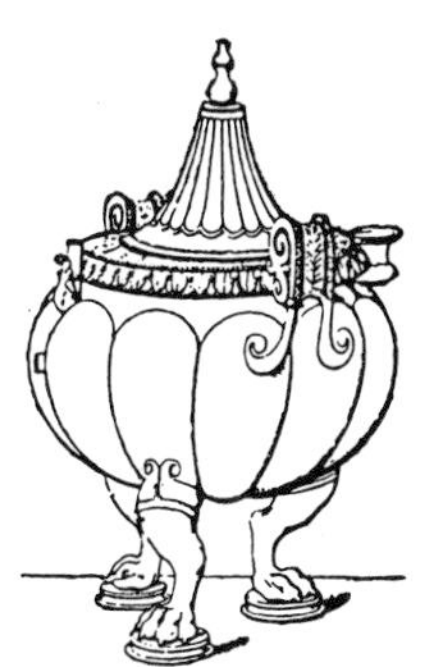

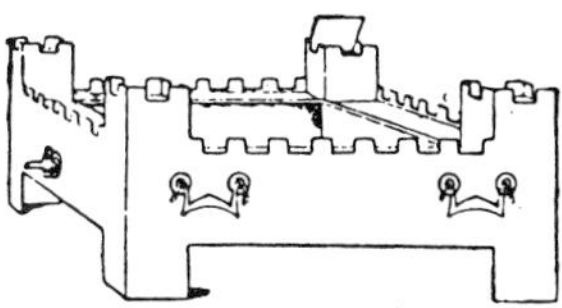

Figure 3.6 a) Mixing bowl, bronce Pompeji; b) Samovar, bronce Pompeji; c) Charcoal base heater, bronce Pompeji
Source: Hellenic and Roman Culture, Stehle J Nordhausen 1891, Museum Bourbon

ceramic platters and dishes, with cheeses and cakes in addition, one could speak of an early, if simple, banquet – the height of ancient gastronomy and a sight to behold.

When the family were on their own, they would eat the main evening meal (*deipnon*) with the older children and ladies of the house present. The Ancient Greeks ate with their fingers from small bowls or platters – only for some soups or stews would a simple spoon or ladle be provided. Bread was particularly useful in the consumption of liquid or dishes with milk, gravies or sauces, and useful to wipe one's fingers on at the conclusion of the meal.

Throughout the meal wine would be drunk, which almost always was mixed with water, usually up to 50 per cent or more, although some special wines were taken undiluted.

When guests were present, the men usually ate on their own, although on special occasions the ladies or elder children may have been present at the beginning of the meal, but would most certainly withdraw before the heavy drinking and discussions of the men began (symposium). In a similar way, ladies in Victorian times withdrew from the dining room when the time came for the men to drink the port and smoke.

Eating and drinking in the country or in more simple abodes took very much the same pattern, even if there was less variety of food, or certain items were scarce or completely unavailable. Add to this the fact that water would often replace wine, and it can be seen that elaborate presentation and ceremony would be superfluous. Yet in the simplest of Greek homes or farmhouses, the men would eat on their own, with the women of the household tending to their needs at the table. The women made sure that the men received the choicest of cuts, or the largest of portions, thus ensuring the well-being of their menfolk for another hard day's work in the fields.

That we know so much more about the presentation of food, eating and types of food consumed, is due to writers such as Athenaeus (see also page 73) and Archetratus, who lived in the fourth century BC and wrote poems about food in hexameter verse.(3.6) These poems and their content seem to have been published and republished under various titles such as *Gastrologia, Gastronomy, High Living, Dinner Lore (Deipnology)* or *Dainty Dishes (Opsopalcia)*. His authority on things gastronomical was so commanding that he became known as 'The Hesiode or The Originator of Epicurus'. Later came two culinary writers and experts of sorts, both named Apicius, one in the reign of Tiberius and one in the reign of Trajans. Their fame survived via Athenaeus to the Middle Ages in a work called *De Reconquinria*, being reproduced in 1929 in Philadelphia with the title of *Apician Morsels*.(3.7)

But none of these ever wrote a cookery book for the simple reason that they were not practising cooks, merely writers on food and dishes, customs and etiquette of eating. Their concern is the presentation of food, the dishes served, the guests present, the latest scandal discussed at table, and the new mistresses brought to the table by various important guests.

The hiatus between the practising cook, unable or maybe too busy to write, and the often superficial writings of food, has remained intact until today.

The meal consumed, washed, and relaxing on the couch, the diners would listen to music, reading of poetry, or watch slave girls dance. Some slave girls would be purchased or were given as bedfellows for the night, or sometimes athletes were brought in to give a display, as were jugglers and clowns. When this performance concluded diners would come to the main aim of the evening – the symposium – the drinking and discussions which would last until late into the night.

Topics of conversation would naturally concern the latest political situation, near or far-away wars, the merits of gods, or just the last bit of poetry or music heard from a pretty girl. The problems with wives or mistresses, or the beauty of one or other, were often subjects of lengthy if not always worthwhile conversation. Both food and wine consumed at the table, or at a dinner a day, days or weeks ago, often became the subject of conversation, particularly when it came to judging the merits of one wine over another.

The Athenians adopted and practised a more refined cookery in the period of prosperity which followed the Persian wars, which has influenced much which we do today. The cooks of Italy and, in particular, Sicily, aided and encouraged by the rich Greeks and Romans, made cookery a fine art and gave it, in many

3.6 *Ibid.*, vol. 1, p. 8.
3.7 *Ibid.*, vol. 1, p. 8.

Figure 3.7 'La chasse est ouverte'
Source: Nestlé Pro Gastronomia Foundation, © 1993

respects, the dignity of a science early in the fifth century BC.(3.8)

The Italians, and Sicilians in particular, by textbook and travel and by insisting on excellence, raised the standards of eating in all its aspects through the Greek *beau monde*. The prominence of the cooks of Italy and Sicily in the ancient communities is attested by the conspicuous role they played in ancient comedy.

They appear among the earliest stock characters of European drama. Later they were again to have considerable influence on European Gastronomy via the French courts. When Catherine de Medici married the Dauphin, later Henry II of France, she brought with her to the French court her Florentine and Sicilian chefs with a whole new attitude to the preparation and presentation of food, which at the time was unique, and has influenced European eating etiquette and custom to this day.(3.9)

3.8 *Ibid.*, vol. 7.

3.9 Bode, W. and Leto, J., *Classical Food Preparation and Presentation*, Batsford, London, 1984, pp. 9–10.

The ancient cooks and their masters may not have understood much of the physiology of eating, but nevertheless they made gastronomy an art. This they did by the construction of a *philosophy du goût* in much the same way as did the French gastronome, Brillat-Savarin, centuries later, who redevised the rules and attitudes of how to dine.

He recognised at all times the importance of the social aspects of eating which made the need to eat a social event and a cultural occasion. The intimate relationship between civilisation and cookery or food eaten in a social and cultural setting has maintained a long tradition through the ages, and must never be underestimated.

Daily Life in Ancient Rome

Life in Ancient Rome was not that different from that of life in Ancient Greece, by which it was influenced for much of its existence. Dress was very simple. The ladies wore skirts, and the men wore loincloths. Over this a tunic was worn, held in place with a belt of various materials with a buckle. On special occasions, the heavy and cumbersome toga was worn. Later the toga was replaced by a lighter and more simple cover called the pallium.

In the morning the man's toilet was soon completed with a simple wash taking very little time. During the afternoon, the men would have a leisurely bath. During the periods when it was fashionable to wear a beard, the men spent long, often painful, sessions at the barbers, having their beards trimmed or shaven. The ladies took much longer and much more care to complete their toilet. With the help of lead-framed mirrors, needles and brooches, ointments, pomades, tooth-powder, tinctures and other make-up, they spend the best part of the early morning adorning their face and body. Some Romans had false teeth, some of which were made from gold.

The interior of the house was relatively simple. Like the Greeks, the Roman men spent very little time in their houses, and when they did, during the evenings, they were lying and resting on the kline which, in the Roman household, had become enlarged so as to seat three people. Three of these klines were placed against a wall each, leaving the fourth wall of the dining hall open or free for a door, through which guests would arrive and food could be brought in and served.

At mealtime, in the average middle-class home, guests would recline on the kline three at a time, making a dinner party of nine or so people the common or normal number. Various foods and dishes were placed on small tables, which could be replaced or renewed with different foods or courses three or four times during the evening. Much has been written about the excesses of the Roman table; what is less well known is that in most cases most meals were really quite simple. Even the better off would start their day with not much more than a piece of bread and, possibly, a little soft cheese, and fruit. This would be followed later by a simple snack lunch either at home with the family or, more commonly for the adult male members of the house, in the city bought from various stalls of the numerous street sellers. Both the first and the second meal were often eaten standing at home or walking along in the street, with often very little ceremony or comfort. For those who had to earn a living, work started at sunrise and lasted until midday. Few worked in the afternoon, but work was usually resumed in the early evening, and often continued late into the cool of the night.

For the better off, after a late rising, the afternoon was reserved to make the necessary household purchases, to meet friends or political colleagues, or walk in the parks. Later, some two hours or so were given to visiting the public bath-houses.

Here one could swim in hot or cold pools, take steam baths or wallow in individual tubs. Slaves were in attendance who often gave massages, and then covered the body in oils and perfumes. Within the complex of the public bath one could partake in games and simple athletics, or simply watch, or visit the restaurants or library or a gaming room to lose a small fortune during the leisurely afternoon.

For the young male of the household, education continued through the morning, but it was on the whole less important and comprehensive than it was in Greece. The subjects taught were limited to reading, writing and some mathematics, and the learning of the *tabulae duodecim* (the twelve books of law).

The young males of the less-well-off households would, at the age of fourteen or so, take an apprenticeship to learn a trade or occupation, usually that of the father, a custom which prevailed in Europe until quite recent times.

The young ladies of the household would be instructed by the lady of the house in duties pertaining to the running of the house and becoming a wife and mother, which was often at sixteen or eighteen years' of age. The type of instruction given would depend on the class of the family. The lady from a well-off family would be trained in maintaining a household with many slaves. In a lesser household with few slaves or no slaves at all, the training would centre on the work involved in carrying out household duties.

In both cases, young ladies seldom had a life very much outside the home. In the early evening, the families would be united for the evening meal which would be taken *en famille*. But when there were guests, it was an affair for the men only, which the ladies joined for an hour or so.

Food and Drink of Ancient Rome

The Romans ate very much what the Greeks ate. Whereas the Greeks relied upon wild-grown produce, the Romans became much more organised about what they put on to their table. Having improved upon the art of the table in respect of the Greeks and others, the Romans soon realised that constant good food, for the development of gastronomy, needed a plentiful and, more importantly, a secure supply of good-quality and varied produce for use in their kitchens. They also gave much thought to the time and labour required to prepare the food, and serve the food at the table. Food was brought every night into the city from the surrounding countryside and by ships from abroad. Slaves provided cheap and plentiful labour.

Rome's greatness was firmly rooted in the cultivation of soil, and much of Rome's wealth was based on crops and flocks. Rome was a considerable agricultural nation, and love for the land, gardens, the countryside and nature was a part of its life and its religion. The many gods in Roman life were considered primarily the protectors of the crops and herds, as well as the elements presiding over the land in which they thrived or died.

The rich, with their estates in the country, produced much of their own food, and this came rumbling in with that for the public market. What Romans could not produce themselves they imported from elsewhere – bees and honey from Greece, mushroom spores from India, wheat from Egypt, peppers from Persia. New plants to be cultivated and rare animals to be reared came from almost anywhere. Not always satisfied with their own flora and fauna, and with many produce expensive to import, Rome began to introduce food plants of many types from all over the known world, to be cultivated more or less successfully in their own soil – an endeavour which has enriched European food until this day.

Rome's system of farm management was profit-orientated. Many estates, besides growing food for the markets of Rome, had mines of various types, quarries, sand-pits and brickworks. In many respects, this made the estates self-sufficient and, at the same time, secured a valuable secondary income. Further away from the large estates would be enclosures for such animals as wild boar, deer, roebuck, mountain goats and gazelles.

With a variety of basic ingredients thus secured, time and thought could be given to the preparation, cooking and presentation of the food at the table. The preparation of the important evening meal became a very serious matter. The operation required, at least in rich and large houses, considerable space – large storage rooms, preparation rooms, and kitchens – and many people. The kitchens had many large fireplaces, which would be fitted with spits, skillets,

Figure 3.8 'Nouvelle cuisine'
Source: Nestlé Pro Gastronomia Foundation, © 1993

gridirons and cauldrons. Pots, pans, jars and bowls, ladles, spoons, knives, moulds, pitchers and much more were strewn around the kitchen.

Specialisation in the preparation of food and dishes was now possible with, in my opinion, much advanced food cookery, and laid the foundation for the kitchens of large houses of later Europe, and for the development of the working of restaurants and hotels many centuries later. Escoffier, for example, clearly being a good historian as well as a very good cook, owes much of his fame to reorganising the kitchens of hotels and restaurants of the nineteenth century.

In the Roman kitchen, various tasks were allocated to particular slaves and supervisors. By doing their work again and again, they gained much skill and confidence, and developed and improved known preparation and cooking methods. With such skills and confidence came a certain respect and authority for a job well done, and a dish well-cooked and presented. In this way, we have the first identification of a *forcarius*, the fire stoker, a much-skilled job in the evolution of the *loctor,* the modern saucier or sauce cook; the *pistor* who prepared the various stuffings and baked the breads and cakes, the forerunner of the *pâtissier*; all guided more or less kindly by the *cogus*, the equivalent maybe of the modern head-chef. These and others in the kitchens intermingled with butlers, water carriers, wine mixers, wine pourers, collar men, and fetchers and carriers of all manner. They were supervised by the *nomenclator*, who was responsible for the display and service of food, as well as the entertainment proffered to guests during the meal.

The meal was divided into basically three different entrées, not as yet called courses. The *gustatio*, representing the modern *hors-d'oeuvre*, consisted of olives, nuts, pickled vegetables and salads of both raw and cooked preparation and proffered with various sauces and dressings, flavoured with fresh herbs and spices of often great variety and dressed liberally with oil and honey. The food was garnished with radishes, celery or palm shoots.

The first entreé was followed by the second called *mensae primae*. This represents the modern main course which embraced all manner of hot dishes not yet categorised and differentiated as fish, flesh or fowl. This service included various soups and stews, some quite spicy, savoury puddings, and forcemeats and sausages of all shapes and flavours made from fish, meat, game and poultry. They included blood, herbs and spices and various grains to bind them. All were served swimming in rich sauces of various types, thin or creamy, light or dark, subtle or sharp, intended to caress the mouth and palate at the same time. This service would include lobsters, crabs, oysters and crayfish, mussels and scallops, again in various presentations and flavours, and roast meats of pheasant, hares, pork, quail, beef and kid served with milk sauces. With this were served dumplings, courgettes, celery and purple asparagus, interrupted with marinated chops, giant steaks, fresh or oiled sardines, omelettes, cabbage, marrows and chestnuts, as well as many types of breads, from pure white to dark brown in appearance.

The third entrée was the *mensae secunde*. The desserts offered sweetmeats, stuffed dates and figs, sweet eggs and egg-custard, honey preserved apples and pears, fresh grapes and pomegranates, sweet cakes and green fresh nuts rolled in salt.

The Romans ate their food with their hands. This was a messy and most untidy affair, and for this reason bowls with warm water were continuously passed around to the guests by serving slaves with towels and napkins. Knives were often seen at the table, more for carving and portioning than for individuals to eat with. The fork was not yet known – only a spoon may have been given for the eating of soups and stews out of small bowls.

At large banquets, guests would be graded and seated according to importance, with the more expensive and rarer dishes nearer to the host and honoured guests, where also the more selected wines would be placed. For this reason, all the lesser guests would get very little, including the most watered down wine.(3.10)

3.10 Winter, W.H., *Eine Kulturgeschichte Europas* (A Cultural History of Europe), Freytag, Verlag, Leibzig, 1891, pp. 56–77.

In Athenaeus' times, considerable understanding and regard was already given to certain types or vintage of wines. Some interested guests would display considerable knowledge and expertise as to which wine they would drink with what food, and those they should avoid. We are led to believe that most wines were watered down to varying degrees.

Here it must be understood that Roman wines were very much stronger regarding alcohol content – up to 16–20 per cent of alcohol – which helped in their storage and would have made guests very drunk very quickly had they not been watered down.

Much has been made of the voraciousness, gluttony, manners and behaviour at the tables of the rich and powerful, but this must be viewed and understood in regard to Roman ethics and moral values.

'However successfully one banishes this rude vision, it no doubt remains that Rome, both under the Republic and the Empire, was a world where it was only agreeable to live if one was very rich, and where the greater part of one's life would have been involved in the pursuit of pleasure – but a kind of pleasure that most of us have never known. Entirely unclouded by guilt it was seen as a good in itself. Its pursuit, the search for different means of gratifying the appetite, not only became a way of life for many, but provided a living for thousands who were "variously but incessantly employed in the service of the rich. In their dress, their table, their houses and their furniture". The favourites of fortune united every refinement of convenience, of elegance and of splendour, whatever could soothe their pride or gratify their sensuality.'(3.11)

'Food and sex to these men were more than just utilitarian means of sustaining and reproducing mankind. They were instruments to procure the supreme felicity. Moreover they were closely bound together in religious celebration, of an orgiastic nature, symbolising fertility and life; they were sensual experiences to be varied and expanded, sometimes, apparently, to be enjoyed simultaneously.'

'The Roman fondness for food is an historical fact. Fortunes were squandered by men who lived for their palates, at whose behest the world was ransacked for delicacies. Even under the comparative austerity of the Republic, such dainties as whole boar, goose foie gras, peacock and Trojan pig – stuffed with all kinds of sausages, vegetables and surprises – were served at the most lavish feasts. A disciple of good living was one who fed on oysters, fattened birds and fish. These facts are supported by the general view today of a Roman kitchen – over-spiced

3.11 Pullar, P., *Consuming Passion*, Sphere Books, London, 1970, p. 3.

with unspeakable zests and extracts, putrid with abominable sauces.'(3.12)

These were the opinions of some, but this next passage conveys equal truth regarding the Roman inheritance to modern day:

'There were people, however, more inclined to make food the object of their desires.'(3.13)

They went along with the epicurean view that the satisfaction of the belly was the root of all good. Mealtimes were oases in long brown days. Yet these are the very meals that are now supposed to have been endless pageants of disgusting, almost inedible, dishes. In effect, this is saying that people of great intelligence and vitality, of cultivated tastes and wealth, patrons who bequeathed to the West wonderful architecture, sculptures, paintings and learning, were only able to produce a kitchen that was worthless and from which it is possible to retrieve nothing that is of practical and historical use.

Is this really the case? Surely not. By unravelling the facts a different truth is revealed. There will always be people like Heliogabalus, a degenerate whose languid appetites could only be roused by the most unnatural and the nearly unobtainable. Gibbon wrote:

'To confound the order of seasons and climates, to sport with the passions and prejudice of his subjects, and to subject every law of nature and decency, were in the number of his most delicious amusements.

'Rewards were offered for the invention of new sauces, but if the new concoction was not relished, the inventor was allowed to eat of nothing else until he had discovered another more agreeable [sauce] for the imperial palate.'(3.14)

The Romans left behind some cookery books which survive to this day. One of these was written by the first Roman culinary gourmet, Apicus. It was said that he poisoned himself when he realised his money was running out and that he 'was unable to continue his lifestyle of continuous banqueting of the highest standards'.(3.15) His writing is of little use today as it does not give any weights or measures, nor mode of preparation. It includes the naming of some foods which remain unidentifiable. There is even some doubt whether the book is all

3.12 *Ibid.*, pp. 17 – 24.

3.13 *Ibid.*, p. 26.

3.14 Gibbon, as quoted in Pullar, P. in *Consuming Passion*, Sphere Books, London, p. 31.

3.15 Levy, J.-P., *The Economic Life of the Ancient World*, Chicago University Press, Chicago, 1967, p. 72.

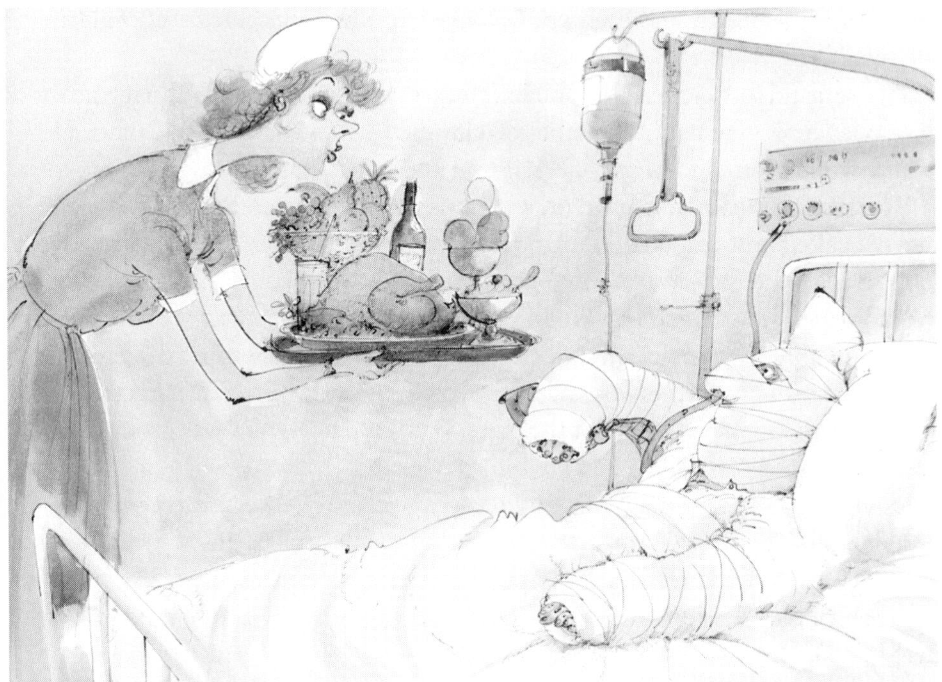

Figure 3.9 'Bon appétit!'
Source: Nestlé Pro Gastronomia Foundation, © 1993

his own work, as some think that it could not have been compiled until some two or three centuries after his death.

The practice of including weights, measures and methods of preparation with the writing on foods was, at least in England, not adopted until the fifteenth century. What can be said with certainty is, the rich Romans seem to have had a deep-rooted dislike for natural foods and food flavours and thus gave their dishes of meat, fish and fowl highly flavoured sauces and dressings.

Among the sauces and seasonings was a mass-produced condiment called *liquamen* or some times *garum*. These were made from salted fermented fish over a period of weeks or months. This resulted in a clear golden liquid which was kept ready in earthenware jars to be added to all manner of savoury dishes during and at the table after cooking, 'giving them a salty, fishy, cheesy flavour'.(3.16)

This appears to be not unlike the use of some modern condiments such as Worcester sauce, soya sauce and Maggi. In large food production methods, the use of monosodium glutamate and hydrolysed vegetable flavouring as flavour-enhancers come close to the Roman condiment.

Roman diners also liked to eat strongly spiced foods. Many spices were

3.16 Tannahill, R., *Food in History*, Palladin, London, 1973, p. 97.

imported from all over the then known world, of which pepper was considered the spice *par excellence*.

The demand for spice in the Roman kitchen was considerable, and it developed into a special trade. From 86 classified goods imported to Rome, 44 were spices imported mostly from Asia and Africa.

However, most Romans lived on an all too often very meagre ration, which Juvenal called 'just bread and much spectacles'. And both ordinary and rich were subsidised by the Roman government in the form of free issues of grain during the many periods of war, famine and other local hardships which befell the Roman Empire. Originally intended to relieve poverty, these issues of free grain increased at times to massive hand-outs, which seriously distorted both the economic and social structure of the state. By 70 BC, free grain was given to forty thousand citizens of Rome.(3.17)

Julius Caesar (101–44 BC) was very pleased to have cut down these subsidies by half to about 150,000 recipients, but during the days of Augustus (63 BC–AD 14), it had reached 320,000 again, almost one-third of the population of Rome. Servus Alexander (356–23 BC) decreed that ready-baked bread rather than grain should be given to the poor.(3.18)

Aurelian (AD 121–180) increased the daily bread ration to one and a half pounds and added pork fat to this to improve 'their meagre rations'. One hard-pressed official exclaimed 'before we know where we are, we will give the plebs chicken and geese as well'.

The giving of ready-made bread was made possible by the improved method of milling – the grinding of grain into flour had never been an easy task, needing much stamina and considerable patience. For thousands of years, the Egyptian quern was used for this purpose and had a grinding motion forwards and backwards. In the fifth century BC, the quern was replaced with a lever-operated, hopper-rubbing millstone, using a side-to-side action. This made the making of flour considerably easier and somewhat quicker. This was replaced by the fully-rotary milling stone in about the third century BC, which could be driven by animals. This gave the miller the opportunity to grind and sieve grain and flour on a very large scale. In the second century BC, the millers took a new step by becoming bakers as well.(3.19)

The new millers became very prosperous. Their prosperity was only interrupted by Caligula in the first century BC when he demanded that all the

---

3.17 Carcopino, J., *The Daily Life of Ancient Rome, the People and the City, at the Height of the Empire*, Yale University Press, Yale, 1941, pp. 28–9.

3.18 Levy, J.-P., *The Economic Life of the Ancient World*, Chicago University Press, Chicago, 1967, p. 96.

3.19 Moritz, L., *Grain, Mills and Flour in Classical Antiquity*, Clarendon Press, Oxford, 1958, pp. 25–7.

animals which powered the mills should be used for war, and when the Goths in the sixth century AD cut off the water supply, with which by then most mills were then powered. As the scale of bread making increased, it was necessary to redesign the ovens in which the bread was baked. The great physician, Galen, whose pronouncements were to remain the foundation of Western dietetic medicine for almost fifteen hundred years, took an interest in the making and baking of bread, concluding:

> *'That bread which is baked in ashes is heavy and hard to digest, because its baking [state of cooking] is uneven. That which comes from small ovens has no room to develop and therefore causes dyspepsia and is again hard to digest. But bread which is baked over a brazier or baked in a pan [early baking tin] owing to the addition of a mixture of oil, is easier to excrete and clean, but the steam from the drying makes [it] wet and unwholesome. Bread baked in larger ovens, however, excels in all the good qualities, for it is well flavoured and thus good for the palate and stomach alike, easily digested and very easily assimilated.'(3.20)*

Athenaeus is a considerable source of much of what is said and known about ancient bread. He gives long lists of types and variations of bread which, today, can no longer be easily identified. His often very vague descriptions of 'bread' must have included other bakery goods as well as cakes. He did not say how they were made and how they were different from one another.

However, what Athenaeus does show us very clearly is the ingenuity the ancient Roman applied to his most basic needs. The basic original diet of the poor of Rome had consisted of a polenta-like porridge made from millet and coarse bread bristling with chaff. Later, additions of oil, suet, honey and cheese, as well as variation of shapes, such as plain loaf, plaited loaves, rings, rolls and biscuits, garnished with nuts, fruits and poppy seeds, all became popular.

The same imagination must also have been applied to sauce making, which were very strong and most likely developed in the more modest households of Rome or possibly in the countryside, and only later mass-produced for everyone.

The very strong sauces in Roman times reflect to some considerable degree the idiosyncrasies and excesses of the rich and, gastronomically speaking, bored Romans. Indeed, some of the excesses of the cuisine of Rome was often one of political expediency, a way to impress, be different or titillate, which more often than not resulted in a ridiculous rather than a gastronomic event.

As Raymond Oliver says:

3.20 Gulick, C.B., *Athenaeus*, *The Deipnosophis*, vol. III, Heinemann, London and New York, 1927, p. 115.

'Money and good appetites are not enough to build real gastronomy, better gastronomy has been born out of necessity ensuring experience, imagination and care for food, rather than wealth.'(3.21)

This sense of experimentation to better or vary the same daily meagre rations by the poor of Rome was to become the very base of the development of European cooking, cuisines and gastronomy in general.

Daily Life in the Silent Centuries

Daily life during the silent centuries, in a vast new realm, with many different peoples, attitudes and values, could not easily be brought to a common denominator. It was, however, a life that was very much dominated by nobility, church and the land. Life for most was dominated by the concern for their 'daily bread', by often very hard work on the land.

Figure 3.10 shows a calendar which depicts the year and duties on the land during the silent centuries. *Ora et labora* (prayer and work) was the motto of the 40,000 or so monasteries of various types which grew up all over Europe. With the influence gained by the church, it was not surprising that this motto became the motivator of the times, and to this day has remained part of the European work ethic.

Work was essential; the trade and commerce of the Roman Empire had broken down and in most regions systems of exchange and barter had taken over. Trading routes had changed to the centres of Baghdad, Constantinople, Russia and Scandinavia. Astrackan, Sarai, Kasan, Novgorod and Kiev had become the new trade centres in the east and north-east. In the south a new route, via Baghdad, the Levantine Coast and Sicily, reached Spain and the Rhône estuary. Mid-Europe was more self-reliant, developing its own skills, crafts and production of goods. This led to what must be considered one of the greatest contributions of the silent centuries – the development of specialisation in the form of craft-skills.

For the first time can be identified craftsmen such as artists, bakers, brewers, builders, carpenters, cooks, cartwrights, coachmen, fishermen, leather-workers, cobblers, shoemakers, millers, musicians, net-makers, potters, painters, soap-makers, stonemasons, turners, trainers of falconry, weavers and wagoners. Most households tried to be self-sufficient and much of the work was done by the

3.21 Oliver, R., *The French at Table, Wine and Food Society*, London, 1967, p. 137.

Figure 3.10 Medieval calendar of month duties in the fields
Source: Vienna National Museum

family – the spinning, weaving, dying and sowing remained for a long time woman's work. But as the demands of the various noble houses, monasteries and churches grew, the development of manual skills and craftsmen also grew, and their skills were much sought after in the building of stone houses, castles, monasteries and churches. It is true that usually the craftsman was bondsman to his master, usually a noble lord, who would send or lend him to friends and neighbours to execute his special skill.

His pay would be in kind or sometimes money, and some percentage of both became due to his lord and master. Gradually, many craftsmen became free. A freemason, for example, did not have a master and could travel throughout the realm to offer his skill and labour to anyone who was willing to pay for them.

But for most the work was mainly on the land, and agriculture was the basis of much of Carolingian life. Everywhere in the north and north-west of the realm, land was developed for new farms and villages. Rye, barley, oats and some wheat were grown; millet, spelt, hemp and flax were successful crops, and from the eighth century AD, hops were grown for the making of beer. All types of vegetables grew well in the rich soil of the river valleys of northern Europe, and the selection of fruit and berries grew wider with the attention paid by the monks to the nurturing of all types of seedlings.

Again from the eighth century onwards, three-field rotation had begun, and with the separation and selection of better seed and seedlings, farming results were surprisingly good. The design of the hoe, harrow, spade and sickle was much improved, and most farmers either possessed or could borrow a plough with an iron blade. When this latter implement was fully developed, it became known as the mold-board plough, slashing vertically and deeply into the earth.

Food production expanded and, as is normal, the population then expanded. In the seventh century, the population of northern Germany expanded fourfold, to that which it had been during Roman times.(3.22)

The new plough and the newly developed two-wheeled farmer's cart, drawn again by oxen or, later, by horses, were expensive to make or buy. At this time, co-operatives were established consisting of several farmers pooling their money to buy, say, a new plough with which to work the fields in turn in a corporate enterprise.

Except for wars and famine, the farmer's life was simple but good. Our forefathers of the Middle Ages lived their short, hard-working lives, fond of drinking and merrymaking. And when religious festivals were not enough, the authorities had no hesitation in adding or incorporating some heathen festivities into the calendar of merrymaking.

During the silent centuries, food was available according to season, famine or good harvest, and could therefore be sparse or plentiful. Sometimes it was in such short supply that even the king and his court moved from castle to monastery and castle again in their search for food. Bad harvests made the poor eat the bark from the trees, or kill and eat the rodents, dogs and cats.

But when the harvest was good, the hunt successful, the deal by the trader or

---

3.22 White, L., *Mediaeval Technology and Social Change*, Clarendon Press, Oxford, 1966, p. 54.

craftsman successfully struck, one ate well. One ate from the available dishes made from fish, flesh or fowl, generously rinsed down with mead, beer or wine, the latter being more commonly drunk in the southern region of the realm.

The new secular and spiritual masters generally enjoyed some considerable social intercourse, meeting at the hunt, banquet and many necessary, or not-so-necessary feasts, in the name of the Lord. The free contacts of bishops, abbots and priests with the ladies was much criticised, especially when, despite cannon laws, they lived in open marriage. The prospering farming communities gradually found life more difficult, first because of feuds and civil wars, and later because of taxes which were the consequence of the wars. More and more farmers had to sell their land to the rich masters and monasteries to whom they were in debt because of taxes or waste.

They either left the land altogether or stayed to work as serfs or bondsmen on the land they once owned. Charlemagne tried to change the injustice by lowering the taxes and contributions from the poorer people, but he was singularly unsuccessful. His kingdom was too large, he lacked the necessary co-operation from his wasteful noblemen and clergy, and his 'civil service', which was essential to him, was either not yet fully established or was corrupt. Nobility and the clergy had become too powerful.

Food and Drink of the Silent Centuries

The highly developed culture of the table, which made the Romans so famous, was always the privilege of the rich few. How much that culture was accepted in the northern parts of the Roman Empire, and now persisted in the Carolingian realm, is not known, but if it was accepted, only a few could have afforded it.

What is known is that the meals of Charlemagne's table were simple and eaten in quiet dignified ceremony. He often ate alone when travelling, and when at home he ate with his family and friends. The meal was served by young courtiers, noblemen who served at the court in an honorary position as butlers, waiters and wine waiters.

A sort of grace was always said at Charlemagne's table before every meal. Much encouraged by priestly teaching, this was a custom practised throughout the realm, from the emperor's table to the most humble meals in the peasants' abode, and it has lasted as a custom in Europe generally until very recent times.

The four-course meal consisted of soup, fish, roast meats, some vegetables, fruits and cheese, and some form of early cake would conclude the meal. One drank little at the table; mostly water, ale, mead or beer or, on special occasions

Figure 3.11 The medieval meal
Source: From the author's collection, actual source unknown

or with honoured guests present, the more expensive wine would be served. Charlemagne loved wine and this was the only distraction he permitted during the average meal. On state occasions, the meal would be served in the splendid setting of the large hall which would be decorated with carpets, small trees and many flowers.

It was on such occasions that the honoured state guests would have sight of some of the treasures of the realm, taken in bounty or received in tribute, when goblets, bowls and plates, candle holders, spoons and knives of precious metals would adorn the emperor's table.

On these special occasions, Charlemagne would bring further culture to the table. After the meal he would allow the reading of poetry, playing or singing of music or, according to his mood, permit his wandering players to perform a comedy or tragedy to entertain his guests.

How the poorer people cooked and ate is open to conjecture. What is known is that at least in the many farmhouses, people ate from a plain wooden table, which would be large enough to seat the whole family. On special occasions, the table would be covered with a linen tablecloth, the proud possession of the lady of the house. Some wooden tables had shallow indentations carved into the table in which the food would be placed. At the conclusion of the meal, the table would be washed down with hot water and scraped, and placed in the sun or near the fire to dry. Such tables were used mostly in northern regions. But even in some better houses, it was common practice for several people to eat and drink from the same cup or bowl. The drinking-horn, similar to that of the Athenians, was passed around the table. It was always held in someone's hand, as its shape did not permit it to be laid down. The ale boot, or yard of ale, today normally made of glass, is the modern equivalent of the old drinking-horn.

Just as simple as the tableware was the kitchenware of the poorer people of the day. Pottery was still the main material for storage or cooking jars, for pots and pans and casseroles. Occasionally, an iron pot or pan could be found in a farmhouse, or a spit for the roasting of meat, and the all-important cauldron, so much a feature of the northern European kitchen in the Middle Ages.

Basic foods and cooking methods varied according to the firmly-entrenched attitudes and customs of the peoples in this vast new realm of Charlemagne. Those who had experienced the full force of Roman gastronomic influences persisted in this mode of food preparation, but it must have suffered when the spice trade flagged. Those in the northern part of the realm, who had never been used to spices, developed their own food flavouring and cooking, still retained today in British, Dutch, German and Scandinavian dishes.

It has often been said that people or nations have the cooking and food they deserve. This often derogatory remark is, in many respects, unfair. Cooking and attitudes to food are mostly developed within the limits of the available technology or resources. For example, the Masai in Kenya cook the little food they have using dried cow-dung – the only fuel readily available to them. The logical application of available fuels, equipment and developed skills to food preparation has contributed to the development of gastronomy, certainly as much as the availability of food.

The climate of an area is also a factor to be considered. In the hot climates of the Mediterranean regions, wood as fuel was scarce. Charcoal-burning stoves of many types and sizes developed and so many cooks of southern Europe became experts with the frying pan or grill.

Figure 3.12 Early inn in the Middle Ages, L Cutts
Source: Freytag Verlag, Leibzig 1881

Most of the best-developed and well-known dishes of Spain, southern France, Italy, the Balkans and Greece are a reflection of the available technology of the time. They are a gastronomic inheritance, still much enjoyed and part of our lives today, although the old fuels may have been changed for more modern ones.

In the northern part of the Carolingian empire, there was no shortage of wood; it grew in abundance and almost anything which was made and built was of wood. 'The big houses of nobility, as most farmhouses and other dwellings, were built of logs right up to the twelfth century.'(3.23) The halls of these log-built houses were heated by enormous blazing wood fires, and all cooking was done on this readily available fuel. The roasting of meat on the spit, the frying of all manner of foods on the hot plate, and the baking of crusty rye-bread in big stone ovens, were all achieved on burning wood. If we add the availability of iron in the form of pots and pans, and a new development, the cauldron, to our

3.23 Derry, T. and Williams, A., *A Short History of Technology from Earliest Times to 1900*, Oxford University Press, Oxford, 1960, p. 172.

Figure 3.13 Medieval early kitchen
Source: From the author's collection, actual source unknown

new arsenal of kitchen equipment, we should not be surprised that the cooking in the north of the realm took a new and somewhat different direction from that in the south.

When he was old and ill, the emperor began to hate his doctors when they told him to change his diet and eat meat boiled or braised, for he loved his roast meats.(3.24) From necessity his poorer subjects relied heavily on a diet of boiled or braised meat for which the new iron cauldron was ideally suited.

Upheavals and civil wars apart, the diet of the silent centuries and early Middle Ages, although simple, was most certainly not monotonous. Game was freely available in the large forests, and the rivers and lakes were full of fish. Even when the local nobleman forbad hunting and fishing by the common people, most, by fair means or foul, would fill their larders with the odd deer or rabbit, or supplement their diet with fish. Domestic chickens, ducks and geese pecked for food on every farm hamlet or village. Most households would feed and fatten their own pig for slaughter in the autumn, with acorns, beech-masts and garden or household leftovers. Many types of sausage were made by filling the pig's intestines with its ground meat and/or offal. They were dried, boiled, salted or smoked and hung in the loft of the house for consumption during the long, cold and lean winter months. A salted side of bacon and one leg, if not

3.24 Grant, A. (ed), *Einhard Eginhard, The Early Years of Charlemagne*, Alexander Moring, London, 1907, p. 38.

both legs, of the pig would be brined and smoked. A leg would be eaten some months later with bread, a most substantial and tasty meal. Even the bones of the pig would be salted in large wooden barrels or earthenware jars to be used later to give flavour and substance to stew-soups. The slaughter of animals for home consumption is still very much a part of the European scene.

The custom of preserving for the leaner part of the year was developed and resulted in one of the major contributions to gastronomy *charcuterie*.

Salt has always been a biological as well as a gastronomical necessity. Gastronomically, however, we must note that there were two basic ways of salting food which gained new impetus and expertise in the Middle Ages. The first method was the barrelling of fish or meat in suitable containers in a granular salt-bed. This was used mainly for fish, in particular, herring. During the long winter when other fish or meats were in short supply, large catches of herring were salted in wooden barrels and were sent inland to supplement the diet of the poor. Second, we have the method of salting using brine, which was better suited for the preservation of meats, in particular, pork.(3.25)

However, salt was very expensive – it added a third or more of the cost to the meat to be preserved. For this reason, only the best meats and choicest cuts would be salted, because the cheaper meats and poorer cuts were 'not worth their salt'. In Scandinavia, these preserving methods have resulted in a considerable array of various fish preparations known as *gaffelbitar*.

The second major method of preservation of food was that of drying (see also page 41). In the silent centuries in northern Europe drying was used for two basic foods: fish with a low fat content, such as cod, haddock, perch and ling; and fruits and vegetables.

When gutted and sometimes boned, the fish were cut open and dried on the rocks of the sea shore, or hung on wooden racks in their thousands as a valuable food reserve for the winter. This resulted in the *stokkefisk* of Norway and the *lutfisk* of Sweden. Today they are eaten in both countries at Christmas time.

Dried apple rings and pear rings are still familiar to us today. But more often the common vegetables, such as beans and peas, would be dried. These would hang in their bushels upside-down from the eves of the farmhouses. Removed from their shelves or pods, they would be soaked overnight and slowly simmered to soften them. Additional flavour and sustenance would be given to these pulses, already relatively high in protein, by the addition of a piece of bacon. Today's equivalent is the *bohnensuppe* of Germany, the yellow *ärtsoppa* of Sweden and the delicious green pea soup, mushy peas and pease pudding of Britain.

Smoking played a not inconsiderable part of the preservation of food throughout the Middle Ages. Mostly applied to fish and meats, it has given us

3.25 Bridbury, C.R., *England and The Salt Trade in The Later Middle Ages*, Clarendon Press, Oxford, 1955, p. 29.

Figure 3.14 'Mise en place'
Source: Nestlé Pro Gastronomia Foundation, © 1993

some excellent delicacies, such as the kipper of Scotland, the smoked hams of northern Europe and the various raw smoked salmons, of Parma, Westphalia, Spain and Hungary.

We can conjure up a reasonable picture of the diets and dishes of the time from archives, inventories, shopping lists and ecclesiastical records. The picture of people scattered over Europe north of the Alps is one of plain living. They lived on a diet of bread, water, ale and, occasionally, wine, supplemented by cheese, fruits and nuts according to season, and a variety of vegetables, such as onions, celery, beets of various types, roots, radishes, lettuce, ridge-cucumbers, and various types of cabbage. The considerable efforts of the people of the Middle Ages to preserve some of these fresh vegetables resulted in a number of pickled foods, which have evolved into today's well-known and much appreciated pickled onions, pickled cabbage, pickled cucumbers and, in a slightly different direction by salting and fermentation, *sauerkraut* and mixed pickles.

The technical development of the iron cooking pot and cauldron made a considerable contribution to gastronomy. I am in no doubt that the cauldron used during the Middle Ages to cook and make some of the above fresh vegetables more palatable represents the real beginning of compositional cookery in Europe. It resulted in the making of soups, the main meal for most people during this period of culinary development, with its vital accompaniment, the bread.

'For hundreds of years soups have represented the main meal, especially for the poor and peasant classes, and there can be no doubt that they are one of the oldest preparations in compositional cookery or in the history of eating. Esau, we are told in the Old Testament, bought his brother's heritage for "a mess of pottage". It is especially interesting how soup dishes compare in importance as a basic diet and similarity of production all over the world, and in particular in European countries, from Får i Kål of Sweden in the north to the Minestrone of Italy in the south, the Irish Stew from Ireland in the west to the Bortsch of Poland and Russia in the east. In all those countries, soup represented the main meal of the day, always popular and easily produced from what was available and cheapest in the garden or in the fields.(3.26)

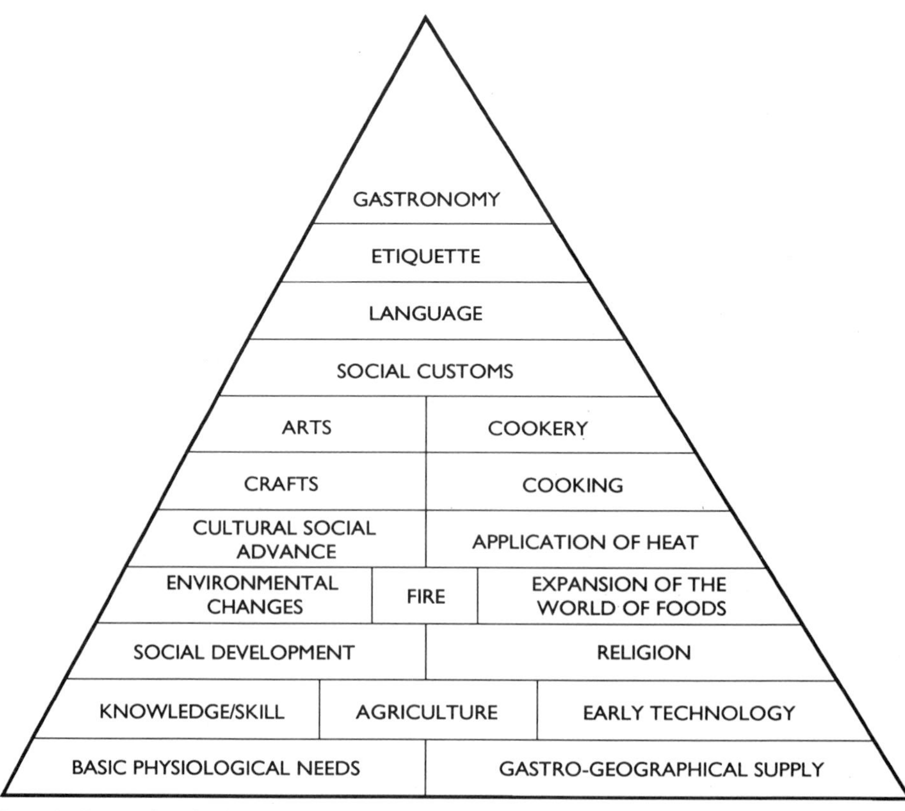

Figure 3.15 Ascending development of the structure of gastronomy
Source: Drawn by James Llewellyn-Smith to instruction of the author

3.26 Bode, W. and Leto, M., *Classical Food Preparation and Presentation*, Batsford, London, 1984, pp. 18–19.

Figure 3.16 Early winged Venetian glasses, Murono, 1710
Source: Austrian Museum for Practical Art, Vienna

Food and Drink of Castles and Towns

In the Middle Ages, all life's behaviour and standards were set by the courts and castles and were emulated by the masses. With the emergence of large towns, traders, travellers and crusaders exposed courts, castles and townspeople to culinary experimentation and practice. From the Islamic cultures via Spain came new 'table disciplines' which had not before played a part in the behaviour at table in the Middle Ages. Some of these 'table disciplines' stated that:

'One should not eat too hastily.
One should not speak with a full mouth.
One should not steal the choicest cuts from one's neighbour at the table.
One should use only three fingers when taking from the bowls and platters to place meats on the trencher (the prototype of our plate).
One should be polite and assist the elders at the table.
One should be gentle and polite with ladies at the table,
One should wash before and after the meal' (3.27)

The new French custom of allowing ladies to be present at the table, freely intermixed or seated in pairs with their spouses or fiancés, was now a widely

3.27 Pullar, P., *Consuming Passion*, Sphere Books, London, 1970, pp.41–2.

accepted custom. It improved the general behaviour at the table, including the language. If in pairs, men and women served and attended to one another, often eating from the same trencher and drinking out of the same cup.

The saying of grace before a meal by the resident priest or host was common practice, as was the thanks to the host and to God by a guest on the conclusion of the meal. Knives and spoons were used to serve and eat the meal. In the better homes, one had for the first time the *trencheur* who stood at the table or sideboard and executed the skilful dissection and carving of roasts and relevées with the aid of a fork and knife. A second new appearance at the table was the 'fore-taster', usually an attendant to the king or prince, who tasted the food before his highness lest it should be poisoned by a rival, or not be to his normal taste or liking. This was especially common in the case of visiting nobility.

The types of foods and dishes had not increased greatly since Carolingian days, but they were more adventurously prepared, better cooked and presented, and there were usually much larger portions. Sideboards for the presentation of foods, tableware and heirlooms, already known in Roman times, made a greatly appreciated reappearance.

The townspeople, through their exposure to increasing numbers of traders, craftsmen and travellers from home and abroad, were influenced by the social, technical and culinary innovations which the castles often missed. The budget for expenditure on the purchase, preparation and presentation of food of some of the rich traders often rivalled that of the nearest court. Whether out of jealousy or growing concern for the poor, laws were passed which were intended to curb the excesses at the table, but they were never obeyed and were never enforced. This was not all that surprising as many members of the aristocracy, including many law-makers, hypocritically partook of the offered 'luxuries' at the tables of the *nouveau riche*. Highly decorative tableware appeared on the tables of the new rich merchants. Knives, spoons, salt and pepper pourers, bowls, plates and goblets made from silver, brass or pewter became quite common and outshone anything the noble house could muster.

Monogrammed cutlery was introduced, bearing the initial letter of the family name. The reason for this was twofold: first, it was to show off and, second, it was to ensure that the tableware could not be stolen easily by the invited guest.

The sensation of the mid-fourteenth century was when a rich merchant family of Augsburg, the Fuggers, invited forty guests to their daughter's wedding, and provided each guest with a knife and spoon skilfully made from silver with which to eat the elaborate banquet. This had never been known before. Other rich noblemen provided cutlery for their family and honoured guests only; the rest of the guests had to bring their own!

Rich, white, linen tablecloths, or even more luxurious, white damask tablecloths imported from Damascus, with matching table napkins, appeared more and more frequently to decorate the tables of the rich nobleman or rich merchant.

More meat was eaten than ever before, certainly in the better off households, but even in lesser households this was the case. Veal, beef, duck and goose were replaced by more common meats, such as mutton and pork. Occasionally, a chicken or duck would be served on a festive occasion, but for most these were more highly prized for the eggs they provided rather than for their meat. Rye-bread was the staple diet, while bread made from wheat flour, crusty and white, would be served as a treat on Sundays or on special occasions. A porridge or gruel made from oats, millet, wheat or rye flour and enriched with cows' or goats' milk also remained a staple food. Root vegetables, such as carrots, turnips and swedes, greens such as cabbage, onions, celery and an early type of leek, were eaten as accompanying vegetables, cooked individually or as mixed vegetables, flavoured with salt and enriched in their flavour with pork or pork fat.

All fats were collected and stored in individual jars according to type and spread as dripping on bread, or added to soups and stews for sustenance. Butter began to appear, but it was very expensive and was usually only on the tables of the rich.

Religious holidays, such as Easter, Christmas and Whitsun, days set aside for the memory of early saints, engagements, weddings and even the birthday of a senior member of the family, or Christening of the newest member, were occasions when even the poor found the food to make a hearty feast.

Many foods and dishes, which originated with these special occasions, are part of our lives today, if sometimes the reason for them is lost in obscurity. A record of a wedding on a farm near Strasbourg gives the following list of dishes served:

> *'White bread of wheat served in thick crusty slices.*
> *A porridge made from millet, served with milk and honey.*
> *A purée of parsnips, rich with fat bacon, so rich that hands and beards shone with fat.*
> *Fried sausages served on a bed of cabbage, counting not less than four types of sausage, all with their own distinct flavour and spices with herbs and lots of pepper.*
> *A brides-mush (oats) served with berries blue and cream.*
> *All during the meal the host freely and generously offered mead and ale, and at the end of the wedding feast, spiced red wine, sweet and hot, which made all the guests, and the bride, quite drunk.'(3.28)*

3.28 Winzer, F. (ed), A *Cultural History of Europe*, Westerman–Verlag, Braunschweig, 1981, p. 118.

From AD 1446 we have the notes on food and recipes for one hundred dishes, written down by a farmer's wife on a farm near Freiburg. Her collection of recipes included: eighteen ways to cook a chicken; seven ways to prepare and cook duck or goose; and sixteen ways of cooking fish, such as boiling, braising, baking and frying, naming beef dripping as the best frying medium. Even the recipe for frying dough or batter is given. She had a recipe for the baking of pike, which included such spices as salt, pepper, cinnamon and cloves. Instructions are given on how best to salt, dry or smoke fish and meats, and more than thirty soups or stew-like soups are included in her culinary repertoire. This is the first-known written reference of the importance of the use of stocks in the making of all soups and sauces, still an important requirement in today's best cookery. An obvious favourite luxury dish of the lady was braised veal, served on a purée of carrots and flavoured and decorated with almond milk and blossoms of fresh violets.

Vinegar was mentioned frequently in her list of recipes, in the preparation and cooking of fish, chicken, pigs' intestines, liver, tripe and the many stuffings she used. More and more French and Italian names of dishes and equipment were an indication of the influence of these countries on the new table culture, the centre for which was the lower triangle of the Rhine, the area which now includes France, Switzerland, Germany and Italy. The influence spread, at least in the better houses, all over the continent, including the British Isles. Most French technical terms in respect of culinary equipment date from earlier times, but an innovation was a mechanical grinder which replaced the mortar and pestle for the grinding of herbs and spices, almonds, nuts, grain, pulse and pepper. With this we recognise the first labour-saving device showing that early technology had arrived in the kitchen. Thus another period and evolving way of life made its contribution to gastronomy.

Food, Drink and Manners of the Renaissance

The fifteenth and sixteenth centuries are considered the age of the Renaissance – a vital period of European life and history which gave rise to new knowledge and understanding. One of the developments of the period was that of a more 'beautiful existence', a cultural advance which manifested itself in the arts of painting, poetry, music and manners, the building of big houses, castles, châteaux and other buildings, and in the food that was eaten and the manners displayed at table. The food in this 'beautiful existence' was relatively simple, but usually much better prepared and presented than before. One now ate two big meals a day, the *desinare* in the late morning, a mixture of breakfast and lunch, and the *cessia* in the early evening. Both consisted of two types of dishes: beef, veal, mutton and pork, hot and freshly cooked in various ways, or, during the summer months, cold as joints; or prepared as a very much larger selection of *charcuterie* such as cooked or smoked raw hams, pâtés, potted meats, and many types of differently flavoured sausages, such as salami, liver-sausage, brain-sausage, ham-sausage and small *saucisson*, some of which may have been served hot. Lettuce, chicory, endive, artichokes, asparagus, peas, beans, onions and an early form of leeks were more often than not served as salads, dressed with oil and vinegar, or with bacon fat, vinegar, salt, pepper and many herbs. In colder climates and during the winter, these vegetables were complemented or replaced by beets, turnips, swedes, cabbages, carrots and dried peas and beans, cooked individually or in mixtures, not unlike the modern mixed vegetables. These were served hot with the meats.

Because of better knives and increased skills, vegetables and salads were cut more neatly and into various shapes for better presentation and to 'please the eye'. On fast days or during Lent, fish and eggs replaced the meat, resulting in a considerable increase in the preparation, cooking and presentation of many new fish and egg dishes.

Whatever the main meal, it was concluded with cheese of many types, shapes and flavours, including some flavoured with spices and herbs. To the selection of fruits eaten at the end of the meal one can now add peaches, apricots, grapes, apples and pears and, in more northern regions, dried grapes in the form of raisins. Nuts completed the selection for dessert.

With all this food one drank the local red and white wine, now stored in wooden casks in cool cellars, which was brought to the table often in straw-covered, club-shaped glass containers, the prototype of the bottle, which is still a feature of some Italian wines today. In the more northern regions of Europe, mead and ale, and also much improved beers, replaced wine on the many feast days. Basic food was much the same, but its presentation again was improved. The best tablecloth was ostentatiously shown off, precious ceramics and the best of the table silver were used and, of course, one invited the most valued guests. The meal would be enriched with more expensive game, refined and decorated sweets and confectionery, and more rare, expensive, selected wine would replace beer in the north, or the local wine in the south of Europe.

With the sixteenth century and the mercantile influences of Spain, France, England and the Netherlands, new food appeared on the tables of Europe. For the first time the flavours of anise and vanilla were used in cooking; in Spain and Italy sweet corn, cauliflower, pineapples and rhubarb were imported and grown; sugar cane and molasses became available, if not in every household, at least in the houses of the nobility and richer burgers.

The availability of this new sweetener led to the production of new types of breads, rolls, cakes and some hot and cold sweets.

It was at about this time that the fork was introduced. A large version had been familiar in the kitchen for some time, used in the various cooking processes. The smaller version was now placed, together with spoon and knife, on the more elaborate dinner tables, for the family as well as for the honoured guests, or was brought to the table by the invited guests as their personal belonging and taken back home after the meal.

Several reasons are suggested as to why the fork made this sudden appearance at the table. One reason is related to the dress which was worn – the wide Elizabethan lace collar became very fashionable, and only by an extension of the hand, via the fork, was it possible to place the food into the mouth. Another consideration may have been that many more sugar-coated or candied fruits were served, making the hands and lips very sticky, and the fork was desirable, if not essential. Others saw the appearance and use of the fork as just another technological advance, which would have happened anyway, and was a natural step in the more refined eating habits and etiquette at the table.

The precious goldware and silverware which appeared more and more on the tables of the rich was intended not only for the service of food and drink, but was also excellent capital investment. On the death of the Duke of Albuquerque in 1515, his executors found no less than 1,400 dozen large platters and plates, 500 large and 700 smaller bowls made from silver, all of which had come from Mexico and Peru.

In time of war and other economic difficulties, many kings and princes of Europe confiscated the silverware in lieu of war taxes. It is thought that this form of tax of war on the culinary decoration of the noble houses of Europe gave rise to the emergence of the glass industries of Europe, as more and more of the table silver was replaced with the less valuable, but not less decorative, glassware for the table.

From the middle of the sixteenth century, Spanish fashion, behaviour, morals and customs of society influenced many of the courts of Europe. An example of how things went to extremes is given by a French lady at the Burgundian court of Karl V, when the writer explains:

'When the infant princess, Maria Theresa, wanted a drink, a page was summoned to fetch the same. When he returned with the beverage the glass was passed to a lady-in-waiting, who, kneeling, offered it to the seven year old princess, a second lady-in-waiting then offered the princess a serviette between each sip of the drink. When the princess had finished, both ladies-in-waiting and page would walk away backwards for at least ten steps. The whole procedure

was overseen by a Lady-of-Honour, in sole charge of the infant.'(3.29)

The glittering ceremony of the Renaissance, with its main attraction being the banquet, owed much of its structure and presentation to the late antiquity. Kings, princes, dukes, bishops, noblemen and even rich merchants and craftsmen tried hard to better one another on these occasions within their respective spheres of life and society. The entrées and accompanying performances were often designed and overseen by famous artists of the day, and were considered to represent a work of art which was intended to satisfy all human senses. The following account of a banquet, given by Nandetto Salutati to the sons of the King of Ferrante of Naples in 1476, is a very good example:

'With the call of sixty trumpets the guests were asked to be seated. As first course, guests were given a small individual silver bowl filled with gilded cakes, flavoured with pistachio nuts and offered together with a silver cup of almond and rose oil flavoured milk.

'The second course was a white galantine of chicken, each individually decorated with an edible coat of arms of the assembled dignitaries including a line or two of his favourite prayer, poem or speech, all presented on most expensive silver platters. Before the next course some table-fountains were brought in spraying a fine spray of orange-blossom water, so that the guests might wash their hands and faces and the room would smell pleasantly again.

'The third course was the much-loved blanc-manger, made from milk, with almond paste, rice and fish, with the whitest of flesh. A second chorus of trumpets hailed the entrance of the main course, with twelve dishes of game, veal, beef, pork, pheasant, partridge, capon, chicken and all manner of vegetables, steaming hot, or salads, according to one's need, duly chilled. All was given in large silver bowls decorated with the most intricate work any silver-smith could design and execute.

'The show course, the pièce de résistance, was one which was not intended to be eaten, let various birds fly with all their colours, from bowls and artificial nests, as it showed man-made peacocks, with golden beaks, filled with strong smelling essence to refresh and amaze the guests.

'Lastly there were brought the courses of sweet dishes, including tarts, torten, pies, marzipan, confectionery of all sizes, colours and many flavours, as there were compotes, and candied fruit and grapes and raisins to leave the mouth sweet-smelling.'(3.30)

3.29 *Ibid.*, pp. 217–18.

3.30 Pullar, P., *Consuming Passion*, Sphere Books, London, 1970, p. 217.

Towards the end of the fifteenth century, it became the custom to raise the dignitaries at a banquet on to a podium, often covered by a baldachin of the finest and brightest material.

At the instigation of King Karl VII, his head chef opened the first cookery school of modern Europe, within the grounds of the palace. Here young men were taught the culinary arts, including the decoration of food, as well as its presentation at the table. Besides young men to be trained as cooks, many young noblemen attended these classes as an introduction to the arts of the table as part of their general education. Both the young chefs and young noblemen were sent out to many courts of Europe, primarily to cook, but also as early diplomats, and their presence laid the foundation for the reputation which French cuisine has retained to this day.

Those young noblemen who were not privileged to attend the school were instructed, along with dancing, fencing and the playing of an instrument, in correct table manners and carving as an important part of the hallmark of an educated young man of a good family. This interest in the behaviour, manners and knowledge of the table reached down to the more average burgers. Erasmus of Rotterdam published a book in 1530 with the title *De Civitate Morum Puerilium*, which concerned itself with the upbringing of children and young people. Much of the fourth chapter of this book concerned itself with table manners. The book was translated into many languages and remained the textbook on manners for many years.

Prosperity and a subsequent interest in all things culinary became part of all strata of society. Many cookery books were published and became the proud possessions of the richer housewife or a much hoped-for wedding gift of the young bride. Many of these books left several pages at the end of the book free of print so that treasured recipes of mother or grandmother could be written down as a culinary heirloom of the family.

The less well off tried to emulate 'good' table manners and behaviour. Sebastian Munster, the well-known German pastor, recorded in his travel papers that:

> *'Even the poorest eat their meal, of bread, porridge, peas, beans and onions, cooked with salted pork, and accompanied only by water or whey, in quiet respect to God and much dignity. Their joy in food was natural and most inventive, for at a wedding I attended in a poor farmhouse, all guests were merry and could eat and eat and eat again from all that field and garden would provide, all in happy enjoyment, and only a gentle indulgence, worthy of, or better than a highly born nobleman.'(3.31)*

3.31 Winzer, F. (ed), A *Cultural History of Europe*, Westerman–Verlag, Braunschweig, 1981, p. 311.

Figure 3.17 An early English country house
Source: The Even Giant Swipe File, The Hart Publishing Inc. 1978

The first books on travel followed the publications of books on manners and cooking. In addition to extolling the beauty of the buildings and countryside of the land visited, these books listed many of the hostelries and inns found along the roads and rivers of Europe. From the comments made on food, we can see that the food provided was always simple and only occasionally good.

Louis XIV of France will most certainly be associated with the lifestyle of Europe during the seventeenth century. He encouraged the arts such as philosophy, architecture, music, poetry and the social art of gastronomy of which he became an ardent patron. The King's interest in food, new dishes and sauces, as well as the best food presentation at the table, is legendary. Life at Versailles was a long list of festivities, banquets and dinners, some of which lasted for two to three days, and some festivities had up to two or three thousand devoted and admiring guests.

Many foreign visitors to France were surprised that even the average French man would spend most of his money on food, and only secondly on accommodation. The delights of the table played a large role for most Frenchmen; one ate with great pleasure and was not afraid to become fat. Indeed, a fullness of the body represented the prevailing ideal of beauty for both man and woman. But one cannot suppose that all Frenchmen had the appetite of the King who ate, so the palatine Princess Liselotte recalls, all the following dishes at a single dinner:

> '. . . *four plates of soup, a whole pheasant, a whole partridge, a big bowl of salad, two large slices of ham, a considerable portion of mutton flavoured with garlic, and to finish, a selection of sweet cakes and fruit.*'(3.32)

Bread and meat were the basis of the diet of the workers, as one can read from the household accounts of the court of d'Audiger which recommended:

> '. . . *that all servants should be served with not less than two pounds of bread and one and a half pounds of meat per day, as well as other complementary foods to make it a reasonable meal, which would allow them to perform their daily duties to the full.*'(3.33)

This clearly shows that the workers on the estate of a rich nobleman at least ate well, and much more than one would consider reasonable today. From the same source we can also find that the free workers of the estate, for example, a carpenter, 'could purchase from his daily earnings two pounds of meat, two pounds of bread, some vegetables and fruit and a fair measure of wine'. It does not say whether the carpenter had all this food for himself or whether he had to share it with a wife or even a family.

The people of the country lived reasonably well, mostly on the produce of the land, with cream, cheese, an occasional chicken, much bread and many fresh vegetables and some fruits. If anything, the poorer people most certainly lacked fresh meat, such as beef, veal, mutton or pork, which they considered their capital investment and which was intended for sale rather than for home consumption. However, their diet was enhanced with the one or two pigs they allowed themselves for their own use. These were eaten in preserved forms, such as hams, various sausages, pâtés, potted meats and salted pork and pork bones. Even the poor began to appreciate good wines with their good food, which, with the establishment of more and better vineyards, had become quite reasonable in price. They enjoyed music from the flute and violin and seemed to live a reasonably happy and contented life judging from the paintings of Louis le Nain.

During the reign of Louis XIV, many new or improved foods were introduced to the diet of the people, which today form very much a part of modern gastronomy. At first these foods, such as coffee, tea, chocolate and potatoes were available only for the rich, but over a period of time they became increasingly available to the less well off inhabitants of Europe.

3.32 *Ibid.*, pp. 112–13.
3.33 *Ibid.*, pp. 114–15.

Coffee

The history of coffee is little more than three centuries old as far as Europe is concerned, but it was known probably in the twelfth century in Arabia and Africa, but not in the form we know and consume it today. Coffee came to Europe in the early seventeenth century. It entered the continent via Venice and the French port of Marseilles, and acquired its name from the Arabian word *gahwah*, or more likely from the Turkish *kahve*, resulting in *café*, coffee, *kafé*, *kafia* or *kaffee*, according to which European language one speaks.

Like so many new foods, it was first enjoyed by the aristocracy and the rich merchants of the time. As coffee became more popular with the establishment of early coffee-houses, attempts were made to discredit it in many countries. For the French wine growers it was a most unwelcome competitor. For the Italians and their early coffee-houses, it was to eradicate the 'social cankers therein', which were considered to be infested with corruption and immorality. Priests made an appeal to Pope Clement VIII to have coffee forbidden to Christians as a 'hellish black brew'. The Holy Father, however, drank coffee a lot himself and considered it a delicious drink. He replied, 'This Satan's drink, as you say, is so delicious that it would be a pity to let the infidel have exclusive use of it.' Coffee also met opposition in Hannover, London, Prussia and Sweden, mostly because of the opposition of the brewers whose beer it was going to replace on an alarming scale, particularly at breakfast. A women's petition against coffee was published in London in 1674, complaining that 'men were never to be found at home during times of domestic crises, since they were always in the coffee-houses' and that 'the hellish brew made them intoxicated and impotent'.(3.34)

England's first coffee-house was opened in Oxford at the Angel in 1650 in the parish of St Peter. London's first coffee-house was opened in 1652 by a Greek called Pasqua Rosea, with the financial backing of two Englishmen, Messrs. Bowman and Hodges, merchants at St Michael's Alley in Cornhill. Within a few years, London had hundreds of coffee-houses of all types and sizes and with varying clientele and professions, but women were barred from them.(3.35)

Arriving at about the same time as the new Puritan rule, coffee-houses were considered an excellent aid to temperance and the fight against alcoholism, particularly in London. Half-way between tavern and club, they were well suited to the new social climate of the day.

Later, a French periodical of the times entitled *Le Café* pointed out the fact that coffee-houses were catering equally for the rich and poor and must be

3.34 Bode, W. and Leto, J., *Classical Food Preparation and Presentation*, Batsford, London, 1984, p. 286.

3.35 Evelyn, J., 'Diary, May 10th 1637', quoted in Tannahill, R., *Food in History*, Palladin, 1973, p. 175.

considered 'very valuable and most democratic in character'. *Le Salon* had always been only for the rich, *le Café* was for all in a more democratic and socially dynamic age. Indeed, it has been said that the French revolution was fermented in the French coffee-house meetings, the *Café Foy* being the starting point of mob spirit on the way to the Bastille.

Gradually, the coffee-house became established in all countries of Europe in one form or another. By the end of the seventeenth century, it was estimated that London had some 2,000 and Paris some 3,000 establishments.

In many parts of Europe, *le Café* became the social centre of the town or village, where one went not only to drink coffee and eat some delicious pastries and cakes, but also to be seen. In Vienna, the coffee-house became a national institution, which to some extent has been retained until the present day. The Viennese coffee-houses undoubtedly became the most elegant in the world, full of young officers and their elegant young ladies, businessmen and merchants, writers, artists and musicians. One of the Strauss brothers was said to have composed one of his famous waltzes on the marbled table top of the famous Viennese café. Others sat for long hours, not just to drink *melange*, the Viennese version of coffee and milk, but to read the many newspapers freely supplied by the cafés on 'stick and hook' – a very common sight even today. One of the more famous Viennese coffee-houses had the proud boast that a particular corner table used to be occupied by a certain gentleman every day 'twixt 4 and 6 pm, except Sundays, for thirty-seven years'.

Thus in the span of less than one hundred years, coffee became part of the life and daily drinking habits of most, if not all, Europeans. The popularity of drinking coffee has never faltered, although in England tea has become the drink for breakfast and afternoon tea. During this century, coffee drinking has had several revivals in Britain, although many lovers of coffee and tea in England have said that of late bad coffee has replaced good tea in many cases and places.

Exactly when coffee first came to be taken at the end of a meal or banquet is less well documented. Its appearance on the written or printed menu can first be traced to the late seventeenth or early eighteenth century. But this means very little, as we know from other sources that in aristocratic houses, at the conclusion of the meal, coffee was taken by the ladies of the house in the lounge or drawing room, while the gentlemen remained in the dining room or moved to the library to smoke and to enjoy their port. The drinking of coffee in the lounge is a pleasant practice reintroduced in the last few years in many hotels and restaurants, not only to sell the dining table for a second time, but for the more relaxed atmosphere. The drinking of coffee away from the dining room may well be the reason why coffee, although printed on the menu, is not considered a course or part of the menu.

Tea

Tea is the oldest man-made drink and was drunk in China as early as the Tang period (AD 618–907). Most likely it was brought into Europe via Japan rather than directly from China. Tea had arrived in Holland in 1611, in northern Germany by 1630 and as a medicinal drug, in England, in 1609.(3.36) At a public sale in 1657, tea was sold for the first time in England, and in 1660 Samuel Pepys tried his first 'cup of tea of which I had never drank before'.(3.37)

At first tea was, like coffee, expensive, but gradually it became a most popular drink for all and was liked especially by the ladies of Europe. In England, between 1770 and 1779, some eighteen million pounds of tea were sold and consumed, much of it having been smuggled. British merchants claimed tea to be the cure for many evils and infallible for illnesses such as apoplexy, catarrh, colic, consumption, epilepsy, gallstones, lethargy, paralysis and vertigo.

The Netherlands, Denmark and northern Germany became important importers, blenders and drinkers of tea. But it was Russia where tea was made the national drink, and the samovar, that charcoal-heated *bain-marie* with the teapot ever-ready on top, became almost a Russian gastronomic emblem. Besides Russia, where tea is served in glasses and flavoured with sugar, and later with lemon, England is the only other real tea-drinking nation in Europe. The drinking of tea with milk was a gradual development which has never been satisfactorily explained, but the English afternoon tea, with all its parts, is one of the country's most civilised contributions to European gastronomy.

Potatoes

When the Spaniards returned from the new world, potatoes were carried as part of the ships' stores. They were grown in Spain most certainly by 1573, when the hospital of de la Sangre at Seville ordered potatoes with other provisions for the feeding of staff and patients.(3.38) In 1601, the potato was common in some parts of Italy and was cooked like other root vegetables.(3.39)

It is most likely that the potato reached England from Italy. For a long time it

---

3.36 Filby, F.A., *A History of Food Adulteration and Analysis*, Allen & Unwin, London, 1934, p. 31.

3.37 Braybrook, Lord (ed, 1825), *The Diaries of Samuel Pepys*, October 1660, Colburn, London, 1825.

3.38 Salaman, R.N., *The History and Social Influence of the Potato*, 1659–69, with particular reference to, Cambridge University Press, Cambridge, 1949, p. 143.

3.39 *Ibid.*, p. 90.

was believed that Sir Francis Drake imported the potato from Virginia to England, but it was not until the 1930s that the geneticist N.I. Vavilow showed this to be an impossibility.(3.40) It is possible, however, that Sir Francis Drake took supplies on board at Cartagena on the Colombia Coast in 1658, among which were potatoes, and some of which were still on board when he returned from Virginia.

The potato became fashionable in mid-Europe, again at the courts and in rich merchants' houses. Dr Tobias Venner thought that 'the nourishment yielded by the potato, although somewhat windy, was very substantial, good, and most restorative'.(3.41) William Salmon claimed that the potato 'stopped fluxes of the bowels, was full of nutrient and cured consumption. Being boiled, baked or roasted, potatoes should be eaten with butter or dripping, some salt, orange or lemon juice, or sugar.' He even gave the potato some aphrodisiacal properties, saying that they 'increased seed, provoked lust and caused fruitfulness in both sexes'.(3.42)

No doubt a marketing ploy was used to introduce many of the new foods to the general public. Today, potatoes are a very popular vegetable in most European countries, but at first it was not accepted as a valuable food, especially by the poor of Europe. The Frenchman Antoine Parmentier (1737–1813), after whom many potato dishes and dishes containing potatoes are named, struggled for many years to convince the French of the delights of the new *pommes de terre*. The French gastronome Antoine Viard was somewhat more successful with his publication of *La Cuisine Impériale* in 1806, which gave some two dozen recipes for cooking potatoes as eaten by the king.

The much-travelled French chef Antoine Beauvilliers published a small recipe book in 1814 which, for the first time in France at least, featured some English dishes in which the *matchepotesse* (mashed potato) was included, indicating that it was already very much part of the English diet before that time.(3.43)

The lack of early acceptance of the potato is a stark contrast to an over-reliance on the potato in the general diet, of which the Irish experience tells a horrific story.(3.44)

3.40 *Ibid.*, p. 52.

3.41 *Ibid.*, p. 104.

3.42 *Ibid.*, p. 106.

3.43 Tannahill, T., *Food in History*, Palladin, London, 1973, p. 259.

3.44 Forster, R. and Forster, R., *Food and Drink in History, a Selection from the Annuls, Economies, Societies, Civilisations*, vol. 5, translated by Forster, E. and Ranum, P., John Hopkins University Press, Baltimore, London, 1979, pp. 31–61.

Sugar

In about 1506, Spain began the cultivation of sugar cane in the Greater Antilles. The growing and production of sugar is a very labour-intensive undertaking, and the physical labour required was not considered suitable work for the conquistadores.

Slavery in Spain was still commonplace – some rich families could have as many as fifty slaves for the household and garden alone. Some of these slaves were Europeans, Greeks, Russians and Turks, but most of them were blacks from Africa.(3.45, 3.46) It is not surprising, therefore, that when Spain needed slaves for the Caribbean sugar plantations, she used strong blacks from Africa.

When the Spaniards became more interested in the silver and gold of the New World, the Portuguese took over the role as suppliers of sugar from their newly-acquired territories in Brazil, to which large numbers of blacks were shipped to do the very hard work, encouraged by Pope Nicholas I who had given his blessing to 'attack, subject and reduce to perpetual slavery the Saracens, pagans and other enemies of Christ'.(3.47) In 1550 there were five sugar plantations in Brazil, in 1623 the number had risen to 350.(3.48)

The Dutch, English, French and Danes, who had taken possession of a number of islands in the Caribbean, soon learned how to plant and produce sugar for the European market, which took all they could produce.

Chocolate

Chocolate is a food native to Latin America, and was discovered by the conquistadores. Drinking chocolate was made by drying and then roasting the beans of the cocoa tree over a fire and pounding them into a paste. In Mexico, the paste was mixed with hot water, herbs and some spices and gulped down:

> '. . . *in one swallow with much pleasure and satisfaction of bodily nature, to which it gives strength, nourishment and vigour, in such a way that those who are accustomed to drinking it cannot remain robust without it, even if they eat*

3.45 Vinces-Vieve, J., *An Economic History of Spain*, University Press, Princetown, 1969, p. 214.

3.46 Barraclough, G. (ed), *Eastern and Western Europe in the Middle Ages*, Thames & Hudson, London, 1970, p. 132.

3.47 Wyndham, R.H., *The Atlantic and Slavery*, Oxford University Press, Oxford, 1935, p. 221.

3.48 Russel-Wood, A.J.R., *Fideagos a Philanthropist*, Macmillan, London, 1968, pp. 53–4.

other substantial things, and they appear diminished (in their vigour) when they do not have this drink'.(3.49)

Spain and Portugal held the territories where the tree grew. But Spain kept the existence, production, consumption and enjoyment of this delicious new beverage almost a guarded secret. By the early seventeenth century, however, large amounts of the new chocolate paste were imported into Europe, in particular to Italy and Flanders from where it reached England and France. The French court was most enthusiastic, especially when in 1659 the French faculty of medicine bestowed its imprimatur on the drinking chocolate. Louis XIV considered it one of his favourites, offering it to all his guests.

As with many new foods and dishes, some strange stories were told about chocolate. One of these was of a pregnant marquise who had continuously consumed large quantities of this dark brew during her pregnancy, who subsequently gave birth to a boy who was as black as the devil!

For three hundred years, chocolate remained a beverage which was drunk both hot or cold, and served after any meal of the day. It was also considered to be an excellent bedtime drink – a custom which is still practised in England today. Gradually, chocolate paste was used in the making of after-dinner sweets, in the form of creams and mousses. It also appeared in the making of confectionery and cakes, as well as in the form of set chocolate pieces with the addition of sugar, cream, butter and other ingredients. These set chocolate pieces were the forerunners of the mass-produced chocolate bars of today. Some of the 'pralines', mouth-size, highly flavoured, artfully decorated and delicious pieces of chocolate, are today very much a part of gastronomy as *petits fours* after dinner, or as chocolates given in friendship or appreciation. Chocolate has become one of the first widely accepted convenient foods.

When *La Belle Epoche* came to its close, nearly all the components of gastronomy, cultural, technical and artistic, were well established, and the periods that followed added only organisational and professional competence to gastronomy as we understand it today.

Food and Drink in Britain

It was during the eighteenth and early twentieth centuries that Britain made its most prodigious contribution to European gastronomy. It is true that this is not

3.49 Carletti, F., *Ragionamenti – 1594–1600*, translated as *My Voyage Around the World*, by Weinstock, H., Methuen & Co., 1964, London, 1965, p. 53.

always recognised or widely accepted by the Continentals, but this contribution is a fact, and a most welcome fact nevertheless.

For most of the continent, the culinary arts on the tables of England were at best considered a laugh. In the 1950s, I planned to come to England to work as a young chef and learn English, but I was advised by those I respected not to stay too long. England was alright to work for a year or two to learn English, they said, but make sure you get into a good hotel with a French, Swiss, Italian or, possibly, a German Head Chef, so that you do not lose any of your culinary skills. On arrival, I found that very few large hotel or restaurant kitchens with a reputation were in the hands of a British Head Chef.

What is normally considered wrong with England's gastronomic attempts is best conveyed by the following tale.

A well-to-do and very cultured French businessman came to England by invitation to stay for a week or so, in the country house of his near aristocratic English business partner, for holiday-come-business discussions. On arrival and on entering the country house with its lovely grounds and gardens, situated in the beautiful Surrey countryside, the French guest was overwhelmed by the grandiose proportions of the house and its hall, the layout, furnishing and general charm of said abode, thinking that only a highly cultured gentleman could live thus.

Taken by his host for a welcome drink into the library, the cultural excitement of our Frenchman grew when he saw a room full of books, on oak shelves from floor to ceiling and furnished with exquisite china, silver, beautiful paintings, and flower arrangements everywhere. Plus the most generous and comfortable chairs and sofas, on which he was invited to relax.

This most pleasant first impression of his host's home reached new heights and expectations when, after a rest and change in his most spacious and immaculate bedroom, he heard the gong calling for dinner.

As he sipped his pre-dinner glass of champagne, proffered to him by a most scrupulously attentive butler, from a silver tray, of a size and quality which, if sold, would place a lot of currency in the treasury of many smaller countries, the guest glanced through the open library dooor leading into the panelled dining-room of the house, where he could see a large polished table, laid for dinner for a party of ten.

This table was liberally strewn with large silver ornaments and a candelabra with large candles, and decorated with the most generous large, as well as individual, flower arrangements.

And it was set with the most delicate of china, exquisite silver cutlery and the most delicate array of crystal for wine, fit for any princely home. When the butler stood in the doorway of the dining-room, bowed reverently to the assembled dinner guests and said with a clear and dignified voice: 'My lords, ladies and gentlemen, dinner is served', the French guest could not be other than most impressed.

The visitor from France had many a breakfast, lunch and dinner during his week's stay in these splendid surroundings. He complimented his host on many occasions on his beautiful home, individual features of the house, its paintings, as well as the selection of wines served at mealtimes. He said nothing about the food or dishes served. Well, almost nothing.

After a few days' stay, he was taken with others for a morning horse ride in the lovely grounds of the country house. The party reached the top of a small hill which allowed a beautiful view over the Surrey Downs. A view which showed hills, fields and villages in the distance, as well as various cottages nearby and churches further afield. A view of the English countryside that delights locals and foreigners alike.

When one of the party asked the French man what he thought of the countryside afore him, he enthused with a mixture of French and English vocabulary, which left little doubt about his obvious delight in what he saw in front of him. After a thoughtful silence, he uttered: 'Please, please never cook it.'

When I came first to England, the feeling expressed by the Frenchman about English cooking still held a lot of truth, but much has changed for the better, and I have proudly cooked British dishes all over the world, with much success, and often with great surprise expressed about the taste and goodness of the dishes.

Well, thirty years or so later, I am still here, and I am convinced that the British have contributed greatly to European gastronomy. As an 'outsider', I should like to list the contribution Britain has made, starting with:

English Roasts

Beef

The best cuts are sirloin, wing-rib, fore-rib and fillet roasted to perfection *à l'Anglaise*, that is to say, slightly pink-rare or underdone and served with a rich gravy, Yorkshire puddings and offered with English mustard and/or creamed horse-radish. To this group also belongs the now classic beef-Wellington, although this is usually served with different accompaniments.

Lamb/Mutton

Here the best cuts are: leg, shoulder, loin, best-end crowns, saddle and haunch. The British invention of mint sauce should accompany this roast, or in the case of mutton, redcurrant jelly. Although not part of the roasts, the demise in the serving of boiled leg of mutton with caper sauce must be regretted.

Pork

Leg, loin and suckling pig are the choice cuts. When served with sage stuffing and a sharp apple sauce, what could be more British?

Poultry

Turkey

Roast turkey served with thyme and/or chestnut stuffing and accompanied by chipolatas, game chips and cranberry sauce is still the British favourite at Christmas. However, it is available in the home and most hotels and restaurants all the year round.

Chicken, Poussin and Capon

These are crisply roasted and served with a slice or two of grilled bacon accompanied by a creamy bread sauce. A slight hint of clove makes these dishes again very British.

Duck/Goose

The popularity of the goose has been overtaken by the duck of late. When crisply roasted and stuffed with a thyme stuffing, and served with a slightly cinnamon-flavoured apple sauce, we have again a typically British dish.

Furred Game

This includes cuts such as the haunch, saddle and leg of venison. Well hung and often marinated in red wine or cider, they represent some of the finest British roasts when served with a rich sauce and accompanied by redcurrant jelly.

Feathered Game

This includes pheasant, quail, snipe, grouse, wild duck and partridge. When served with game chips, fried breadcrumbs, reduced game gravy and redcurrant jelly, British feathered game is the finest in the world.

Small English Sauces

The next important contribution to international gastronomy must be the so-called small English sauces. These fall into two groups:

Hot	*Cold*
apple	cranberry
butter	Cambridge
bread	Cumberland
caper	gooseberry
cranberry	mint
parsley	Oxford
celery	horse-radish
egg	Worcestershire

Hot sauces are most commonly served with boiled or poached meats, fish or egg and vegetables; the cold ones with cold meats or fish and hot roasted meats. The cold ones are also used to flavour stews, soups and sauces.

Puddings and Pies

Puddings

There are two types of pudding: steamed savoury puddings, such as steak pudding, steak and kidney pudding, steak, kidney and mushroom pudding, steak and mushroom pudding and steak and oyster pudding; and steamed sweet puddings, such as vanilla sponge, chocolate sponge, treacle sponge, date sponge and mixed fruit sponge.

Puddings such as Christmas pudding are excellent when served with various sweet sauces, such as egg-custard, lemon sauce, brandy sauce, chocolate sauce or double cream. Although very different in its preparation, the bread and butter pudding must be included here as one of the classics.

Pies

Pies are found on the menus of hotels and restaurants all over the world.

Savoury Pies

The luncheon main course savoury types are the same as that for steamed puddings (above).

Sweet Pies

These include apple pie, apple and blackberry pie, apple and blackcurrant pie, rhubarb pie and gooseberry pie. Served with a good egg-custard or clotted or

British steamed pudding

Pie crust, top only

Flan crust, bottom only

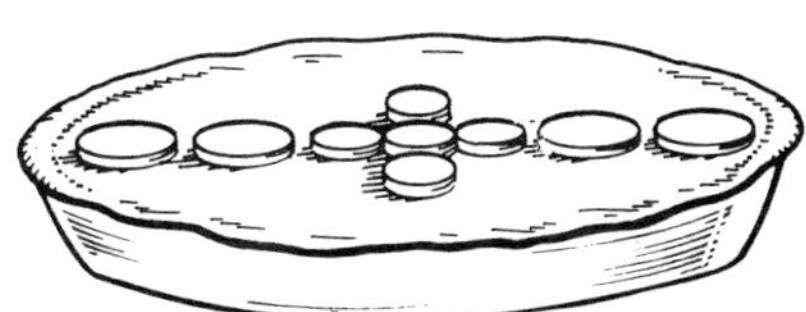

Tart on plate, crust top and bottom

Figure 3.18 Puddings, pies, flans and tarts
Source: The Even Giant Swipe File, The Hart Publishing Inc. 1978

double cream, or even vanilla ice-cream, they are popular sweets wherever you travel.

I recall the serving of a warm apple and blackcurrant pie with double cream at a banquet for 120 gourmets in Stockholm. It was the sensation of the meal, discussed for a long time by the guests, sixty of whom requested the recipe. Truly a great compliment to those very simple but superb British sweets.

It is with some regret that fewer and fewer puddings and pies appear on the menus of British hotels and restaurants. And if they do, they are more often than not manufactured in factories.

There seems today to be still some confusion as to what is a pudding and what is a pie, and the names are wrongly used.

The Silver Grill

Long before one thought much about healthy eating, the better British hotels and restaurants devised a mode of eating which is exemplified by the Silver Grill or Grill Room. The Grill Room and its service can be found in various forms all over the world. Here assorted cuts and portions of flesh, fowl and fish are displayed in chilled cabinets for the guests to choose from. The cuts are cooked to order while the guests consume their first course. The cuts are served with a salad or vegetables and potatoes which change with the season.

The most suitable cuts are:

* lamb: chops, cutlets, kidney;
* pork: chops, cutlets, escalopes, sausages;
* beef: fillet steak, sirloin steak, tournedos, minute steak, T-bone steak, porterhouse steak, rump steak, fore-rib steak and sausages;
* poultry: spatch-cock chicken, spit chicken, breast, legs of chicken, poussins;
* mixed grill: consisting of 1–2 lamb cutlets, 1–2 pork sausages, 1–2 slices of bacon, 1 lamb's kidney and served with straw potatoes, watercress, and a slice of parsley or other savoury herb butter. The mixed grill is also known as the London mixed grill, and is an invention which was introduced in the late nineteenth and early twentieth centuries when the Silver Grill became established;
* fish: the successful cooking of fish over grill bars had to be limited to the smaller, whole-fish types, such as Dover sole, small whole plaice or flounders, lobsters, trout, herrings and mackerel, or larger fish steaks from salmon, halibut, turbot or cod.

Afternoon Tea

In my opinion, the afternoon tea is the most prestigious contribution by Britain to the world of gastronomy; whether it is served with full due ceremony at the Ritz or in a simplified form in a Devon tea room, it is and has remained a classic of its kind.

This service should include:

* freshly made tea served with extra hot water, cold milk or lemon, sugar and the best of china. At least three to four different choices of teas should be available, such as Earl Grey, Darjeeling, Lapsang Souchong and Orange Pikco;
* sandwiches: one to three varieties on different breads and without meats or fish, such as cucumber, tomato, egg and cress, watercress, fish spreads, meat spreads, marmite and jam with bananas (for children's parties);

Figure 3.19 Afternoon tea
Source: The Even Giant Swipe File, The Hart Publishing Inc. 1978

- scones: one or two buttered scones, offered with different jams and whipped or double or clotted cream;
- fancy cakes: one piece of cake from a selection, such as fruit cake, Battenberg, Victoria sponge, madeira cake, chocolate cake, eclairs, or English small fancy cakes;
- toasted cakes: one of the following which may be changed on different days of the week, such as toasted teacake, toasted muffin and toasted crumpet.

In the better establishments, and most certainly when an afternoon tea dance is offered, it is good policy to offer two or possibly even three fresh pots of tea during the afternoon.

Naturally, there are many other valuable contributions made by Britain to what is good to eat and drink – the above represents my idea of what is the best in British gastronomy. However, many famous British dishes are for some reason served only at lunchtime, and this makes it difficult to write menus with typical English dishes when it comes to formal banquets and dinners.

Although much has changed for the better in what is now available on the British table, and Britain now supports some very fine restaurants headed by some excellent young British chefs with good, even worldwide reputations, the experience of the French visitor sadly still holds a truth. This being that the superb setting and service for British gastronomy in hotels, restaurants, banquet halls and town and country hotels as well as private homes is nearly always much better than the care with which the food is presented and served.

CHAPTER 4

Development of the Modern Classical Menu Structure

Introduction

It could be said that the rich of Europe showed little if any regard for the poor in their midst in any age. With very few exceptions, it was the rich who were well educated and well informed, and this gave them the opportunity to be the leaders of all things new.

The life-style of the rich of the eighteenth and nineteenth centuries was no different from that of any age before. Not only were they concerned, if only for their own profit, with all commercial, technical and scientific advances of the times, but also they supported and encouraged the arts, such as music, architecture, poetry, literature and the theatre.

One of the 'new arts' was the art of comfortable living. Having sold their big houses in London at considerable profit and assured themselves of a yearly income from capital or enterprise, the rich aristocrats, bankers or merchants moved into the beautiful English countryside. Some had ancestral homes to occupy; others built themselves country houses incorporating all the new technical advances of the age.

These houses were often situated in the most beautiful settings and surrounded by lovely gardens. First in the Italian style, then in the French style and then in a style all of their own, the gardens of English country houses became famous and were admired all over the world.

Inside, the country house would be finished with the most elegant decor, furnished with the most beautiful furniture, the best of paintings and the most collectable *objets d'art* from all parts of the world. To show the house off, the owner would invite relatives, friends and business associates for a long weekend, or even a week or two, at various times of the year.

This gradually resulted in a continuous social intercourse requiring breakfast, luncheons, picnics, teas, dinners and even banquets for house-guests. In this way, the patrons of large houses did much for renewed food availability, food preparation, cooking, food presentation and the new 'art of eating' in selected company. The whole operation required some considerable organisation both at the back and the front of the house.

Menus were known during the times of Athenaeus at about AD 200, but these were just lists of the items of food to be served. In the following centuries, the menu evolved in various ways. But now came the modern classical menu, which had its origin in the courts or princely houses of the European aristocracy of the late seventeenth, eighteenth and nineteenth centuries.

Only kings, queens, princes and princesses of the many European principalities had the leisure and means to indulge in the development and service of the most exquisite foods. They employed an army of servants to prepare and serve dishes at any time of the day or night. Pomp and ceremonial living was considerable. Hunting, eating and drinking were the main distractions of the idle rich, with occasionally a small war thrown in for added excitement and general amusement.

The day started with a late, long and considerable breakfast and ended with a late, long and substantial dinner, with a wide variety of dishes and many courses. Eating was interrupted only by copious drinking, which often led to bouts of sleep at the table between courses. Much care was taken not to break this continuing indulgence in either food, drink or sleep lest a prolonged period of consciousness brought the realisation of the folly of such ways.

The gastronomic requirements and culinary excesses of the aristocracy were made possible by considerable culinary developments in the skills and arts of the French chefs of the day. When Catherine de Medici married the Dauphin, later Henry II of France, she brought her Florentine cooks with her to the French court. These introduced to the kitchens of the court many new dishes and the use of many oriental herbs and spices. The culinary knowledge and skills of her chefs very quickly found an appreciative following and participants in her newly instigated style of good living among the courtiers and their ladies.

What was more important, Catherine brought with her an attitude to the preparation and presentation of food which was, at that time, unique. With this attitude went a grace of manner and etiquette which had not been experienced at any French court before. Catherine brought to France much new tableware not seen before, including forks and very fine glass. This made dining extraordinarily elegant.

From these embryonic beginnings in the early sixteenth century, it took the *maîtres de cuisine* and *maîtres de table* of France less than a hundred years to build a culinary reputation which has lasted to this day. The excellence of their food and the elegance of their service has been imitated by others, but has never been surpassed. It was the favourable gastro-geographical climate of France and natural sources of supply and, above all, the natural flair and finesse of the

French with anything concerned with the preparation and presentation of foods and wines, which made their reputation all over Europe and, later, elsewhere in the world.

Any court or grand house of the many principalities or dukedoms of Europe, mindful of their proud name and jealous of their reputation for hospitality, had at least a French *Maître de Cuisine* and, in many cases, even a *Maître de Table*. The courts and other large houses quickly tried to outdo one another as to the choice, splendour and delicacy of their dishes *à la française*, and considerable sums were paid for the artistic skills and services of French chefs. This gave the chefs much encouragement and helped in the development of many culinary innovations, both in the form of new dishes and in technical advances in the kitchen.

With this background of development and newly won fame and reputation, it is not surprising that these chefs regulated the order in the kitchen and *etiquette sur la table*. Here we find the source of the gradual building of the classical French cuisine and its menu construction and sequencing, which led to the so-called *service français* of the mid-eighteenth century. This consisted of three types of service with several courses and choices as shown below:

Service 1

2–3 *Potages* (soups)
2–4 *Hors-d'oeuvres chauds* or *entrées volantes* (hot, small *entrées*)
4–6 *Relevés* (large joints)
4–6 *Entrées chaudes* (small cuts)
2–3 *Grosses pièces sur socle* (centre courses)
2–3 *Rôtis et salades* (roasts with salad)
2–3 *Entremets de légumes* (vegetable courses)
2–4 *Entremets sucres chauds* (hot sweets)

Service 2

2–3 *Rôtis et salades* (second different roast and salad)
2–4 *Entremets de légumes* (second different vegetable course)
2–4 *Entremets sucres chauds* (second different hot sweet course)

Service 3

2–3 *Entremets sucres froids* (cold sweets)
2–4 *Grosses pièces sur socle* (highly decorated mounted sweet course)
Fruits, compotes, desserts (fruits and compotes of all types)

All dishes in each service, which on special occasions could be increased in number, would be presented and displayed for the edification and delectation of the guests. When they had admired the dishes and their gastric juices were suitably aroused, the dishes would be removed for carving, dissection and portioning, and would then be served in order of importance to the now seated guests. The hot dishes were kept warm, according to type, on red-hot charcoal trays or hot-water *bains-marie* (water baths), often built into the design of bowls and dishes on which the foods were presented. But, in time, the *service français* was changed and was replaced by the so-called *service russe*, or Russian service.

The Russian type of service is used today as the basis for the correct sequencing of dishes and courses on a menu, whether for a glittering or more simple occasion. The *service russe* has the following construction and sequence:

1 *Hors-d'oeuvre froid* (cold appetiser)
2 *Potage* (soup)
3 *Hors-d'oeuvres chauds or entrées volantes* (hot appetisers or small entrées)
4 *Oeuf et farineux* (egg or farinaceous dish)
5 *Poisson* (fish course)
6 *Entrée chaude* (hot entrée, garnished)
7 *Relevé ou pièce de résistance – ou grosses pièces* (main course, joint of meat or poultry with garnish of vegetable and potatoes)
8 *Entrée froide* (cold entrée)
9 *Sorbet* (water ice flavoured with liqueur)
10 *Rôti et salade* (roast course with salad, poultry, game, some meats)
11 *Entremet de légumes* (hot or cold vegetable course)
12 *Entremet chaud* (hot sweet course)
13 *Entremet froid* (cold sweet course)
14 *Entremet de fromage* (cheese savouries, hot or cold, cheeseboard)
15 *Dessert* (selection of fresh fruit)
Café (coffee, Cona, filter, mocha, Turkish, etc)

The structure of the *service russe* above is represented by the following fifteen-course menu:

Sample menu

1 *Cantaloup frappé* (chilled cantaloup melon)
2 *Coupe de terrapin au xérès* (clear turtle soup in cup with sherry)
3 *Bouchée Montglas* (square puff-pastry case filled with goose liver, tongue, mushroom and truffle)
4 *Oeuf poche à la Barcelonnaise* (poached egg on half-cooked tomatoes, peppers, Espagnole)
5 *Darne de saumon poche* (poached salmon steaks)
6 *Noisette d'agneau Duroc* (small steaklets of lamb, new potatoes, chasseur sauce)
7 *Selle de veau Orloff* (saddle of veal in the style of Orloff, onion, cheese, celery, cheese sauce)
8 *Mousse de poulet Perigord* (chicken mousse with truffles)
9 *Sorbet au Grand Marnier* (water ice with Grand Marnier)
10 *Faisan rôti sur canapé, salade d'endives* (roast pheasant on canape, chicory salad)
11 *Asperge de lauris, beurre fondu* (lauris asparagus with melted butter)
12 *Soufflé Rothschild* (hot soufflé flavoured with spirits, salpicon of fruit)
13 *Bombe Sicilienne* (ice-cream bomb, of lemon and praline ice-cream, almonds)
14 *Bâtons de Venise* (puff pastry sticks with cheese)
15 *Corbeille de fruits en saison* (basket of fruit in season)
Café (coffee)

A closer look at this new Russian-type service reveals that all the basic elements of the French menu and its service are present – only the order and flow of the courses, the nature of some of the courses, and the organisation behind the scenes have actually changed. In the kitchen, the various foods are now arranged directly on to silver flats and dishes for service direct to the guest. The food requiring dissection or carving is very skilfully dissected and carved in the kitchen ready for a quick and easier service when taken into the dining room. Under the *service français* a whole salmon would be dressed as the fish course, but with this more modern service, salmon steaks, or suprêmes, would be cut expertly and cooked individually, ready as a portion for service. The full service style of *service russe* still exists in many hotels and restaurants all over the world, particularly in the case of royal occasions, diplomatic dinners or traditional company dinners. Even so, the number of courses will usually not exceed eight to ten and the presentation, if still sometimes elaborate, is most certainly more modern.

Only the changes and developments of the classical menu have so far been dealt with in respect of the grand households of Europe where it originated, but there were other influences which brought considerable change to the classical menu, and all manner of eating styles in the various strata of the evolving society.

Establishment of the Great Restaurants and Hotel Restaurants

The provision of food and drink by so-called food or bakers' shops (the forerunners of the restaurant) as well as the provision of food, drink and shelter by inn-type establishments (the forerunner of hotels) had, by the late eighteenth and early nineteenth centuries, been established in Europe for many years. In most cases, they provided a service to pilgrims, clergy, soldiers and other travellers. The service was simple, down to earth and sometimes primitive, and the food and beverage offered was similar to the diets of the peasantry, consisting of local produce, always wholesome, sometimes good, but seldom fancy. At the end of the scale were the new restaurants of, for example, France, which were anything but down to earth or simple in either the organisation behind the scenes or at the table.

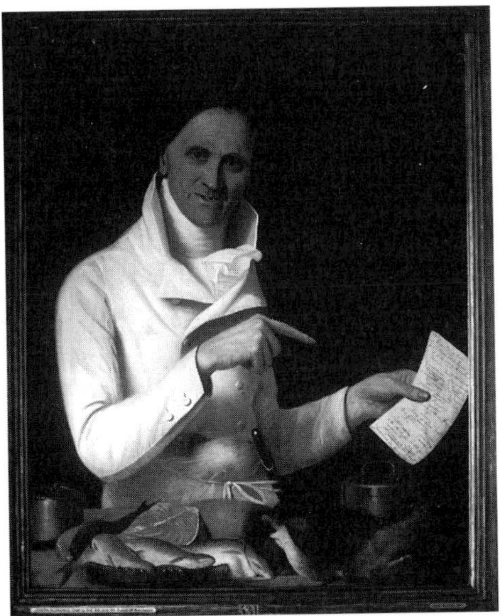

Figure 4.1 Joseph Florence, 1817, Chef to the 3rd, 4th and 5th Dukes of Buccleuch
Source: In the collection of the Duke of Buccleuch and Queensberry KT

Figure 4.2 The chef at the Hotel Chatham by Sir William Orpen
Source: Royal Academy of Arts, London

Most of these restaurants were launched by now-famous chefs or *maîtres de table*, who had gained their experience in the aristocratic kitchens or dining rooms of Europe. Some of these restaurants had much style and splendour. Their elegance owed much to the emulation of the living surroundings of their princely patrons whom they intended to serve.

Rooms with high ceilings, marbled walls, paintings and mirrors and other decoration, plus elegant furnishings and much exquisite tableware, abounded. The new restaurants became famous throughout Europe as centres of good eating and living, and they brought fame and fortune to some exponents of *haute cuisine*.

However, as more and more of the chefs of royal households opened more and more restaurants and other eating houses, there resulted a glut of places where people could eat in royal style, and which could not be supported by the aristocracy or even commercial patronage. Many restaurants went out of business, others lowered their standards in the hope of attracting a wider clientele, yet others specialised in local and regional foods, or limited their offerings to dishes for which they could become famous.

Wars and other economic difficulties did not help the new restaurants either. One could argue that to some extent the very excellence and splendour which

Figure 4.3 Café Restaurant Pierron, Paris 1852
Source: Lippheidesche Bibliothek, Staatliche Kunstbibliothek, Berlin

had brought the *cuisine française* to the forefront of fame and repute within the royal households, could also be the cause of its later malaise. It is one thing to prepare and present long, exquisite and expensive menus in an aristocratic house where the patron will foot the bill, but it is another matter to transfer the same into the commercial field where eventually it must pay its way and make a profit.

Changes had to be made for economic reasons and because of a more enlightened attitude to food and living eating habits generally. Thus, gradually, the classical menu (see page 110) changed and contracted – a trend which has continued to this day. The changes were never in the quality of the food, at least not in the better household and restaurants. The changes which took place affected the quantity of the food (both portion size and number of courses) and the presentation of the food, which was becoming less elaborate.

Despite the changes, the sequence of courses on a menu has remained intact. We still eat the *hors-d'oeuvre* or soup at the beginning of our meal, and the gâteau or cheese last. The balance of our meal from light to heavy and back to light has remained. Both the sequence of courses and balance should apply whether we are eating in a four-star restaurant or a Wimpy Bar. The following examples and comments follow our sample menu (page 112) and show how this may be reduced within the correct sequence, and why.

Sample menu: first variation

1 *Cantaloup frappé*
2 *Oeuf poche à la Barcelonnaise*
3 *Darne de saumon poche*
4 *Selle de veau Orloff*
5 *Sorbet au Grand Marnier*
6 *Faisan rôti sur canapé, salade d'endives*
7 *Asperges de lauris, beurre fondu*
8 *Bombe Sicilienne*
9 *Bâtons de Venise*
10 *Corbeille de fruits en saison*
Café

Figure 4.4 Café Française, Leibzig 1842
Source: Lippheidesche Bibliothek, Staatliche Kunstbibliothek, Berlin

Here, from the original menu's fifteen courses, only ten are now left, as the soup, the hot *hors-d'oeuvre*, the *entrée*, the cold *entrée* and the hot sweet have been removed. However, the menu is still quite considerable by any standards and has lost nothing of its balance.

A further reduction has been made to the second variation below, where only eight courses from the original fifteen remain as the cold *hors-d'oeuvre*, the hot *hors-d'oeuvre*, egg course, *relevé*, cold *entrée*, vegetable course and cold sweet have been removed. This results in a still quite substantial meal with a very good balance. In this way, further reductions in courses to be served can be made without loss of balance and with a more reasonable number of courses akin to modern eating habits.

Sample menu: second variation

1 *Coupe de terrapin au xérès*
2 *Darne de saumon poche*
3 *Noisette d'agneau Duroc*
4 *Sorbet au Grand Marnier*
5 *Faisan rôti sur canapé, salade d'endives*
6 *Soufflé Rothschild*
7 *Bâtons de Venise*
8 *Corbeille de fruits en saison*
Café

Sample menu: third variation

1 *Coupe de terrapin au xérès*
2 *Oeuf poche à la Barcelonnaise*
3 *Selle de veau Orloff*
4 *Mousse de poulet Perigord*
5 *Faisan rôti sur canapé, salade d'endives*
6 *Bâtons de Venise*
7 *Corbeille de fruits en saison*
Café

This third variation on the original menu is without a sweet course. Often a menu of this type is offered when the dinner guests are gentlemen only or when a savoury rather than a sweet is asked for. Even the sorbet has disappeared, but the delicate chicken mousse will still give a nice break between the *relevé* of the saddle of veal and the roast pheasant.

Sample menu: fourth variation

1 *Cantaloup frappé*
2 *Darne de saumon poche*
3 *Noisette d'agneau Duroc*
4 *Sorbet au Grand Marnier*
5 *Faisan rôti sur canapé, salade d'endives*
6 *Bombe Sicilienne*
7 *Bâtons de Venise*
Café

Still with a good balance, the fourth variation is a somewhat lighter menu, suitable for a mixed gathering or ladies only.

Two further variations on the basic theme are as follows:

Sample menu: fifth variation

1 *Coupe de terrapin au xérès*
2 *Selle de veau Orloff*
3 *Sorbet au Grand Marnier*
4 *Faisan rôti sur canapé, salade d'endives*
5 *Soufflé Rothschild*
Café

Sample menu: sixth variation

1 *Cantaloup frappé*
2 *Coupe de terrapin au xérès*
3 *Faisan rôti sur canapé, salade d'endives*
4 *Bombe Sicilienne*
5 *Bâtons de Venise*
Café

In this way the original menu could be reduced further to three or four courses, and many other combinations are possible. It is perfectly feasible to start the meal with a hot *hors-d'oeuvre*, but this is usually done only at dinners or banquets on cold winter days. When just three or four course menus are served, the separate vegetable course should not be included and it is advisable to serve some vegetables or potatoes with what will be the main course.

The last menu variation here is a good example. The pheasant has become the main course and, as this was originally served with salad, a suitable potato, say *pommes noisettes* or *pommes châteaux*, may be added to accompany the roast pheasant. This is not necessary in the case when a *relevé*, such as the saddle of veal Orloff, becomes the main course. *Relevés* by their very nature of presentation usually have a considerable garnish, which can take the place of vegetables and potatoes normally associated with a main course in England. The braised celery and creamed potatoes which make up the garnish Orloff, if served generously, would suffice.

I make no excuse for using the French-based model and French language or orientation for all matters appertaining to food and cookery. Just as the language of commerce is English and the language of music is Italian, the language of food is, without doubt, French. It might perhaps be considered old-fashioned and irrelevant in modern gastronomy, but undoubtedly French is nevertheless unifying and has provided a well-tried and tested code which for many years has lead to a wider understanding of food preparation and presentation, and gastronomy in general.(4.1)

When one considers the development of the modern classical menu, one must recognise several individuals who have in their various ways contributed to the modern menu and to the professional development and elevation of gastronomy on a considerable scale. This list could be long, but for the purpose of this book six names must be mentioned. Like some personalities in literature or science, they tower high above others because of their personal contribution and commitment to the art, and to the scientific as well as social understanding of gastronomy in the twentieth century.

The Old Masters

Marie Antonin Careme

Born in Paris on 8 June 1784 and died there on 12 January 1833, Careme was a king of the chefs, who was able to administer to the tastes and requirements of Talleyrand, Rothschild, the Emperor Alexander of Russia, King George IV and

4.1 Bode, W. and Leto, J., *Classical Food Preparation and Presentation*, Batsford, London, 1984, pp. 9–18.

many other famous men of his time. His family was poor and large, and when he was still a child he was abandoned by his parents and forced to earn his living by knocking on doors trying to find a job, food and shelter. Destiny led him to a small restaurant and he began work as a kitchen help. He had a passion for working and learning the secrets and resources of cookery. His initiative led him to the celebrated *pâtissier* Bailly, who had the famous diplomat Talleyrand as his client. This diplomat cleverly made gastronomy serve his political ambitions. He was the gentleman who declared to Louis XVIII, the gourmet king, on leaving for the Congress in Vienna, 'Sir, I have more need of casseroles than of written instruction.'(4.2) Careme acknowledged Bailly for the ability and experience he gained when he wrote:

'I was with M. Bailly as his first tutor, the good master showed a lively interest in me. He allowed me to leave work in order to draw in the print room. When I had shown him that I had a particular vocation for his art, he confided to me the task of executing pièces montées for the Consul's (Napoleon's) table.'(4.3)

Careme had associated confectionery with architecture and he wrote, quoted by Anatole France: 'The fine arts are five in number, one of them being architecture – whose main branch is confectionery.'(4.4) He entered the service of M. de Lavalette, who kept a famous table and who entertained most of the distinguished men of his day in politics, the army, the arts and sciences. Here he worked, as he put it, to further the union of delicacy, order and economy. He stayed twelve years with Talleyrand whose table, he declared, was furnished at once with grandeur and wisdom.

Next Careme was appointed to the office of chief cook for the Prince Regent in England, where he stayed for two years. Every morning he explained the properties of each individual dish to the Prince who one day said: 'You will kill me with a surfeit of food. I have a fancy for everything you put before me. The temptation is really too great.' Careme's reply was: 'My great concern is to stimulate your appetite by the variety of my dishes. It is no concern of mine to curb it.'(4.5)

He returned to France because the English fogs depressed him. When the Prince Regent, later King George IV, asked him to return, he declined the offer, giving the reason that London was 'all too sombre' and he wished to finish

---

4.2 From teaching notes, facts, comments, gathered over 30 years, sources now unknown.

4.3 From teaching notes, facts, comments, gathered over 30 years, sources now unknown.

4.4 From teaching notes, facts, comments, gathered over 30 years, sources now unknown.

4.5 From teaching notes, facts, comments, gathered over 30 years, sources now unknown.

writing his book with the time he had left. Careme fell gravely ill and died at the age of 49. His life is a model of probity and nobility. Money meant nothing to him. His art alone was important. Careme should be regarded even today as the founder of *la grande cuisine*, classic French cookery.

Antonin Augustin Parmentier

Born in Monndier in France in 1737, Parmentier wrote numerous works on food, especially on the popularisation of potatoes, which were scorned as food in France before his time. He not only introduced this edible root into France, but also persuaded his countrymen to accept it as a food. At the same time he taught them more than twenty different ways of preparing it for the table. Some alleged that it contained poison or that it would produce skin disease, and that it was generally fit only for pigs' food. In some French provinces the cultivation of potatoes was forbidden.

Louis XVI professed such esteem for the great philanthropist that he interviewed him and Parmentier explained how nutritious the food was, being an economical substitute for bread. In France at this time there was a great famine. The king was so impressed with Parmentier's earnestness that he subsequently conferred on him a title and then chose for him a crest, which was, appropriately, a potato flower.

In addition, there was a royal proclamation that 50 acres of uncultivated land should be devoted to the cultivation of potatoes. It is on this land that the town of Neuilly now stands. After this there was a mania for potatoes and everyone in court was wearing a potato flower in his button hole.

Parmentier died in 1813 at the age of 76 and was interred at Pere la Chaise cemetery. Around the monument erected to his memory is a small garden, planted with the vegetable for which he loved and laboured so much.

Alexis Soyer

Born in October 1809 at Meaux-en-Brie in France, Soyer was dedicated by his parents to the service of the church. At the age of nine, he was sent to the cathedral church as chorister in order that he could earn free instruction for the priesthood. Alexis urged his parents to let him do something different. The story is told that he enforced his desire to leave the church by tolling the big bell of the cathedral and giving an alarm of fire in the middle of the night. Because of this the inhabitants were scared from their slumber and the garrison placed them under arms until the culprit of this escapade was found. His dismissal from the choir of the cathedral followed as a matter of course.

For some years the future was very undecided, and it was not until he was sixteen that he made any move at all towards selecting a career. Then his brother, Philippe, introduced him to cooking, and accordingly he was apprenticed at Gripnon in 1826. Having completed his apprenticeship with éclat, he was engaged by Douix, the well-known restaurateur in the Boulevard des Italiens, with whom he remained for three years during which time he became head of the kitchen when he was little more than seventeen. In 1830, he was appointed to serve in the Foreign Office as second cook. After only a few weeks a revolution broke out and the kitchen was stormed. Soyer saved himself from rough treatment by singing *La Marseillaise* with all his might and beating time with a spoon. This led to his being carried off in triumph by the mob, while all his *confrères* were ill-treated and some were shot.

Soyer fell in love with a Miss Emma Jones, the stepdaughter of one M. Simonau, a Flemish artist in Fitzroy Square. They were married in 1837 at St George's church. That same year he accepted the post of head cook at the Reform Club. It was said that at all times he was merry and full of fun and no man loved a practical joke more than he.

One day, Lord Melbourne was inspecting his kitchen at the Reform Club, and laughingly observed to Soyer that his female assistants were remarkable for their good looks. 'Ah, my lord', replied Soyer with a knowing smile, 'we do not want plain cooks here.'(4.6)

During the famine in Ireland in February 1847, he went there to help feed the thousands with his soup-kitchens. He is also known for his good work during the following years in the east of London and in the Crimea, where he worked at the same time as Florence Nightingale. Whereas Miss Nightingale was concerned with the appalling conditions of the sick and wounded of the Crimean War, Alexis Soyer was equally appalled by the lack of arrangements for feeding the troops. He devised a simple drum stove from materials found on the battlefield, which would allow groups of soldiers to provide themselves with a simple but hot meal. The construction of this simple Soyer cooking stove has seen some technological changes, and has been redesigned into larger and smaller versions, but its basic simplicity and effectiveness has not really changed. The British army acknowledges this fact and still calls it the Soyer stove today. Most army cooks still prefer the Soyer stove to more modern appliances when cooking in the field. 'You can trust it in all conditions and it is so adaptable to any fuel' (Capt. R.M. Knowles, 1983). Alex Soyer died on the night of 5 August 1858 at the age of 49.

4.6 From teaching notes, facts, comments, gathered over 30 years, sources now unknown.

Charles M. Elme Francatelli

Francatelli was born in London in 1805 (his father was Italian). He was educated in France but was destined for a career as a chef. In France he met Antonin Careme, who was becoming a 'king' in his profession. It has been said of Francatelli that he taught the Prince of Wales to eat macaroni, and her Majesty the Queen to value the flavour of pistachio in sweets and confectionery.

He was the first culinary artist in this country to advocate the dinner *à la russe.* Of cooking he wrote:

> *'Simplicity is as essential an element in cooking as it is in other arts. Excess in the quantity and variety of spices and condiments – the bane of English cookery – is especially to be guarded against.'*(4.7)

Francatelli was appointed chef de cuisine to the Earl of Chelmsford and Dudley, Lord Kinnaird and Mr Rowland Errington of Melton Mowbray (this town is famous for pork pies made from a recipe provided by him). As a manager of the celebrated Freemasons' Tavern, he did much to ensure the exceeding popularity of that house, which it maintained for many years. He was employed by Queen Victoria for several years as *maître d'hôtel.* As an author on cookery he had few equals. His first work, *The Modern Cook*, appeared in 1845 and ran through twelve editions. In 1861 he produced *The Cook's Guide and Butler's Assistant*, and shortly afterwards *Cookery for the Working Classes* and *Royal English and Foreign Confectionery Book*. Francatelli died in 1876 at the age of 71.

Alfred Suzanne

Born in Normandy in 1829, Suzanne's father and grandfather were remarkable chefs. He studied in Paris, but at the age of eighteen he abandoned his studies and returned to his father's profession and carefully read the works of the immortal Careme. He started as an apprentice in the kitchen of the Earl of Clarendon, then Lord Lieutenant of Ireland, and at the end of six months he was promoted to the honourable position of head pastry cook at Dublin Castle, a position which he held for four years. He then went into the service of the Earl of Wilton as *chef de cuisine* for the following twenty-eight years. He is acknowledged to be a great authority on culinary matters. In his book, *Egg Cookery*, he describes more than two hundred different ways of converting eggs into dainty and appetising dishes.

4.7 From teaching notes, facts, comments, gathered over 30 years, sources now unknown.

During his retirement he and his wife lived in the charming Parisian suburb of Neuilly. He was still active and he was a gentleman who was regarded with admiration and respect on account of his geniality and undoubted abilities. His personal accomplishments were many: a musician, artist and an amateur photographer of some repute. His works included the Earl of Bradford, the Marquis of Hastings, Baron Rothschild and Prince Edward of Saxe Weimar. He is well known for his portrait of Fred Archer in hunting dress, taken at Melton Mowbray where the Wilton family have their seat.

Auguste Escoffier

Born in October 1846, in Villeneuve-Loubet on the French Riviera, Escoffier became an apprentice at the Restaurant Français in Nice at the age of 13. During the Franco–Prussian war in 1870 he was *chef de cuisine* of General McMahon. Later he directed the kitchens of the world's finest luxury hotels, such as the Hôtel de Paris in Monte Carlo, Hotel Schweizerhof in Lucerne and the Hotel Adlon in Berlin. In Monte Carlo he met the greatest hotelier of all time, Caesar Ritz, the creator of the Savoy and Ritz Hotels in London, who brought Escoffier to the city. Together they established their fame – Ritz as the hotelier genius, and Escoffier as the master of the culinary arts. Not only was he a chef, but he was the creator of world-famous dishes, such as *Filet de Sole Waleska*, *Pêche Melba* and many others. He was a great charmer – a celebrated gastronomic food writer said: 'He has the face of an artist or statesman, had he been a man of the pen and not a man of the spoon, he would have been a poet.'(4.8)

He was an extraordinary organiser, and in the kitchen he carried out time and motion studies (before the term was known) to get the best of food from his chefs and specialists. He radically reorganised the modern restaurant kitchen into the partie system, which divided the kitchen in large hotels and restaurants into so-called corners, or sections. In a French partie, a specialist with some assistants were concerned with certain tasks and dishes on the menu only. Performing these special tasks of food preparation and presentation repeatedly many times a day, the specialist would become even more skilled in the execution of his art. On this basis, Escoffier built up a hierarchy and expertise in the kitchen which in its effectiveness has never been surpassed. It became the model of every first-class hotel in the world and has lasted to this day in the best of them with only minor modifications.

4.8 From teaching notes, facts, comments, gathered over 30 years, sources now unknown.

It most certainly gave new impetus to the gastronomical advances of the last hundred years or so. Escoffier's kitchen organisation and hierarchy looked something like this:

Maître de cuisine (Administrator, head chef)
Sous chef (leading practitioners, second chef in command)
1 *Chef de partie saucier* (head sauce chef)
Demi chef saucier (second in command)
Commis saucier (several) (assistants, to improve)
Aprenti (several) (apprentice, learner).
2 *Chef de partie rôtisseur* (head roast chef)
Demi chef de rôtisseur (second in command)
Commis de rôtisseur (assistants)
Aprenti (apprentice)
3 *Chef de partie poissonier* (head fish chef)
Demi chef poissonier (second in command)
Commis de poissonier (assistants)
Aprenti (apprentice)
4 *Chef de partie entrementier* (head vegetable chef)
Demi chef d' entrementier (second in command)
Commis d' entrementier (assistants)
Aprenti (apprentice)
5 *Chef de partie potager* (head soup chef)
Demi chef de potager (second in command)
Commis de potager (assistants)
Aprenti (apprentice)

Two section chefs had particular responsibility, and because of their specialised work, headed a kitchen within a kitchen with special expertise and equipment. These were:

6 *Chef de partie garde-manger* (head larder chef)
Demi chef de garde-manger (second in command)
Commis garde-manger (assistants)
Aprenti (apprentice)
Chef de partie hors-d'oeuvrier (specialist for starters)
Commis d' hors-d'oeuvrier (assistant)
Saladier (salad maker)
Commis saladier (assistant)
7 *Chef de partie pâtissier* (head pastry chef)
Demi chef de pâtissier (second in command)

Commis pâtissier (assistants)
Aprenti (apprentice)

Where the size of the kitchen and volume of business warranted, the chef pâtissier would have under his direction:

8 *Chef boulanger* (head baker)
Commis boulanger (assistants)
Chocolatier (chocolate maker, sugar work, *petits fours*)
Glacier (ice-cream maker)

The organisation of the restaurant mirrored that of the kitchen with:

Maître d'hotel (head waiter)
Chef de rang (section chief)
Commis de rang (assistants)
Aprenti (apprentice)

A *chef de rang* would be responsible for a number of tables and guests in a restaurant operation, with some *commis de rang* to assist him and to fetch and carry the various dishes and courses from the kitchen to the sideboard or table.

Sommelier (head wine waiter)
Commis de sommelier (assistant)

These would be considered a must in any first-class restaurant proud of its wine cellar. The name *sommelier* was originally applied to a priest in a monastery who was responsible for the making of wines, ales and beer and for the service of these to the monks at various meal times. The *sommelier*'s duties were adapted to the needs of the emerging restaurants: to assist and advise guests to choose the right wines to accompany their meal, and to serve these wines in the best condition.

Except for knowing what is available from the wine cellar, and possibly the purchase of new wines, the duty of the modern *sommelier* is one of advice and service in the restaurant rather than in the wine cellar.

Trancheur (carver)

This was often considered a necessity in first-class hotels and restaurants where a considerable amount of carving, filleting, dissecting and *flambé* work at the table was part of the operation. It would be executed by a waiter with these particular skills, or sometimes this task would be undertaken by a smartly dressed chef in white, released from the kitchen for the purpose of carving at table.

The admirable British contribution to the mystique and service of gastronomy, the much-admired English butler, is, in fact, a combination of a *maître d'hotel*, *sommelier* and *trancheur*, aided by two typical British virtues, unflappability and understatement. Yet who can resist the character at his best, his obvious expertise and dignity, or his pronouncement in the door of an oak-panelled dining room when he says: 'My lords, ladies and gentlemen, dinner is served.' Surely, both in expectation and dignity, this is still one of the finest moments of European gastronomy, experienced alas less and less often.

Although much rationalisation has taken place in both restaurants and kitchens, many of the terms and aims of Escoffier still have considerable meaning, in particular, when one looks at advertisements for posts in first-class restaurants and hotels all over the world.

The Language of Gastronomy

One other aspect in the development of ritualistic and gastronomic eating must be considered, and that is the evolving language related to all aspects of gastronomy.

Let us first consider the word 'gastronomy' and how it was derived. In the *Oxford Dictionary* (Oxford Press, 1901) we find:

Gastrologia
derived from the Greek words, *gaster* (belly or stomach) and *logia* (system of governing or knowledge regarding a given subject).

Gastronomy
derived as above from the Greek words *gaster* (belly or stomach) and *nomas* (Greek for law of a subject).

The same source gives the word 'gastrologia' as a title of an early poem by Athanaeus on the delights of food. The American *Webster's Dictionary* (London–New York, 1961) gives much the same source of the two words, but credits the poem *Gastrologia* to the fourth century BC Greek poet Achetratoes, which he wrote after a tour of the then known world and the culinary delights he encountered during his travels. Clearly, we have some confusion here, but in both cases the source of the words is Greek.

In relation to this, the *Oxford Dictionary* continues to give some further definitions and conversational use of the words and some of their derivatives in the English language as follows:

Gastronomy

'The art and science of eating . . . the banquet was according to all the rules of gastronomy . . .' (Sir R. Wilson Private Diary II, p. 345, 1814)

'. . . the march of improvement will one day we hope, induce the professors of gastronomy to elevate their calling . . .' (M. Donovan, *Dom. Econ.*, II, p. 379, 1843)

Gastronome

'A judge of good food and eating . . . a conversation on the mysteries of the table, a modern Gastronome might have listened to with pleasure . . .' (Scott Perivel, XXXVII, p. 48, 1823)

Gastronomer

'. . . an analogy with astronomer . . . he became a philosophical gastronomer of European reputation . . .' (*Black Watch Magazine*, LLXXI, p. 747, 1828)

Gastronomic, gastronomical, gastronomically

'Her Ladyship proposed tickets or lots, which each 'ere inscribed with some article of the supper table. Nothing could excite the amusement more, which the lottery gastronomic thus produced . . . being initiated into the gastronomic mysteries of the kitchen . . .' (H. Angelo, *Reminiscences*, p. 297, 1828)

'It would take less time to acquire and cultivate a gastronomic taste, than any other . . .' (F.R. Hawthorn, *Journals*, 1, p. 24, 1850)

'. . . it is not easy to understand the mechanical, physiological and gastronomical intricacies and difference of fish, flesh or fowl . . .' (*Frazer Magazine*, XLIV, p. 208, 1851)

'. . . he duely qualified as a graduate of the gastronomical College . . .' (W.S. Seton Carrin Haileybury, *Observer*, V, p. 10, 1842)

'. . . gastronomically speaking the whole feast was most satisfactory . . .' (*Dasent Vikings*, II, p. 81, 1875)

Gastrophil, Gastrophilite, Gastrophilist

'. . . the glutton practices without regard to the beautiful art of good eating and we call him a gastrophil or gastrophillite . . .' (*School of Good Living*, p. 84, 1814)

'. . . which the sturdy gastrophilist can not fail to endure . . .' (*ibid*, 1850)

Gastrophilism

'. . . no one can say that the spirit of gastrophilism has never found its way into the Vatican . . .' (*ibid*, 1850)

Gastronomist

'. . . we may talk to Beauvillier and all such gastronomists and tell them they are all but men . . .' (*Quarterly Review*, XXXII, p. 434, 1825)

Gastronomous

'. . . fervent and gastronomous he was, the very apostle of gluttony . . .' (*The Examiner*, pp. 708–2, 1828)

These English definitions and use of words give us a fair understanding of their meanings in everyday use, but this is only one language and its understanding, it would be helpful to look at other European languages. Surprisingly, languages such as French, Italian and Spanish do not add anything more detailed to the understanding of the definitions of gastronomy; the two languages which do are German and Swedish.

GERMAN

Gastronomie

gastronomy

Feine Kochkunst

the fine art of cooking

Feinschmeckerei

the appreciation of good food

Gerwerbliche Kochkunst

professional art of cooking

SWEDISH

Gastronomi

gastronomy

Högre Kokkonst

higher art of cooking

Gastronom

gastronome

Matkännare

one who knows about good food

Sybarit

sybarite

Vällevnadsman

one who eats and lives well

Njutnigsmeniska

one who lives for pleasure only

The German definitions seem to add a professional aspect to the understanding of gastronomy, with the reference to *gewerbliche Kochkunst* (the professional art of cookery) suggesting that when it comes to the higher art of the subject, gastronomy should be in the hands of the expert or professional.

The Swedish definitions refer to the possible sybaritic nature of the subject, or the dangers of over-eating and drinking. But, as the very nature of good gastronomy is not excess but respect for all we eat and drink, it will do no harm to be reminded here of the possible dangers of an over-indulgence in anything we do. A well-known wise and true old English proverb makes this point when it states that 'a little of what you fancy does you good'.

Of all the various definitions given by individuals, the best is that of Jean Brillat-Savarin written in his book *The Physiology of Taste*, also known as *The Philosopher in the Kitchen* (1825). His definition reads as follows:

Gastronomy

is the reasoned comprehension of all that relates to the nourishment and well being of man.

Gastronomy

aims to procure the preservation of man, by means of the best possible nourishment.

Gastronomy

only, should give guidance according to certain principles, to all who seek, provide and prepare that which may be turned into good food.

Gastronomy

is in fact the motive force behind:
the farmer
the wine-grower
the fisherman
the butcher
and the cook
(the food technologist)
(the food scientist)
or however their title or qualification may disguise their work as gatherers, growers or preparers of food for mankind with care.

Gastronomy

pertains to history, physics, chemistry, (nutrition), psychology, physiology, and considerable aesthetic values to be shared with our families and friends. Last but not least it is an Art.

I have taken the liberty to add words (in brackets) to this quotation, which

Jean Brillat-Savarin would surely have included had they been known to him.

There are two aspects of gastronomical language to be considered. The first is the technical language of gastronomy, which is of immediate importance to the host, innkeeper, restaurateur, hotel manager, head waiter and chef. This includes the naming of new equipment, machinery and service utensils, developed and used in the preparation and service of food and wine.

As this has been very much led from France, it is not surprising that many technical developments have a French name, for example, *assiette* (plate), *rondeau* (a particular type of round, low saucepan) and *terrine* (a special container, usually earthenware, in which food would be both cooked and served). Some of these names are of interest to the guest because they could appear on the menu, for example, *assiette de légumes* (plate of vegetables) and *terrine de porc* (*terrine* or *pâté* of pork served in a dish). Both denote a way of preparation and presentation which could be important when the guest makes his or her choice.

The second aspect is that of menu language. When this is good, straight French, written on the menu, either at a country house of old or in a restaurant today, there was, and is, no problem – the upper class or those who frequented country houses or restaurants usually spoke French well and were quite comfortable with a menu in French. In more modern times, the French written menu is often explained on the menu itself, or the head waiter is at hand to help with the translation. However, when gastronomic and culinary French is found on menus, it can be very flowery, artistic and even theatrical, as it can be full of hidden meanings. Consider the following examples:

Straight translation

Crême de carottes (cream of carrot soup)
Crême d'asperge (cream of asparagus soup)

Gastro-geographical reference

Crême de Crécy (cream of carrot soup)
Crême d'Argenteuil (cream of asparagus soup)

These examples make reference to two parts of France: Crécy, which is famous for the quality of its carrots, and Argenteuil, in northern France, where asparagus grows exceptionally well in its sandy soil and has attained a European-wide reputation. Many other such regions or towns of France appear on the menu, identifying ingredients in common use in these parts of France. For example:

Normande – the use of cream, apples, cider, calvados and seafood.
Provençale – the use of garlic, olive oil and tomatoes.

Bourguignon – the use of wine from Burgundy; *boeuf Bourguignon.*
Lyonnaise – the use of onions; *pommes Lyonnaise, foie de veau.*

Famous persons, occasions, restaurateurs or chefs, often with a historic significance, can also appear on the menu. This group is by far the largest and needs some considerable knowledge of history, but even then we may not understand the content of the dishes or the mode of their preparation. Some of the best known are considered in 'The Origin of Names of some Famous Dishes and Garnishes, and Historical Culinary Terminology' at the end of this chapter.

Evolution and Definition of the Various Courses of the Modern Classical Menu

The Starters (Les Hors-d'Oeuvres)

In composing a modern menu, the cold *hors-d'oeuvre* always takes first place except in certain cases such as on a cold winter's day when hot soup may be preferred to a cold starter. In its present form, the *hors-d'oeuvre* was developed by French chefs in Russia in the seventeenth century and they combined good Russian food with French skill and finesse.

In the days of great mansion houses or palaces, aristocratic high society held frequent receptions and dinners. It must have been a fine sight to see the lords and ladies arrive by coach and horse; the ladies in high-fashioned gowns with crinoline skirts, the gentlemen in tight breeches and buckled shoes, topped with white powdered wigs. Thus the reception and dinners were a matter of much

Figure 4.5 The first contact, the menu by G Nairn
Source: © W Bode and M Leto

pomp and ceremony and it often took hours for all to assemble. During these lengthy receptions the guests could not be left to wait standing around until all had arrived. Invariably, an orchestra played for amusement or dancing, and great amounts of vodka and champagne were freely served and consumed. This had the disadvantage that most guests became somewhat unsteady on their feet, if not positively inebriated, before the actual dinner began.

At this time, French culture and language were very prominent in Russia – as elsewhere in Europe – and the *cuisine française* was highly regarded as part of good culture and good living. French chefs were accustomed to the highest praise for the composition of their dishes, the skill with which they combined flavours, and the absolute artistry and splendour of their service and presentation. Alas, however elegant, a rather drunk assembly was unable in its somewhat shaky state to appreciate the food presented. Nor were the guests able to offer due praise and make the compliments to which all French chefs had become accustomed.

A method had to be devised quickly to ensure that as sober an assembly as possible sat down to dinner and was able to appreciate the offered delicacies. To stop the generous service of vodka and champagne would not have been hospitable. The chefs had the idea of serving the early arrivals with something to eat – something, so it was hoped, which would give them some base for drinking, some lining for their often empty bellies. Hopefully, the guests would then sit down to dinner somewhat more sober and consequently more appreciative of the delights of *la cuisine française* to come.

Figure 4.6 Delights to come by G Nairn
Source: © W Bode and M Leto

Thus the *hors-d'oeuvre* was born. At first it was a simple piece of bread with some cold meats, game or fish and cheeses, and possibly some salads, plus some titbits, for example, olives, nuts, onions, eggs and gherkins. Gradually, the *hors-d'oeuvre* became established, and fashionable chefs competed with each other in the varieties offered. From this competition, *hors-d'oeuvres* became finally quite substantial and almost a meal before a meal.

The translation of the French term *hors-d'oeuvre* (literally meaning 'outside the main work') into other languages is not easy and it is interesting how many different variations there are. In England the terms 'starters', 'appetiser', 'prelude', 'overture', etc. are used. 'Side dishes' is probably the most common. Originally, *hors-d'oeuvres* were served from the side tables of the reception room, or in the anteroom before the guests entered the large dining hall.

Modern Service

Today, the *hors-d'oeuvre*, cold or hot, is just another course on the menu, and it is more often than not served at the table. Busy restaurants serve cold starters directly on plates, or from trays or trolleys built especially for this purpose, but in recent years the plated service has predominated.

In some restaurants, the customer may help him or herself to *hors-d'oeuvres* from a table situated prominently in the room – a type of service which is particularly suitable for those types of establishment which wish to make their side dishes a feature of the restaurant. When the customer has helped him or herself to the first course from the offered delicacies, he or she will sit down and the subsequent courses will be served by waiters and waitresses. Just as the manner of serving the *hors-d'oeuvres* has changed, so have the reasons for eating them. We do not eat this course today as a base for drinking, but to titillate our palate. Appetiser may, therefore, be a very good word for this course, especially if we remember that the *hors-d'oeuvre* may only be one course of several and it should be served in modest portions.

As an appetiser, side dishes should at all times be colourful, appetising, piquant, varied and suitable for the time of year, occasion and meal. Most important of all, they should, whenever possible, be fresh, mouthwatering and attractive. There is little doubt that a well-presented *hors-d'oeuvre* will set the tone for the ensuing courses. Seldom has the chef opportunity to make such a good first impression. A colourful and appetising starter will be the prelude to subsequent good courses.

Since the humble and somewhat restricted beginnings of the *hors-d'oeuvre*, the varieties have steadily increased and new dishes and compositions are added almost daily. There are now a variety of 10,000 foods or dishes suitable for

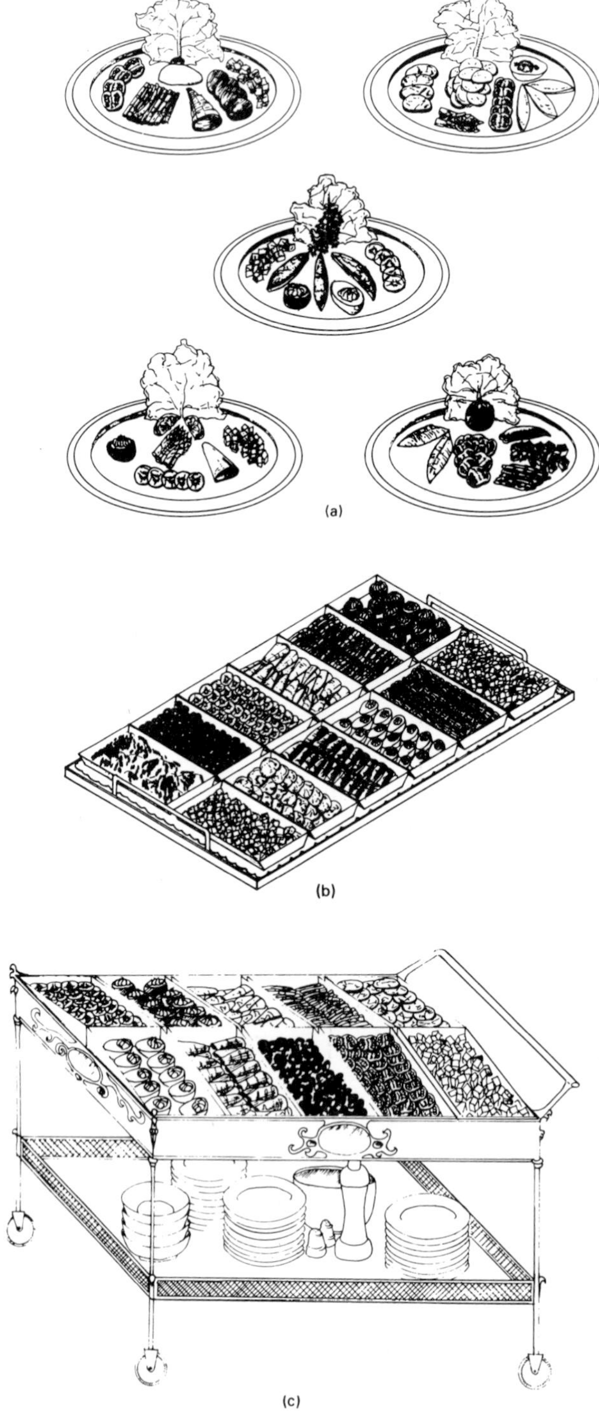

Figure 4.7 The service of hors-d'oeuvres. a) Plated modern service; b) Selection on tray; c) The silver service hors-d'oeuvres trolley
Source: Drawn by James Llewellyn-Smith to instruction of the author

serving as an appetiser or starter to a meal, and these are classified into the following types:

Hors-d'oeuvres simples (single side dishes)
Hors-d'oeuvres variés (selection of side dishes)
Hors-d'oeuvres chauds (hot side dishes)

Single side dishes (hors-d'oeuvres simples)

These should be of one type of food with only a little garnish and maybe categorised in the following ways:

Fruit based
Avocado pear with various fillings or dressings
Grapefruit halves chilled, grilled cocktails or juice
Melons chilled as portion, as halves, cocktail some fillings
Oranges as cocktail alone or with other fruits, juice
Pineapples as cocktail alone or with other fruit, juice
Salads, various fruit based, for example, Waldorf, juice
Tomatoes, with various fillings, fish, poultry, meats, juice

Egg based
Stuffed eggs with various fillings or garnishes
Egg mayonnaise in various presentations or garnishes
Egg salads in various presentations or garnishes
Cold poached eggs in various presentations, even aspic
Cold eggs in a cocotte in various presentations, garnishes
Plovers, lapwing, peewit eggs in various presentations

Fish based
Smoked fish, herrings, mackerel, salmon, sprats, trout
Fresh pickles, soused, Dieppoise, Portugaise, Hongroise, in mustard, in cream or in herb sauces
Bottled or tinned sardines, herrings, pilchards, tuna, Rollmops, Bismarck, potted fish and shell-fish
Fresh shellfish, lobster, crab, crayfish, oysters, mussels, cockles
Fish cocktails of lobster, prawn, crab or poached fish
Fish mousses, from salmon, prawn, lobster, white fish

Meat based
Smoked, various hams, turkey, chicken, venison
Charcuterie, liver sausages, liver pâtés, various hams cooked or raw, salamis of German, Dutch, Italian or French origin, for example, garlic sausage, beef sausage, tongue sausage, ham sausages, Mortadella

Meat preparations, pies of pork, veal, ham, poultry, pâtés of goose, chicken, veal or pork liver, parfaits, mousses, mousselines, brawn, potted meats, rilettes, etc

Salads

These may be based on fruit, vegetables, meats, fish, shellfish or a combination of these, for example:

Fruit compound salad: Waldorf – a mixture of apples, celery, walnuts bound with mayonnaise

Fish compound salad: *Fécampoise* – a mixture of poached fish, prawns, cucumber dice and fennel, bound with mayonnaise

Meat compound salad: *provençale* – a mixture of strips of cooked beef, gherkins, onions, red peppers, garlic and flavoured with tomato dressing.

Vegetable compound salad: Russian – a mixture of diced cooked carrots, turnips, beans, peas bound with mayonnaise and garnished with mounds of caviar

Mayonnaise: only made of white meats, for example, cooked chicken dice and the addition of pineapple or asparagus tips and bound with mayonnaise; or white cooked fish dice or shellfish pieces again bound with mayonnaise, with additions such as cooked champignons, asparagus tips or red pepper dice

Selection of side dishes (hors-d'oeuvres variés)

This is simply a selection of chosen starters from the list of single side dishes above. Which of the above and how many are included is simply a matter of cost, but should not be less than four – eight to ten are a normal number.

This may be presented in advance on a plate joining, for example, a stuffed egg-half, a little tomato salad, some asparagus tips, a sardine, some slices of pâté and a little Russian salad. The choice is wide, but the combination should be colourful, appetising and changing with the seasons.

If the predetermined selection is simple, the selection of starters may be offered on a tray or silver *hors-d'oeuvre* trolley according to the standard of the restaurant.

For hot starters (*hors-d'oeuvres chauds*) see page 140.

The Soups

According to the composition and ingredients used in its preparation, the second item on the classical menu is the soup or *le potage*. The terms *consommé*, *purée*, *velouté*, *crème* and *bisque* may also be used. Although soups occupy second place on a menu, they are of much older origin than the *hors-d'oeuvres* which occupy first place.

For thousands of years, soups have represented the main meal, especially for the poor and peasant classes, and there can be no doubt that they are one of the oldest preparations in compositional cookery and in the history of eating generally. Jacob, we are told in the Old Testament, bought his brother's hermitage for 'a mess of pottage'. It is especially interesting how soup dishes compare in importance as a basic diet and similarity of production all over the world and, in particular, in European countries from the *får i kål* of Sweden in the north and the *minestrone* or *minestra* of Italy in the south, to the *Irish stew* from Ireland in the west and the *Bortsch* of Poland and Russia in the east of Europe. To all, soup represented the main meal of the day, always popular and easily produced from what was available and cheapest in the garden or in the fields. Mostly vegetables, potatoes, barley and rice were used, as well as pulses. If times were good, a piece of meat, poultry or bacon or sausage would be added to give the soups substance and flavour.

Attempts to make this simple everyday meal more palatable and varied gave rise to the use of seasonings, herbs and spices on a wider scale.

The soup would be made in the manner of *pot au feu*, literally 'pot on the fire'. A piece of meat or poultry (*poule au pot*) would be placed in an iron or earthenware pot (casserole) together with various vegetables in season, some barley, rice and pulses; then it would all be covered with water. After having been brought to the boil and seasoned with herbs and spices, the pot would be placed on the side of the stove, or in the hot ashes of a fire, to simmer gently for hours.

In the evening, when the peasants returned from their hard work in the fields, the soup-stew was ready to be served. First, the thin broth was ladled into the bowl or plate to be eaten as soup; thereafter the thicker part, of vegetables, potatoes, rice, pulses and meat if any, followed as the main course. Fresh fruit or dried fruit or a *compote* in the winter, or home-made cheese concluded this simple meal.

In this, we can see the beginning of the structure of our three course meal. Modern developments in catering in hotels and restaurants over hundreds of years have lessened the importance of soup to just one of many courses in a meal. The stocks are now strained and called *bouillons* or *consommés*; the vegetables may be sieved for purée soups or cut with the meat into meat dice or strips for *paysannes* (peasant soups).

The strained stock may be poured on to a roux, for binding to produce *velouté* soup. Modern catering and cookery has devised many new soups, such as *Kaltschalen*, *Bisques*, turtle, shark-fin and bird's nest soup, with basic materials and recipes from all over the world.

This development will no doubt continue, although some are of the opinion that it may have gone too far already. We can now buy soups in small packets or cubes, needing less than 5 minutes cooking or, as in the case of 'Cuppa Soups', require no cooking at all. What they have in common with the old hearty and real soups is left for the individual to judge.

A great many soups are used in international gastronomy, and they are grouped into basic types which can then be used as a basis for selection according to the season, type of meal, special occasion or banquet. These basic types are as follows:

Consommés (clear soups)
Bouillons (broth soups)
Paysannes (peasant soups)
Purées (purée soups)
Veloutés (thick soups)
Crèmes (cream soups)
Bisques (shellfish soups)

There are a few others which are less easily classified – there are over two thousand soups to be found in the European repertoire of cooking, some of which are considered suitable only for lunch, others are suitable for lunch, dinner and supper.

The Hot Starters (Les Hors-d'Oeuvres Chauds)

This group of hot *hors-d'oeuvres*, sometimes also referred to as '*petites entrées*' or '*entrées de volantes*', are, besides being hot starters, not prepared in the *hors-d'oeuvre* section. They are all prepared and cooked in the various kitchen sections according to the type of starter. So why are they not seen as main courses? For example, we may use creamed prawns, creamed veal or creamed chicken, which are all to be considered fish or meat courses. But by placing them into a pancake, a *bouché*, or a strip of puff-pastry, we have changed their emphasis to *crêpes* (pancakes) and they become hot *hors-d'oeuvres.*

Thus we can list two types of hot *hors-d'oeuvres* all served hot with various types of fillings and garnishes:

True hot starters
Fond d'artichauts, asparagus, *brioche*, quiches, croquettes, *concombre farcis*, pizzas, *ragout fins*, *petits soufflés*, *tomate farcis*, etc

Figure 4.8 Café Restaurant, mid-18th century, by an unknown artist
Source: Staatliches Kupferstich Kabinettes, Dresden

Disguised hot starters
Allumettes, *barquettes*, *bouchés*, *canapés chauds*, *crêpes*, *crêpinettes*, *croûtons*, *croûtes*, *dartois*, *duchesse*, *fondantes*, *tartlettes*, etc

Selection of Hot Starters *(les Hors-d'Oeuvres Chauds Variés)*

In some speciality restaurants, we may find occasionally a selection of hot side dishes. Modern eating habits, the increasing cost of food and the need to eat more quickly in these hurried times have re-classified many of the original hot *hors-d'oeuvres* as *entrées* and many of these are now often served as main courses.

In the British Isles, the so-called savouries served after or in place of sweets are, in many respects, similar to some of the savoury hot *hors-d'oeuvres* above.

The Egg (les Oeufs) and Farinaceous (les Pâtes et Farineux) dishes

Egg and farinaceous dishes represent some of the oldest and most basic foods and dishes of compositional cookery, and occupy the third or fourth places on the classical menu. When this was devised over a period of time, most dishes had an emphasis on fish, meat or poultry. When one compares menus with a dozen or more courses, it was considered proper to include some of these often simple, but very old and stable, foods for the sake of variety and balance. It is interesting to note, however, that even in a menu comprising a dozen or more courses, only one of these types of food will be included. Should the menu include an egg dish, a farinaceous dish is usually avoided, and vice versa.

Hens' eggs above all play the most prominent part in egg dishes. Eggs can be cooked and presented in many ways, and are found on every type of menu from breakfast to late supper. This is not surprising for they are nutritious, satisfying and versatile. The relatively low cost of eggs, compared with other equally nutritious foods, makes it understandable that more and more egg dishes are today accepted as a main meal dish, especially for lunch. However, with the exception of Britain, where richly-garnished egg dishes are served for breakfast, it is more common to serve egg dishes plain or with only little garnish for early breakfast. Egg dishes with richer garnishes and accompaniments are usually served for a late breakfast or luncheon. Very few egg dishes are served for dinner, but all are acceptable again for late supper. *Larousse Gastronomique* includes some four hundred compositional egg dishes.

Farinaceous dishes can be considered of equal importance to, and interchangeable with, the egg dishes described above. For this reason several farinaceous and egg dishes are placed side by side on an *à la carte* menu, inviting the customer to make a choice. On a *table d'hôte* menu a choice is usually given of one of each, either one or the other, according to the custom of the establishment and, possibly, price range. On a set or banqueting menu, the choice is usually made for the guest in advance, taking into account the host's wishes, time of year, type of function and, of course, general balance of the menu composition.

The term 'farinaceous' is derived from *farina*, the term for flour, ground from any type of cereal or corn. The word comes from the Latin word for corn. When the flour is mixed with a liquid it naturally forms a paste, pâte or pasta. This must not be confused with pastry, however, although it is rather difficult to say where one should draw the line. One could say invariably pasta is cooked by boiling, whereas pastry is usually baked, but even this is not always the case – suet pastry can be boiled or steamed, for example. On the other hand, one can fry some kinds of pastas, for example, noodles, and bake some types of farinaceous dishes such as rice. While not fitting into the category outlined above, rice is nevertheless placed in the list of farinaceous dishes because it is a starchy cereal and is used as a savoury dish more often than as a sweet dish. Thus one might consider that farinaceous dishes are different from pastry dishes because the former are of a savoury nature and are used as main course dishes or as *entrées*, or as accompaniments or garnishes for *entrées*; pastry, however, is usually sweet and used for sweet dishes only.

But this yardstick cannot be said to be always accurate. For example, savoury flans do not rate as farinaceous dishes, nor do cheese straws, macaroni or vermicelli puddings, even though they are prepared from what must be accepted as being paste. One can, therefore, apply only the yardstick of tradition supplemented by a number of guidelines.

Farinaceous dishes can be divided into two categories. First, those prepared from flour and made into a paste by the addition of a liquid, usually water, some seasonings, and sometimes eggs and a little oil. They are shaped by rolling and cutting into various widths or shapes. Examples include noodles, lasagnes, canneloni and ravioli (the latter two being filled or stuffed). Others of this type are shaped by extruding through special plates and then drying, for example, macaroni, spaghetti and vermicelli. Second, those prepared from cereals, such as rice, to produce pilaff and risotto dishes; maize flour producing polenta or semolina for *gnocchi romaine*; potatoes for *gnocchi piedmontaise*; or choux paste for *gnocchi parisienne*.

All the above dishes are served with either melted butter and cheese or with various sauces and presented in various ways. They are a very welcome addition to good cookery of any standard and type of gastronomic outlet. Again, in *Larousse Gastronomique* some four hundred or so farinaceous dishes are listed.

Figure 4.9 Stocks and sauces, the bases of all culinary delights by G Nairn
Source: © W Bode and M Leto

The Fish Course (Les Poissons)

In most parts of the world, fish has always been a valuable source of protein and, indeed, in some parts it has been the only source. For the catering industry, it has provided an excellent change from the normal meat diet and has been of great value for special diets and meals for the sedentary worker. In addition, most fishes have until recently been, weight for weight and value for value, cheaper than meat, an important factor for those catering establishments with a limited budget. Fish dishes have also appeared on the menu for religious reasons and customs, particularly on Fridays and throughout Lent. Recent developments, such as the pollution of rivers and the sea, and concern for over-fishing followed by the imposition of fishing limits, have made fish now as expensive – in some cases more expensive – than most types of meat.

Nearly all good cookery books give almost as much space and consideration to the preparation and presentation of fish dishes as they do to meat. Although these recipes are numerous and varied, it is true to say that most of them are limited to the most popular types of fish. In the British Isles these are cod, haddock, herring, turbot, halibut, plaice and sole, as well as salmon and trout, and shellfish, such as crab, lobster, oysters and mussels. On the continent, especially in land-bound countries, many lake and river fish are included on the menu.

The increasing cost of fish has made it necessary to consider fish which have not been so popular in the past. An interesting example is sea bream. Because of its resemblance to goldfish, it has not been very popular in Britain. However, it is larger than goldfish and has excellent flesh, flavour and a firm texture.

Considering the valuable source of protein fish represents, it is not surprising that all the cooking methods listed in Chapter 2 have been applied to the cooking and presentation of fish dishes, and many garnishes and sauces have been added to the service of fish as a main course, or in the framework of the classical menu, as the fifth course on the menu. Some 1,500 ways of preparing, cooking and presenting fish are known in modern gastronomy.

The Small Main Course (Les Entrées)

In the sixth place on our menu is the *entrée*, and there is no doubt that this course contains the best-known dishes in historical and modern cookery. The range of dishes served under this heading is vast; many different foods are used as well as many different methods of cooking and presentation. The term *entrée* in French means 'entry', and the popular misconception that the *entrée* course means the 'entry' or first course offered at a meal is, therefore, not without logic. This is derived from the times when formal banquets or feasts consisted of two services or courses only: the *entrée* and the *relevé*, or remove course. *Larousse Gastronomique*, however, contradicts this and states that the term *entrée*, in menu language, has no specific connection with its particular place on the menu. If the course has any place at all on the menu, according to this authoritative publication, it should be the third course after the soup and fish course.

In effect, in the past, the first part of the meal or service was made up of a variety of dishes which included soups, whole fish, joints of meat, whole poultry, etc, elaborately and artificially displayed to delight the ravenous gourmets when they entered the dining hall, their appetites already adequately stimulated with liquid refreshment. The debris following the demolition of these set pieces would then be cleared away or removed, hence the term *relevé* or removal course, which was followed by an equally vast variety of small and delicately presented morsels of foodstuffs, including sweetmeats. These dishes were intended to re-awaken jaded appetites before the now satiated guests finally passed out. It could be argued, therefore, that this second service or course would be the course which we now relate to the *entrée* course, in fact, to the entry of the dish or dishes following the removal of the set dishes or pieces.

When those expansive days drew to a close, the menu began to be formulated along the lines of the Russian service recognisable today, and although meals for special occasions continued to be sumptuous, the various kinds of dishes and the various methods of cooking and presentation were divided into distinct courses. These broadly followed the pattern given in the introduction to the menu and its development. It may be thought at this stage that I have wandered somewhat from the subject of the *entrée*, but one should be quite clear as to the place occupied by this course on present-day menus. Regrettably, the *relevé* course has been gradually merged with the *entrée* course in modern menus, and is now commonly known as the *entrée ou relevé* course. This is perhaps a retrograde step as the kind of dishes in each of these categories are entirely different. The purpose, therefore, is to define the *entrée* and to offer guidelines as to where and how they differ from the original *relevés*.

In order to clarify the issue, by '*entrée*' I mean the meat, etc, course, which is served in the middle of the meal, either for luncheon or dinner and occasionally for supper, and which might be served before, or in lieu of, the *relevé*. Probably the most important yardstick and best definition of an *entrée* is that the meat, game, poultry or offal for this course *must always be cut or portioned or prepared prior to cooking*, as distinct from the *relevé* which should be cooked either whole or as a large joint and carved or portioned after cooking. This would appear to offer further evidence for the argument at the beginning of this chapter that the *entrée* course, made up of small cuts or morsels, should follow the main course rather than precede it. But, as the accepted rule for menu composition is to proceed from the lighter courses to the more substantial and then back to the lighter dishes, this would appear to indicate that, in many instances, notably where the *relevé* course is the main or centre course, the *entrée* could logically be served before the *relevé*.

Another aspect of the *entrée* course is that it should be complete in itself. That is to say, it should be served with or in its own sauce and/or garnish and, therefore, not need vegetables or potatoes other than those which go to make up the dish or recipe. This has enabled the 'chefs' – originators of the recipes which make up the repertoire of *haute cuisine* dishes – to have a free rein in the choice of garnishes and sauces. Served with each individual dish, they produce an almost limitless variety of dishes.

Decorative garnishes, as well as contributing to the overall dish, also determine the specific classical recipe. National and regional produce, as well as seasonal fruit and vegetables, play an important part in these recipes and are instrumental in the creation of distinctive preferences and tastes, particularly among gourmets, who, in the past, were delighted to allow a particular dish to be dedicated to them and named after them.

In the course of time, certain traditions have evolved as to which of the *entrées* are most suitable for which menus. For example, it would not be considered suitable to offer stews, boiled or steamed puddings, pies, etc, on a dinner menu, while *vol-au-vents*, *tournedos*, hot mousses or *soufflés*, etc, are not considered to be suitable for luncheon menus.

From the foregoing it will be appreciated that the subject of *entrées* can be a very complex one. Most methods of cooking given in Chapter 2 are applied for the preparation and presentation of *entrées*, and more than 5,000 dishes of this type are known.

The Removal Course (Le Relevé)

The term '*relevé*' means the course which is removed to make way for the ensuing one, and it would appear logical to assume that there must be some foodstuff left to remove and not just the crockery and cutlery, otherwise all courses could be said to be '*relevé*'. If one accepts this assumption, the type of dish served for this course will become immediately apparent. It must be a large piece of foodstuff, such as a joint or, possibly, an entire carcass, or a whole bird, which, after portioning at the table or sideboard, will be cleared away and will provide 'leftovers' which form the base of the *réchauffé* or reheated dishes. Possibly the best description of this course is to be found in the typical English

Figure 4.10 Les relevés by G Nairn
Source: © W Bode and M Leto

restaurant or dining room where one is invariably offered a 'cut from the joint with two veg', this course always being served with vegetables and potatoes. In the household, too, it was, and still is, common practice for the Sunday joint to be removed after the midday meal to provide cold or hot meals for the early part of the week.

In many good class restaurants, the joint of meat or whole bird is portioned from a hot trolley or *guéridon*, which is wheeled to the table by the carver or *trancheur*, and served with accompanying garnish, sauce or gravy, and vegetables and potatoes. The ideal method of service for the *relevé* course does not lend itself to every kind of meal. At banquets, for example, when there are large numbers of diners occupying many tables, it would be unrealistic to provide a carver for each table. Quite apart from the number of staff, most of these functions have a strict timetable to observe if the meal is not to be prolonged over the course of many hours. In these circumstances, the *relevé* course is carved, portioned in the kitchen and dressed with its attendant garnish, the number of portions on each dish corresponding with the number of diners. It is then served at the table by the waiter or waitress.

Figure 4.11 Café d'Orsay, Paris 1847
Source: Lippheidesche Bibliothek, Staatliche Kunstbibliothek, Berlin

Vegetables and potatoes are served separately in appropriate dishes, and sauces and gravies are set up in sauce boats. This complete set of carved meat or poultry, vegetables, potatoes and sauces is known as a 'service' in banqueting terms.

A banquet for 500 people could be broken down into fifty services of ten, that is to say, fifty tables seating ten guests at each table, for which fifty dishes each containing ten portions of the *relevé* course with vegetables, potatoes and sauces would be set up in the kitchen. Some 400 or so dishes could be classified as *relevés* and they play a particularly important part in British gastronomy.

The Cold Buffets (Les Buffets Froids)

In all European countries, a cold buffet is served for such functions as weddings, christenings, birthdays, business or association luncheons, dances and late night suppers. On such occasions as Christmas, New Year, Easter, Spring Bank Holiday and other holidays, a buffet might also be served as a special attraction, complementing the normal *table d'hôte* menu or *à la carte* menu.

When serving a buffet, the average hotel is able to cater for a larger number of

Figure 4.12 The cold buffet by G Nairn
Source: © W Bode and M Leto

guests than is normal for a sit-down meal. Even the number of extra waiting staff can be reduced in proportion, for one of the attractions of a cold buffet is for the guests to help themselves to the delicacies on display. In England we differentiate between three types of cold buffet.

Finger Buffet

As the name implies, this is a type of buffet made up of cold or even sometimes hot foods which can be eaten with one's fingers. It is often presented at receptions and occasions where guests eat standing up.

Fork Buffet

This is like the finger buffet but the foods proffered are usually somewhat more substantial and a fork may be needed to eat the food more easily. Usually guests remain standing, but seats are sometimes provided. Often a fork buffet is provided at wedding or company receptions.

The Classical Buffet

The classical buffet has been and remains a highlight of gastronomic practice and usually unsurpassed culinary skills. Possibly a throwback to the times when man ate his food cold (but not necessarily uncooked), a really good cold classical buffet presented simply or elaborately, has always occupied a very special place in

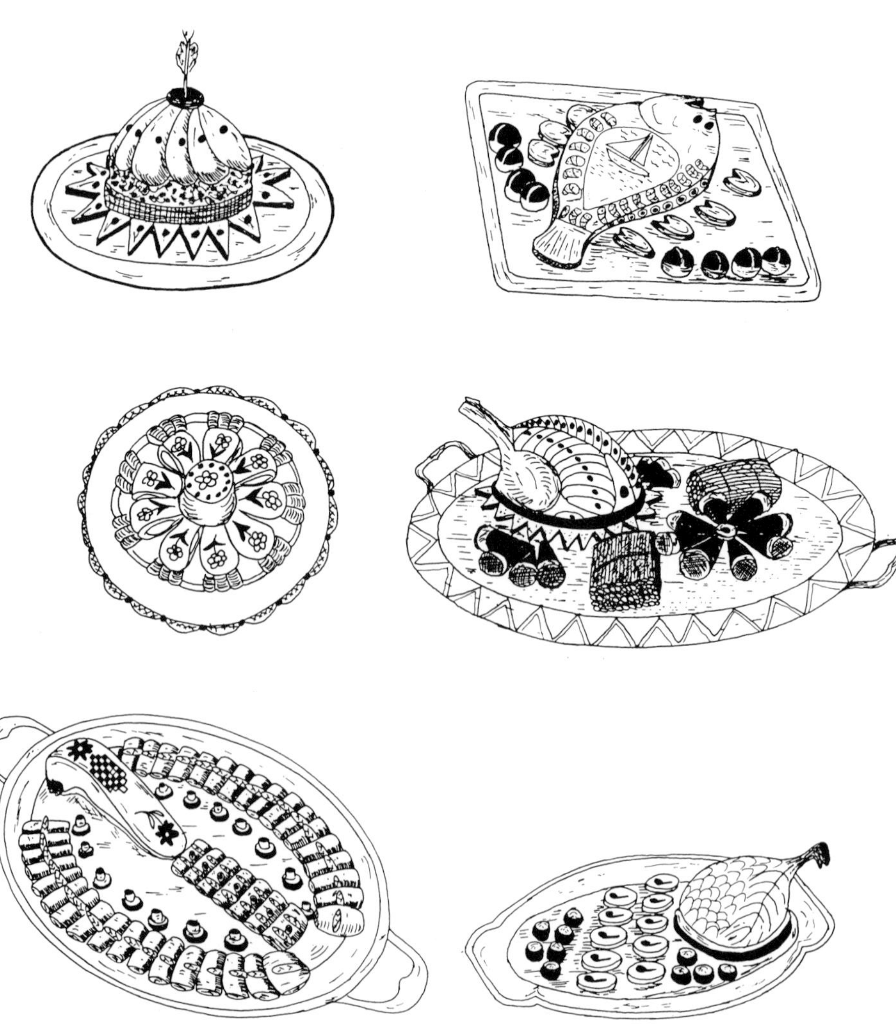

Figure 4.13 Highly decorated classical buffet pieces
Source: Drawn by James Llewellyn-Smith to instruction of the author

the minds of people who enjoy their food. Whether presented on glittering state occasions, high diplomatic receptions, international meetings or simply family ceremonies, the popularity of the cold classical buffet has remained constant.

The cold buffet represents an expression of culinary skills which cannot readily be repeated in many of the other hot courses on the classical menu. The large roasted joints of beef, saddles of lamb, turkeys, baron of venison, haunches of veal, whole salmon, boiled hams and delicately wine-poached trout in natural jellies, all highly decorated, garnished and colourfully presented, are a mouthwatering sight. These main dishes are further complemented by an array of colourful *hors-d'oeuvres* of all types, and simple and compound salads of many origins, combinations and flavours, as well as many cold sauces and dressings. A smartly-dressed chef in white may help with the carving of the particular joint or joints of our choice.

If the cold buffet remains a meal for special occasions, it is nevertheless represented in the structure of the classical menu in the form of a cold course. In our sample menu, this is seen in the eighth course in the form of the chicken mousse with truffles, giving a tasty but delicate cold experience in the sequence of mostly hot dishes.

In most hotels and restaurants, the cold buffet is represented on the menu with the offer of some cold meats and salads in place of hot dishes.

The Sorbet

Once the classical menu with its fifteen-course sequence was well established, it was thought that a break should occur which would refresh the palate and put a pause into the proceedings. For this reason, a cold, invigorating water-ice laced with wine or spirits, a so-called sorbet, was served.

This pause was extended when the custom of smoking a Russian, Turkish or Egyptian cigarette had become widely accepted. A sorbet should, however, really only be served when the menu has not less than five courses, warranting the break.

This break was, in Britain at least, used by the host or guest of honour to give the main speech of the evening. And, as it is a common custom in the British Isles to call for a 'Royal' or 'Loyal Toast', this toast should be made before smoking and speech-making begins. However, smoking during or after a meal is now more and more frowned upon, and so only the sorbet is likely to remain.

The Roast Course (Le Rôti)

This course, which follows the sorbet on classical banqueting menus, reintroduces the diner to the serious part of the meal after the pause and refreshing of the palate. It will be appreciated that at this stage of the dinner the appetites of most of the guests will have been well satisfied, with the possible exception of the inveterate gourmet.

The dinner will have culminated in the serving of the principal and heaviest course of the meal, namely, the *relevé* or the *pièce de résistance*. From here on the remainder of the meal should now be tapering towards the lighter and more delicate dishes, and the roast course could be said to be the beginning of this process.

No more elaborate garnish, no more rich sauces, no more bulky vegetables and potatoes to add volume to the food on the plate, just the youngest and most delicate poultry or game birds, the most tender roast of butcher's meat, the choicest parts of furred game. Thus the saddle, loin, fillet, best-end, etc, could be considered to be suitable for this course, accompanied by an attractive, colourful, light salad.

As the term implies, the method of cooking applied is roasting, which is the application of radiant heat to meats in order to seal the outer surface of the food instantly and, therefore, retain all the natural juices within the joint or bird. The degree of cooking is determined by the time allowed for the heat generated on the surface to be conducted to the centre of the food. It follows that the fiercer the heat applied to the surface, the greater the risk that the area of the foodstuff most exposed to such heat will scorch or carbonise – therefore, heat control and frequent basting and movement of the food to be roasted are crucial for a good result.

There is no doubt that the method of cooking described above originated from the cooking on a spit over an open fire, or over the red embers of an open fire. The radiant heat generated by the hot embers could be controlled by the distance between the fire and the food, and could be directed by building a screen of stones or bricks to prevent diffusion of the heat, and to reflect the heat to the point required.

The spit can usually be rotated so that different areas of the food are continually being presented to the heat source. A bowl, tray or trough placed under the food will catch the drippings which are used to baste the food. It then only requires the necessary experience to determine the time a particular size of joint or bird requires to be cooked to the desired degree to satisfy all considerations. The professional cook is able to determine by the colour and consistency of the juices seeping from the food the stage of cooking that the food has reached at any particular time. For many years the use of an oven has replaced the spit, although in some circumstances modern spits or 'rotisseries' are still in common use. These are very much more sophisticated pieces of apparatus than the original charcoal or log-fired spits used in the past. In the main, electricity now provides both the heat and the power to rotate the spit. In some cases, gas may be used to provide the heating.

The conventional oven is still by far the most common method of roasting food, and today oven roasting has come to be accepted as the norm. It is, of course, a much more convenient way of roasting than the spit, particularly if one is catering for large numbers. To the purist, however, cooking in an oven with the food sitting on a roasting tray, in fat or meat juices, with a certain amount of steam generated which seldom has any means of escaping, and in convected heat, is not roasting in its literal sense. Because of this, many chefs add the term *à la broche* (spit roast) to the roast course on their menus, even though their kitchen is not, and never has been, equipped with a spit or rotisserie. If food is offered as *rôti à la broche*, one should ask whether this is poetic licence or if the food is genuinely roasted on a spit, or at the very least a rotisserie.

The roast course should be served as soon as possible after cooking, as it will deteriorate very quickly if kept warm for any length of time. The reheating of any roast meats in gravy is, in my opinion, a capital crime. By the very nature of the cooking operation, it is desirable that the roasted food is tender.

The days when bullocks were roasted whole are long since past. Whole deer, lamb or pigs are seldom now presented for this course. Possibly the only exception is cold set pieces on buffet menus for special occasions, or for traditional festivals when old-time spit-roast carcasses are still very much in demand. One does occasionally come across the odd suckling pig on some menus, but this is the exception rather than the norm.

It is far more common these days to use joints of meat, poultry or game birds for this course. Possibly the largest cut of meat now encountered is the 'baron' of beef, traditionally served at the Lord Mayor's banquet in the City of London. Otherwise, ribs of beef, wing-rib of beef, fillet of beef, etc, are the joints most often found on menus today. Even then, the larger joints of beef are usually found only on luncheon menus. Only sirloin and fillet could be considered suitable for the roast course at a formal dinner or banquet. All the above joints are naturally prime joints, that is to say, the best and most tender parts of the animal.

With veal in particular, the fleshy part of the thigh, the cushion, under-cushion and thick flank, are probably the most sought after cuts. In lamb or mutton, both the leg and the shoulder are suitable for this course, as is leg of pork and haunch of venison. However, the only cuts suitable for the roast course at a formal dinner are the loin or saddle, the best end of neck and under-fillet.

Poultry and feathered game, however, are the real standbys of this course. Turkey, duck, goose and chickens, ranging from the plump cockerel or capon to the poussin, are the most popular type of food for this particular course. The many game birds – grouse, partridge, pheasant, quail, plover, woodcock, snipe, to mention but a few of the better known – should be added to the list of birds suitable for the formal meal, dinner or banquet.

The side salad may be green salad, simple salad, mixed salad or compound salad. With the roast is served gravy, watercress and game chips or wafer chips, as well as an accompaniment, such as cream horseradish (for beef), mint sauce (for lamb), apple sauce and stuffing (for pork and duck), bread sauce (for chicken), and redcurrant jelly (for roast mutton).

The Salads (Les Salades)

Salads are, in the truest sense, not really a course. However, on the classical banqueting menu, where a piquant, crisp salad may break the sequence of courses, it makes a refreshing interlude. In the last few years, the Americans in particular have composed many new mixed compound salads and dressings

Figure 4.14 The salads by G Nairn
Source: © W Bode and M Leto

which have found much worldwide popularity. There is no doubt that in the last ten years or so the availability and service of all kinds of salads in every type of catering establishment has gained a now long overdue importance. Modern eating habits, with an emphasis on weight control and the desire for more balanced diets generally, have made the service of various salads at all meal-times very popular. In the early and mid-summer months, when most fresh vegetables are not yet available, many types of salads could and should take the place of frozen vegetables. It is ridiculous to serve frozen vegetables in early summer when fresh salads could take their place, often at a fraction of the cost of the more conventional, early or frozen vegetables.

The classical menu differentiates between five types of salad:

Green salads (salades vertes)
One only of various types of lettuces, endives, watercress, mustard and cress, sorrel, green peppers, chicory, etc.

Mixed green salads (salades vertes panacheés)
A combination of several of the green salads above.

Single salads (salades simples)
One only of such as beetroot, celeriac, tomato, cucumber, cabbage, french beans, potato, radish, red pepper.

Mixed salads (salades panacheés)
A combination of green and simple salads.

Compound salads (salades composés ou salades Americaines)
Various combinations of fruit and vegetables, with rice, pasta, fish, meat and poultry, bound with mayonnaise or dressings.

Dressings

All salads are served with a dressing, which might be based on a vinaigrette or French dressing, using different oils, vinegars and seasonings, acidulated dressing of cream, lemon juice and seasonings, mayonnaise, thousand island dressing or herb dressing. The repertoire of international cuisine lists some 300 salads and more than sixty dressings of various types.

A salad would not be a salad without dressing. Indeed, the various dressings allow the same salad combination to become a different salad, different in taste, because of the dressing used.

Salads are used in the presentation of simple *hors-d'oeuvres*, mixed *hors-d'oeuvres*, in many varieties on all types of cold buffets, as accompaniments to the roast course, and as courses in their own right when serving a multi-course menu.

Vegetables and Potatoes (Les Légumes et Pommes de Terre)

When considering the composition of the menu, all too often the chef or gastronome is apt to minimise the importance of vegetables in the meal being planned, and yet these foods play a major part in the preparation and presentation of every course on the menu. Vegetables, potatoes and, in some instances, fruit can contribute to every course of any menu.

Vegetables are the basis of many of the *hors-d'oeuvres*. They provide an aroma and garnishing for fish dishes and for the liquor in which the fish is poached. They are a standard accompaniment for most *entrées* and the *relevé*. The grills are invariably served with some vegetables surrounding them. The roast course likewise is often garnished with potatoes, watercress and, in some instances, with a herb or fruit sauce. Even many of the sweets and sorbets will contain fruit or fruit juices.

Figure 4.15 The vegetables and potatoes by G Nairn
Source: © W Bode and M Leto

Taking this into account, it will be seen that the vegetable and potato element in good cuisines is of some importance and should be given due consideration. In addition, many essential vitamins are obtained from vegetables and potatoes or fruit, notably vitamin C as well as some vitamin A and thiamine (vitamin B). From every aspect, therefore, we should use vegetables freely in cookery and take every care to ensure that they are properly cooked and attractively served, and not to expose them to prolonged heat after cooking, as this has the effect of destroying the essential vitamins.

Generally speaking, all vegetables are either boiled, steamed, baked, stewed, roasted, pan-fried or deep-fried in oil or fat. Methods of cooking are frequently cultural, that is to say, people prefer vegetables cooked in a manner to which they are accustomed. In some countries, vegetables are flavoured with pork or bacon fat, in others with olive oil or butter. Some people like their vegetables boiled or steamed, while others prefer to braise them in stock, sauce or cream. Some people like them well-cooked while others serve them undercooked and crisp. In good cuisine, we like to adopt whichever method of cooking is best suited to the specific vegetable and its suitability to the particular meat dish which it is intended to accompany.

High on the list of priorities is the method of cooking which will produce the most attractive service, for it would be of little use serving vegetables containing an abundance of nutrients if they were so poorly presented that the guest would be inclined to refuse to taste them, or at best accept only the smallest amount consistent with good manners.

Whichever method of cooking is adopted, the object is to break down the cellulose structure of the vegetable, to soften its tough fibres and to gelatinise the starch, thus making it more palatable and digestible. The amounts of cellulose and starch in vegetables vary a good deal and will often determine both the cooking time and the best method of cooking to adopt. Vegetables contain different pigments which determine their natural colouring: green vegetables owe their green colour to chlorophyll; carrots owe their distinctive colour to carotene; cauliflower and other white vegetables owe their whiteness to flavone; and beetroot, red cabbage, etc, owe their redness to anthocyanins. All these vegetables require different treatment if their natural colours are to be retained or even emphasised.

The green colours are best retained when cooked in an alkaline medium or 'soft' water, whereas the white, red and carrot colours are best retained if the cooking medium is slightly acid. Many vegetables are naturally slightly acid and this can have a detrimental effect on chlorophyll, but as these acids are water soluble and volatile, care in cooking should result in their dispersal in the cooking water, and in the steam generated by the boiling water. Of course, if the method chosen is other than boiling, the colour of the greens will have to be sacrificed in favour of particular flavours. Under no circumstances should chemicals such as soda be used to make the cooking water for green vegetables alkaline, as this would have the effect of making the vegetable soft and mushy, as well as destroying the nutrients. Boiling salted water, which should not be allowed to cease boiling for too long when the vegetables are added, should suffice to retain the colour if they are cooked with the lid off, and they are drained and served, or chilled (refreshed) as soon as cooking is completed. The addition of a little acid, in the form of wine, vinegar or lemon juice, to the red carrot or white vegetables, will be beneficial in retaining the natural colours of these vegetables, and should do no harm.

While most people are apt to think of vegetables in terms of leaf or green and roots and, perhaps, *légumes* and pulses, the edible part of the plants we serve as vegetables can be classified under a variety of categories, and it is useful when composing menus to be aware of these categories. The following is a broad classification of the types of vegetable normally used on menus:

Leaves: all types of cabbage, sprouts, spinach, lettuce
Flowers: all types of broccoli, cauliflower, globe artichokes
Légumes: beans of all kinds, peas, including mange-tout
Fruit: tomatoes, egg plant, marrows, squashes, pumpkin, courgettes, cucumber
Stems: asparagus, sea kale, celery, cardons, chicory, chard
Roots: carrots, parsnips, swedes, turnips, celeriac, salsify
Bulbs: onions, shallots, leeks, garlic, fennel
Tubers: potatoes, Jerusalem and Japanese artichokes
Fungi: mushrooms, *cèpes*, chanterelles, *morilles*, truffles
Pulses: the dried seeds of *légumes* – peas, beans of all types, lentils

The texture of the vegetable will often indicate the best method of cooking to apply to it, and it follows that vegetables are at their best when freshly cut or gathered. Over-long storage will have the effect of causing discoloration and limpness, particularly in leafy vegetables, with consequent loss of valuable nutrients.

In the past, the choice of vegetables for the menu was dictated by the season and the speed of the transport from field or garden to the kitchen. The advent of quick freezing and fast air transport has very largely changed all that, and it is now possible to buy practically any vegetable at any time of the year, but the cost can be prohibitive. Some vegetables do not lend themselves to processing, and some do not warrant the cost involved; therefore, fresh vegetables in season are still the cheapest and best.

With current costs being what they are, the caterer or chef is turning more and more to deep-frozen vegetables and, when well prepared and presented, these can very often solve the problem of choice for the menu. It cannot be emphasised too strongly, however, that if the best is required, freshly cooked fresh vegetables should be the aim, and to this end technology has provided some very effective equipment, such as high-pressure steamers, which permit the vegetables to be cooked to order in a matter of minutes.

Some hundred or so vegetable preparations are used in European countries, and some of the most popular of these are cooked and presented in many and varied ways. In most cases, vegetables as salad represent an accompaniment to the main course, be this fish, flesh or fowl. But on the special banqueting menu, we often find some vegetables, or vegetable dishes, served as a course in their own right, such as artichokes with hollandaise sauce.

When I arrived in England some thirty or so years ago, what was done to vegetables in the name of cookery was criminal. However, today the variety of vegetables available, and the care in their preparation and cooking, has improved enormously.

The Sweet Course (Les Entremets)

The term *entremets* is made up of the two words, *entre*, which literally means 'between', and *mets*, a dish or article of food. Thus *entremets* could be understood as items served between the principal dishes or courses, and we have here again French applied to culinary terminology which bears no relation to the spoken or written French.

In the past these foods by the name *entremets* consisted of vegetable preparations, a fact that is confirmed by the title given to the chef responsible for vegetables preparation in the *brigade de cuisine*, namely, *chef entremetier*.

With the development of the elaborate banqueting menus which were so popular in the nineteenth and beginning of the twentieth centuries, special preparations of rare, early-season or out-of-season vegetables were offered as a light course towards the end of the dinner, and this came to be listed as the course we now call *entremets de légumes*.

Gradually, however, it became fashionable to name the individual vegetable preparation proffered for this course, such as *asperges*, truffles, *artichauts*, *primeurs* or *bouqetière de légumes* and *soufflé de champignons*, and it became a course in its own right, represented by course number eleven on the menu (see page 111).

For whatever reason, the word *entremets* came to be applied to the selection of hot and cold sweets which were always popular in Britain. The old term of

Figure 4.16 The sweet course by G Nairn
Source: © W Bode and M Leto

entremets de légumes is retained for special vegetable preparations. So, for the purpose of this section, when talk is of *entremets*, one is dealing with the vast variety of sweets applicable to this course and not the vegetable variety.

The department or *partie* responsible for preparation of the sweet course is the *pâtisserie*, which is under the control of the *chef pâtissier*. *Pâtisserie* means, in effect, pastry work, and reflects the fact that in French cuisine the bulk of sweets as well as fruit had a pastry base.

In the very large and busy establishment which employed a large and specialist kitchen staff (*grande brigade de cuisine*), it became usual to subdivide the pastry department into specialist departments which dealt with a particular aspect of sweet preparation. We thus had the *pâteur*, who was employed in the main with all pastry work, the *boulanger*, who dealt with all yeast work, the *confiseur*, who was concerned with sugar work, chocolate and sweetmeats, and the *glacier*, who produced ices, ice puddings and all cold sweets. The *chef pâtissier*, who was required to be skilled in all the various branches of work in his department, dealt with all other miscellaneous work concerned with the sweet course, such as soufflés, sweet sauces and pancakes, as well as supervising the work of the department overall. Where the amount of work warranted it, he would be assisted by one or more *commis* and almost invariably by apprentices. The bulk of catering establishments now usually employ one *chef pâtissier* who deals with all the work and specialities described above, with assistants, in accordance with the volume of work in the particular establishment.

Let us now take a broad look at the *entremets*. Many are of British origin and are not really translatable into French. For this reason, they may be found in their original English on most menus, but the classical *entremets* themselves are many and varied.

The sweet course may be hot or cold – in winter a hot sweet is preferred, in summer the reverse might be the choice. At banquets with a large number of courses, both a hot and cold sweet may be served. In this case, the hot sweet course is always served before the cold sweet.

Sweet courses may be categorised under the following types:

Pies, tarts, flans, puddings, gateaux.
Crèmes, mousses, *bavarois*, *soufflés*.
Fritters, pancakes, croquettes.
Ice-creams, *bombes*, *coupes*, *parfaits*, sorbets.
Stewed fruits and compotes.
Fresh fruit and fruit salads.

Some two thousand or more sweets are known, plus many and various sauces and creams which may accompany them.

The Cheese Course (Les Fromages)

Cheese is possibly the oldest man-made food. There is pictorial evidence of cheese-making from Mesopotamia in 3500–2800 BC. A relief of Al-U-Baid and a stamp seal from Jemdet Nasr also clearly show the Sumerians milking cattle and using the milk for cheese-making. Other archaeological discoveries have been made in Africa, France, Spain and the Libyan Sahara, suggesting milk processing and possibly cheese-making as long ago as 20,000 BC. At the height of the Greek and Roman empires, cheese was most certainly well established and very much part of the daily diet. Only in the Far East, particularly India, were milk and cheese considered 'a liquid or sickly excretion unfit for human consumption' and this for religious reasons.

For the invention and making of cheese, man needed two obvious gastro-geographical conditions: a landscape more suitable for cattle, sheep and goats

Figure 4.17 Cheese and savouries by G Nairn
Source: © W Bode and M Leto

than growing crops, and a warm climate which facilitated the curdling of milk (by accident rather than design). Milk was stored in large earthenware jars for daily use in what cannot then have been the best of hygienic conditions. These prerequisites for the invention and making of cheese were most strikingly fulfilled in the hilly country around the Mediterranean. It is not surprising, therefore, that the earliest and some of the best-known cheeses have their origins in this part of the world.

Wherever early cheese was made, it was very much a hit-or-miss affair, only gradually improved by trial and error over many thousands of years. The making of cheese was very much a family, or possibly a village, concern, with the technique jealously guarded in the remote valleys or high alpine meadows in which it was produced and enjoyed. Until quite recently, it was no more than a cottage industry in all parts of the world. Only in the eighteenth century did the making of cheese become a controllable industry as a result of the work of Justus von Liebig, a famous German chemist and instigator of laboratory work in respect of medical and bacteriological research, food poisoning and hygiene, and, later, of Louis Pasteur, a famous French chemist with a particular interest in pasteurisation of food, milk and cheese. Unlike other foods, cheese has never been considered suitable at one particular meal-time only. It is eaten at any time of the day.

Some cheeses are better eaten raw, others are more suitable for cooking, and some are suitable for both purposes. To understand the enormous quantities and varieties of cheese suitable for table service, the following looks at five types of cheese and gives some examples of each.

Soft Fresh White Cheeses *(Fromages Blancs)*

These types of relatively young cheeses (not left to mature) are made all over Europe from curd. Some of them have cream or butter added, while others have herbs and spices, for example, Cachat, Demi Sel, Petit Suisse, cottage cheese, quark and crème fraiche.

Soft Cheeses *(Fromages Mous)*

Into this group fall some of the best-known soft cheeses in the world, for example, Brie (*le roi des fromages*) and Camembert (*le prince des fromages*). They are probably the most imitated cheeses in the world and now produced in most European countries. But there are considerably more cheeses of this type than these two, which are usually sold in wooden or cardboard cartons. They include Aunise, Brie, Cambasola, Crème Château, Livarot and Pont l'Evèque.

The Blue Cheeses *(Fromages Bleus)*

Under this heading we find the popular mould-fungi cheeses, with blue, green, orange-red coloured mould growth. These cheeses can vary from soft to semi-hard and mild, as in the case of Roquefort, to sharp as in the case of Danish Blue. With the world famous Stilton, Britain has added one of the great cheeses to this list. Others are Bleu des Causses, Vinney, Dorset Blue, Dolcelatte, etc.

Semi-hard Cheeses *(Fromages Fondus)*

Fondues or *fromage fondu* is a term referring to semi-hard cheeses, and has little to do with the famous Swiss cheese dish of the same name. Nearly all of them have a strong, marked flavour and smell, often referred to as 'stinkers', and when placed on a cheese-board in a restaurant they should be covered by a cloche. They are available in all manner of shapes and sizes and include Limburger, Harzer, Port Salut and Nataise.

The Hard Cheeses *(Fromages Durs)*

In the classification of the hard cheeses we find some considerable difference from one country to another – some are almost bullet-hard while others are moist and crumbling (Cheddar). Other cheeses are Parmesan, Caerphilly, Edam, Emmental, Gouda, Gruyère, Leicester, Gloucester and Tilsiter. These cheeses are ideal to cook with.

Cheese on the Menu

Cheese is found on all types of menu in Europe, from breakfast to late-night supper. At some point in the past, cheese became part of the classical menu and the accepted conclusion to the meal. The research into many old menus does not show cheese used as a course at the conclusion of a meal before the mid-nineteenth century. Therefore, the cheeseboard should be considered a relatively new contribution to the menu, more suited to the restaurant with small parties rather than to the set *table d'hôte* menu used for functions and banquets. This is not surprising as the service of a selection of four to six cheeses for hundreds of guests would be a most time-consuming and difficult undertaking. Thus, at large banquets only one cheese is served, Camembert or Stilton for example, with possibly a few blue grapes, or many of the popular hot cheese preparations, such as fried cheeses, puff-pastry filled with cheese, mille feuilles au Roquefort or Pailles au Gruyère, or choux pastry filled with cheese such as Duchesse de Bresse bleu or Duchesse de Stilton. Another possibility is to serve a hot cheese *soufflé* – always a popular choice.

In *Le Livre des Menus*, published in 1912 and edited by Escoffier, there is a selection of several hundred famous menus of grand occasions, but only very few have cheese included as a course at the conclusion of the meal. The earliest is on an 1870 menu of the Café Voisin in Paris, which concluded with '*fromage Gruyère*'. A 1910 luncheon menu '*en l'honneur de M. Escoffier*' in the Waldorf Astoria Hotel, New York, concluded with '*fromage Camembert*'.

A luncheon given on board HMS *Medina* in 1911 ends the meal with '*fromage et beurre*' and from the same selection of menus from the *Medina* we have a 1912 menu which ends with '*choix de fromage*'.

The earliest cheese-board I have found on old menus was a selection of cheeses at a Paris luncheon (1916), which gave '*Roquefort, Port Salut, Gruyère*' as the concluding course. When cheeses are served, they should include some or all of the different types of cheeses which, in the case of the last example, includes

Roquefort (blue) Port Salut (semi-hard and smelly) and Gruyère (hard).

The French often serve cheese before the sweet course, whereas in England and most other European countries it is more often served at the end of a meal. However, there are no hard and fast rules, therefore it should always remain a personal choice.

Savouries

Savouries are essentially an English addition to a meal or menu, and as such they do not qualify as an additional course on the classical menu, but may take the place of the cheese course. Escoffier, in his *Guide Culinaire* writes:

> '. . . *we suggest that the use of savouries in the classical menu is contrary to gastronomic practice and that there is no reason why they should feature on the classical menu*'.(4.9)

Nevertheless, in Britain, savouries have become a popular alternative in place of cheese on the menu, particularly when the function consists of gentlemen only, who consider the service of a savoury item preferable to that of a sweet, especially when we take into account the British custom of 'passing the Port' which more easily follows cheese, or a savoury dish, rather than a sweet.

Dessert

With this term we have generally some confusion – the general public often bands all sweet courses under this heading. Dessert, however, should only be a basket of fresh fruit offered as the last course at a banquet and no more. To this may be added, during the winter and Christmas time, a selection of nuts, dried figs and dates.

Coffee (le Café)

This is not counted as a course on the classical menu, but is a very recent addition which has become the final and, for most, a pleasing conclusion to a good meal.

4.9 From teaching notes, facts, comments, gathered over 30 years, sources now unknown.

Figure 4.18 The coffee and port by G Nairn
Source: © W Bode and M Leto

Changing Menu Language

Menu language is always changing. Figure 4.19 shows a menu of a popular type of chain restaurant found all over England. Here the *hors-d'oeuvre* is given as 'tummy tempters'; the *potage* is given as 'from the kitchen cauldron'; the *oeufs* is given as 'omelettes'; the *poisson* is given as 'from deep waters'; the *entrée*, *relevé*, and *rôti* have become 'from the grill; the *entremets* is given as 'sweet shop'; and the *fromage* has become 'cheese board'.

The language of the menu will continue to change in order to be more relevant to the consumer and to reflect changing eating patterns. What is pleasing to see is the fact that despite these changes the structure of the classical menu is still much the same.

FROM THE TAVERN

Why not enjoy a subtle draught to prime your palate? Martini, Campari, Sherry or your favourite drink. Wine by the glass or carafe. Lager, beer or ale.

Tummy Tempters

Chilled Fruit Juice
Orange or grapefruit, freshly squeezed

Smoked Fillet of Mackerel
with creamy sharp horseradish

Paté en Croûte
Pork and chicken liver, spiced

Egg and Tomato Vinaigrette
Refreshing lemon dressing

FROM THE KITCHEN CAULDRON

The Daily Pot
Chef's fresh soup of the season

French Onion Soup
Based on the finest stock. Served with cheese gratinated croûtons

Pea & Ham Soup
A true winter warmer

OMELETTES

The Bagpiper
Filled with spinach and smoked salmon

Ham

Mushroom

THE PANCAKE SHOP

A speciality of France, choose from the following fillings:

Seafood

Chicken

Beef

WHOLESOME SALADS

The Californian
Mixed salad with cottage cheese

The Mermaid
Mixed salad with crabmeat

The John Holiday
Mixed salad with chicken strips – a meal in itself

From DEEP WATERS

Fried Fillet of Plaice

Baked Mackerel *with Capers*

Grilled Cod Steak
with Parsley Butter

All served with a choice of salad and potatoes

FROM THE GRILL

Minute Steak 6oz

Salisbury Steak 10oz

Tenderloin Pork 8oz

Beefy Burgers ***single or doubles***

cooked as you wish and served with salad and French frys.

SANDWICH CORNER

Ham

Beef

Chedder

Chicken

Crabmeat

Danish blue

Freshly made to order

Sweet Shop

Crême Caramel

Sherry Trifle

Fresh Fruit Salad

Selection of Ice Creams and Sorbets

CHEESE BOARD

A selection of fine English and imported cheeses

With crackers or french bread and celery

BEVERAGES

Coffee ***(cup or pot)***
Pot of Tea ***(various brands)***
Glass of milk ***(hot or cold)***
Minerals
Juices

Figure 4.19 Popular restaurant menu in modern language
Source: From the author's collection, actual source unknown

The Modern Menu

We do not eat fourteen courses any more. Modern attitudes to eating and a more hurried lifestyle make most of us do usually with a snack for lunch, and possibly an evening meal with two or three courses. On festival days, dinner parties or possibly Sunday lunch, we still might eat three or four courses. This is for most of us the limit to the number of courses we eat, even if we include the much discussed business luncheon or dinner.

Four to six courses are still quite common for large banquets, dinner dances and conferences and club dinners. On menus for government, diplomatic, gastronomic, or company or club banquets, six to ten courses are often served. On these occasions the classical menu gives guidance as to the correct sequence and content of the courses and menu.

For the modern guest in an hotel, or the occasional night out for a good meal in a restaurant, the classical menu has evolved into more modern types of menus:

The *table d'hôte* menu – the 'host's table' or 'no choice menu'.
The *à la carte* or *grande carte* menu – the 'large choice menu'.
The *menu à choix* – the 'limited choice menu'.

Figure 4.20 In consideration of the next menu by G Nairn
Source: © W Bode and M Leto

The Table d'Hôte Menu

The translation of *table d'hôte* means the 'host's table' but it also means a 'set menu' with no choice, as would be the case if we were invited to a dinner party in a private home.

The *table d'hôte* menu is found and used on both the lower and higher gastronomic spectrum. In the small hotel or boarding house, breakfast, lunch and dinner is the same for all the guests. Naturally the menu changes every day. Figure 4.21 shows a hand-written set menu with five courses for lunch at the Hôtel du Pilon, Auron, France. Similarly, in the case of a large formal banquet with 200 to 300 guests, it would be impossible to serve each of the guests something different.

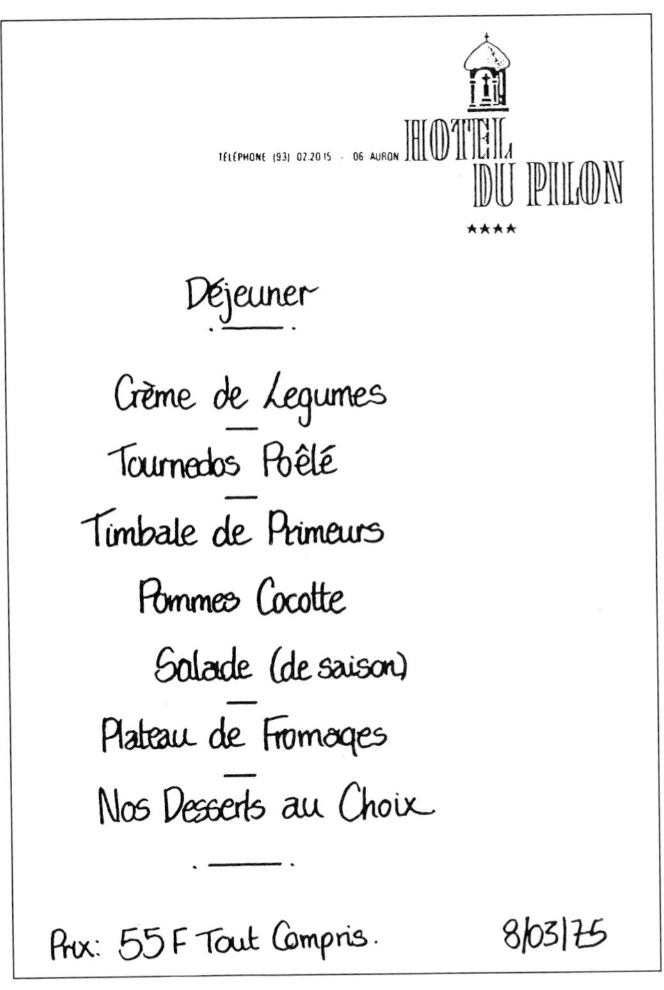

TÉLÉPHONE (93) 02.20 15 · 06 AURON HOTEL DU PILON ★★★★

Déjeuner

Crème de Legumes

—

Tournedos Poêlé

—

Timbale de Primeurs

Pommes Cocotte

Salade (de saison)

—

Plateau de Fromages

—

Nos Desserts au Choix

Prix: 55 F Tout Compris. 8/03/75

Figure 4.21 Simple handwritten *table d'hôte* menu
Source: From the author's collection, actual source unknown

What, however, does change for the formal banquet menu is its presentation and layout. As this is often a special occasion, much care is taken in the production of these menus. Figure 4.22 is a good example of a specially printed menu, produced by students of the Catering Department at Bournemouth College.

The staff and students

of the

Tourism, Hotel and Catering Department

extend the season's greetings

to their patrons

29th, 30th November
1st, 2nd, 6th, 7th, 8th December

BOURNEMOUTH COLLEGE OF TECHNOLOGY

Figure 4.22 Printed *table d'hôte* menu
Source: Bournemouth College of Technology, from the author's collection

Figure 4.23 overleaf is of the same type, but gives further information, such as the royal toast, special guests or speakers, response and vote of thanks, as well as the wine which will be served during the meal.

DEJEUNER DE NOEL

Les crevettes roses en gelée au Chablis

La coupe de terrapine au Xérès
Paillettes dòrées

La suprême de flétan Mirabeau

Le dindon rôti à l'anglaise
Les boutons de Bruxelles Limousin
Le celeri braisé à la moëlle
Les pommes Champignol ou royale

Le pouding de Nöel, beurre Cognac
Mince pies

Le panier de fruits frais
Les noix et noisettes

Le moka

Toasts

LOYAL TOAST

P. C. J. Kendall

OUR GUESTS

H. Ingate

RESPONSE ON BEHALF OF GUESTS

Mr. P. R. Mereweather

Grosvenor House

VOTE OF THANKS

J. C. R. Lewis

Figure 4.23 Printed *table d'hôte* menu for banquet
Source: Bournemouth College of Technology, from the author's collection

Menu

Melon au Marasquin

~

Delice de sole hôteliere

~

Pintade poelee Falconnet Elizabeth

~

Poire de Comice

Rocher de glace

~

Cafe

~

WINES

Caseler Berg 1961

Santenay 1957

The à la Carte or Grande Carte Menu

Before the Second World War, *à la carte* menus could have a selection of as many as a hundred or more dishes, often as many as ten to twelve choices in each

DEJEUNER A LA CARTE

Hors-d'Oeuvre

Honeydew Melon £0.60
Huitres Natives £1.10 ½ doz. Escargots de Bourgogne £0.90 ½ doz. Mortadella di Bologna £0.60 Foie Gras £2.20
Mousse Yorkaise £0.50 Crevettes Cocktail £0.80 Homard Cocktail £1.50 Jambon de Parme £1.15 Caviar £2.30
Grapefruit Florida £0.40 Saumon Fumé £1.15 Potted Shrimps £0.60 Poire d'Avocat £0.50 Garnie £0.90
Terrine Maison £1 Truite Fumée £0.80 Smoked Eel £0.90 Dressed Crab £1.20 Crevettes Crystal £0.90

Potages et Oeufs

Consommé en Gelée £0.30 Vichyssoise en Tasse £0.30
Consommé aux Pâtes Fines £0.30 Crème de Volaille £0.50 Potage Paysanne £0.40
Crème de Tomate £0.40 Oeuf en Cocotte au Jus £0.50 Omelette aux Champignons £0.60
Oeufs Brouillés aux Rognons £0.60 Oeufs Pochés Florentine £0.60 Spaghetti à la Bolognaise £0.70

Poissons

Délices de Sole Caprice £1.10 Saumon Grillé, Sce. Béarnaise £2.10
Scampi Sautés aux Fines Herbes £1.50
Truite de Rivière aux Amandes £0.95 Sole Meunière, Grillée ou Colbert £1.20
Merlan Frit en Colère £0.70 Hareng Grillé, Sauce Moutarde £0.85
Médaillon de Turbotin Riviéra £1.10 Gratin de Saumon Duchesse £1.50
Coquille St.-Jacques Bercy £1.10 Friture de Blanchailles au Citron £0.80

Plats du Jour

Curry de Poulardine Madras £1.40 Côte de Boeuf Rôtie à l'Anglaise £1.70
Foie de Veau Sauté am Lard £1.10 Hamburger Steak Coquetière £1.20
Timbale de Rognons Turbigo £1.00 Chump Chop Grillé Vert-Pré £1.20
Emincé de Poulardine à la King £0.90 Gammon Grillé Manhattan £1.00
Emincé de Filet Smitane £1.10 Chop de Porc Grand'Mère £1.00
Poussin Grillé Américaine £1.00 Médaillon de Veau Majestic £1.50

Grillades et Rôties

Minute Steak £1.30
Côtelette d'Agneau £1.00 Filet de Boeuf £1.50 Sirloin Steak £1.20 Poulet de Grain (3 cts) £2.10 Pork Chop £0.90
Mixed Grill £1.30 Rognons au Lard £1.00 Poulet Reine £3.10 T-Bone Steak £2.10 Châteaubriand £2.20
Côte d'Agneau Double £1.00 Lamb Chop £1.20 Gammon Steak £0.90 Chump Chop £1.00 Aile de Poulet £0.90

Buffet Froid

Veal & Ham Pie £1.40 Délice de Sole Eden Roc £1.10 Salade de Homard £2.00 Dinde £0.90
Jambon d'York £0.90 Sirloin £1.20 Langue £0.80 Selle d'Agneau £1.00 Aile de Poulet £0.90
Salade du Chef £1.10 Demi Homard Garni Riviera £2.00 Suprême Jeannette £1.40

Légumes

Artichauts £0.40 Chou-fleur £0.30 Courgettes £0.50 Epinards £0.30 Carottes au Beurre £0.30
Endives £0.30 Haricots Verts £0.40 Aubergines £0.50 Céleris Braisés £0.30 Petits Pois à la Française £0.30
Pommes Persillées Frites Sautées £0.30 Pommes Soufflees Croquettes £0.30

Les Entremets

Trifle à l'Anglaise £0.50 Meringue Glacée Chantilly £0.50 Compôte d'Orange £0.50
Eclairs au Chocolat £0.50 Custard Pudding £0.50
Café Filtre £0.20 Caffein-free Coffee £0.25

Jeudi 18 Février 1971

Figure 4.24 A *la carte* menu for lunch, 1971
Source: From the author's collection, actual source unknown

course of the classical menu structure. Today the number of courses is much reduced, but, in some larger and better hotels and restaurants in Europe, one can still count as many as forty to fifty or more dishes on the menu.

On the *à la carte* menu, each dish is individually priced and the guest is invited to make his or her own choice from the large selection of dishes.

Figures 4.24–4.26 are examples of *à la carte* menus from some famous London hotels, and one can see there is considerable choice, be this for lunch or supper. Individual dish prices are clearly shown. So that no guest sits down to order only a soup, many restaurants stipulate a minimum charge for served food, or state that not less than two courses must be consumed. The prices here should be ignored, as these menus are quite old.

Figure 4.26 shows an unusual *à la carte* menu that features three set or *table d'hôte* menus: the *Menu de Santée* is a menu for the health conscious; the *Menu d'Affaires* is a menu for businessmen and women; and the *Menu de Soirée Galante* is a romantic or dinner with friends menu.

Figure 4.27 shows a menu that breaks the accepted rule of what an *à la carte* menu should be by stating no prices at all. This is the so-called 'Ladies or Guest Menu'. Only the host will normally be given the *à la carte* menu which shows the prices, so that the guest is free to choose whichever dishes she likes without being influenced by the cost.

The Menu à Choix or 'Limited Choice Menu'

This latest, relatively modern addition to our menu types, which is derived from the old classical menu, reflects the modern eating-out situation. Here the restaurateur wished to avoid the limitation of the set or *table d'hôte* menu, or the expensive production and provisions of the large *grande carte* or *à la carte* menu, yet still allow some limited choice. The limited choice menu is therefore a compromise between the *table d'hôte* and *à la carte* menus.

It is often found in the smaller, more moderate restaurants, and also in some of Europe's better hotels and restaurants. The handwritten limited choice menu shown in Figure 4.28 is from a small but good restaurant on the south coast of England. Here the restaurateur offers a limited number of starters and main courses, including a vegetarian dish, and sweets. They vary from four to eight dishes in each course, which in this example are priced individually. There is one choice of vegetable and potato to accompany the main course, and this is included in the main course price.

DINER A

Les Hors d'Oeuvres

L Assiette Charcutière 16/6 — Les Crevettes Crystal 17/6
Le Melon Charentais 12/6 — La Terrine Maison 15/6 — Le Dressed Crab 22/6
La Mousse de Jambon 10/6 — Le Jambon de Parme 17/6 — Le Caviar 40/-
Les Crevettes Cocktail 12/6 — Le Pamplemousse Florida 6/6
Le Homard Cocktail 22/6 — La Truite Fumée 12/6 — Les Potted Shrimps 12/6
Le Foie Gras 40/- — Le Salami 12/6 — L'Anguille Fumée 16/6
La Mortadelle de Bologne 12/6 — Le Saumon Fumé 19/6
La Poire d'Avocat 8/6 Garnie 12/6

Les Potages et Oeufs

La Crème Agnés Sorel 6/6 — Le Consommé aux Raviolis 5/6
Le Potage Cultivateur 6/6 — Crème de Pois Rafraîchie 6/6 — La Petite Marmite 7/6
Le Consommé en Gelée 5/6 — La Gaspacho Andalouse 6/6 — La Tasse aux Ciboulettes 5/6
Les Œufs Pochés Bénédictine 10/6 — L'Omelette Yorkaise 12/6
Les Œufs Brouillés Meyerbeer 12/6 — Les Œufs en Cocotte à la Crème 10/6

Les Plats du Jour

La Selle d'Agneau Rôtie aux Pommes Mireille 25/6
Le Cœur de Filet Massèna 27/6 — Le Caneton d'Aylesbury Rôti Caprice 22/6
Le Jambon Etuvé aux Epinards 20/6 — Le Suprême de Volaille Princesse 22/6
La Noisette d'Agneau à la Chartres 24/6 — Le Vol-au-Vent Toulouse 19/6
La Grouse d'Ecosse Rôtie sur Canapé 55/6 — Le Poussin Rôti Charcutière 18/6
Le Médaillon de Ris de Veau Maréchale 25/6
L'Escalope de Veau Viennoise 27/6 — L'Emincé de Poulardine à la King 22/6

Les Poissons

Les Délices de Sole Grand-Duc 19/6 — Les Filets de Plaice St. Germain 17/6
Les Scampis Sautés aux Fines Herbes 21/6 — La Truite de Rivière Cléopâtre 16/6
La Truite Vivante au Bleu 17/6 — La Sole Meunière, Grillé ou Colbert 21/6
Le Médaillon de Turbotin Coquelin 19/6 — Le Demi Homard Thermidor 35/6
Le Filet de Haddock Monte Carlo 16/6 — Le Gratin de Saumon Mornay 18/6
Le Crab Meat Maryland 25/6

Figure 4.25 A *la carte* menu for dinner, 1970
Source: From the author's collection, actual source unknown

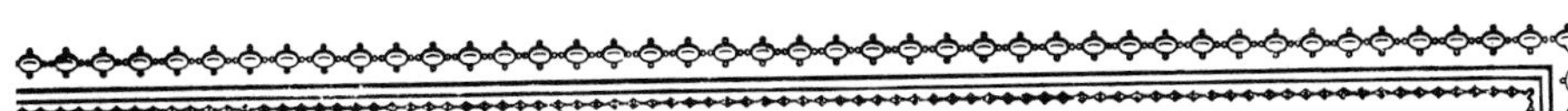

LA CARTE

Jeudi 21 Août 1969

Sur le Grill

T-Bone Steak 40/- Filet de Bœuf 25/6 Sirloin Steak 22/6 Gammon Steak 16/6
Rognons au Lard 13/6 Mixed Grill 25/6 Pork Chop 15/6 Côte d'Agneau Double 19/6
Côtelettes d'Agneau 19/6 Lamb Chop 21/6 Chump Chop 19/6
LES ROTIS : Poulet de Grain (3cts) 52/6 Poulet Reine (4cts) 62/6
Aile de Volaille 18/6 Poussin 18/6 Châteaubriand 40/-

Le Buffet Froid

La Dinde du Norfolk 18/6 La Langue Ecarlate 14/6 Le Jambon d'York 17/6
L'Aile de Poulet 18/6 Le Supreme Jeannette 24/6
Grouse Pie Balmoral 27/6 Le Contrefilet 19/6 La Selle d'Agneau du Dorset 20/6
Le Chicken Pie 22/6 Le Veal & Ham Pie 25/6
Le Demi Homard Garni Rivièra 35/6 La Salade de Homard 35/6
Les Délices de Sole Antiboise 19/6 Salade du Chef 22/6

Les Légumes

Les Artichauts 6/6 Les Aubergines 8/- Les Haricots Verts 6/6
Le Céleri Braisé 5/6 Les Endives 5/- Les Carottes au Beurre 4/6
Les Choux de Bruxelles 5/6 Le Chou-fleur Mornay 5/6
Les Epinards en Branches 5/6 Les Petits Pois 5/6 Les Courgettes 8/-
Les Pommes Persillées, Sautées, Frites 4/- Les Pommes Soufflées, Croquettes 5/-
LES SALADES : Niçoise 5/6 Japonaise 5/6 Panachée 5/6 Verte 4/6
Mimosa 4/6 Rachel 5/6

Les Entremets

Les Quartiers de Pêches Bar-le-Duc 9/6 Le Soufflé au Citron 9/6
La Coupe Nesselrode 9/6 Les Crêpes au Confiture 9/6
L'Ananas Frais Paillard 9/6 Les Petits Fours 5/-
LES GLACES Vanille, Orange, Café, Chocolat Fraise Citron 5/-
La Corbeille de Fruits en Saison

Savouries

Le Canapé Baron 6/6 La Croque Monsieur 6/6 Le Canapé Diane 5/6
Le Canapé Ivanhoe 6/6 Le Canapé Menelik 5/6 Welsh Rarebit 6/6

FROMAGES AU CHOIX 9/6
Cheddar, Ementhal, Gorgonzola, Brie, Roquefort, Camembert
Mr. Fromage, Gervais, Petite Suisse, Edam, Pont l'Eveque
Port Salut, Bel Paese, Stilton, Boursin aux Fines Herbes

Café Filtre 3/- Caffein-free Coffee 4/6

Les Hors d'Oeuvre

Salade de Pigeonneau aux Truffes
tender young pigeon breasts dressed on french leaves with a truffle sauce
£6.50

Sorbet aux Fruits de Mer avec Safron
water ice mingled with saffron served with an array of seafood
£7.50

Crevettes Roses Glacées Broyées
large mediterranean prawns accompanied with four very distinctive and different national sauces
£6.45

Poire d'Avocat au Prince
sliced avocado pear with lobster and garnished with a dill flavoured sauce, served cold
£4.95

Terrine de Coquille St. Jacques au Poivre Vert
a light terrine of scallops flavoured with green peppercorns
£3.95

Petit Omelet Chasseur
a small omelette filled with mushrooms, shallots and parsley served with a madeira sauce
£4.50

Assiette de Fruits à l'Arc-En-Ciel
a rainbow of fresh fruits
£5.75

Saumon d'Ecosse Fumé
oak smoked Scotch salmon with brown bread
£7.95

Les Potages

Crème Agnès Sorel
chicken and mushroom stock finished with cream, julienne of tongue and white of chicken
£2.80

Soupe de Poissons à la Mode du Cap Ferrat
a delicate fish soup with fresh mussels, lobster, goujons of sole, mushrooms and garlic straws served apart
£3.80

Crème St. Germain Relevée
cream of mange tout with a twist of curried cream
£2.80

Consommé de Lapin au Romarin
rabbit consommé infused with rosemary and garnished with small vegetables
£2.80

Les Poissons

Crêpe de Trois Poissons et Céleri
small pancakes topped with shellfish, white fish and a fish mousse coated with three sauces
£12.80

Suprême de Saumon Sauce Mousseline
suprême of salmon served on a bed of hollandaise sauce garnished with quenelles of cream
£13.10

Paupiettes de Sole au Poivre Rouge
rolled fillets of sole poached in white wine, served on a red pepper sauce, with a garnish of prawns and asparagus
£16.50

Filet de Truite Saumonée Cressonnière
fillet of sea-trout served on a watercress sauce
£13.25

Filet de Sole de Douvre Grillée au Beurre Noisette
fillets of Dover sole grilled with nut brown butter and lime juice
£15.75

Steak de Lotte aux Noisettes et Vermout
boneless steak of lotte fish marinaded in vermouth and nuts
£14.50

Les Entrées

Escalope de Veau Forêt Sauvage
escalope of veal with cèpes, morrels and field mushrooms, finished in a cream and brandy sauce
£14.30

Médaillons de Venaison Poire William
small marinaded venison steaks served on a rich red wine sauce and garnished with fresh poached pear, redcurrants and chestnuts
£15.60

Mignons de Boeuf Duroc
two mignons of beef with parisienne potatoes, diced tomatoes, chopped shallots and field mushrooms
£14.50

Ris d'Agneau Braisé Soubise
lamb sweetbreads set on a bed of spinach with leek and onion sauce
£11.70

Magret de Caneton Vallée d'Auge
boned breast of duckling with sliced apple, cream, calvados and hazelnuts
£12.00

Suprême de Pintade aux Nouilles
boned breast of guinea fowl cooked in butter set on black noodles with chestnut and cranberry purée
£11.75

Les Grillades et Rôtis

Blanc de Volaille Grillé
boned breast of chicken grilled with herb butter then garnished with smoked ham and sage
£10.10

Filet de Boeuf avec Sauce Choron
char grilled fillet of beef served with fresh tomato concassé in a béarnaise sauce
£12.95

Entrecôte de Boeuf aux Deux Moutardes
chargrilled sirloin of beef offered with two mustards
£11.30

Foie de Veau Grillé aux Prunoise
grilled calves liver garnished with prunes and madeira sauce
£10.40

Les rôtis de la voiture sont preparés et changes à chaque repas. Demandez au maître d'hôtel le choix de jour.
The roast trolley features a different dish each service
Ask the Restaurant Manager for details

Les Légumes

Assiette de Légumes et Pommes du Jour
individual dish containing three different vegetables and today's potato choice
£[illegible]

Salade au Choix
choice of salads
£2.60

Figure 4.26 A *la carte* or *grande carte* menu, 1985
Source: From the author's collection, actual source unknown

Les Desserts

Voiture du Pâtissier
sweet trolley
£3.25

Plateau de Fromages
cheeseboard
£3.25

Glacés au Choix
choice of ice-creams
£2.95

Spécialité du Pâtissier

Petit Gâteau à la Tour de Londres
an individual chocolate gâteau layered
with chocolate creams, and garnished
with nut biscuits
£3.80

Sorbet de Fruits aux Passion
passion fruit sorbet served
in a meringue nest
£3.15

Bordure aux Figues Farcie et Kirsch
nest of figs filled with creamed
rice laced with kirsch
£4.80

Café ou Thé et Petits Fours
coffee or tea with sweetmeats
£1.95

Menu de Santée

This menu is devised for the health conscious and therefore we think suitable for everyone and features the very best seasonal produce

Sorbet de tomate à la salade verte
fresh tomato sorbet set on a salad made from
crisp garden greens

Teillage de poissons aux légumes parisiens
lattice of salmon and lotte poached in
cucumber stock garnished with vegetables

Petits pommes de terre duchesses
small duchesse potatoes

Haricots verts a l'anglaise
french beans english style

Poires au vin poivré
baby pears poached in wine
scented with pepper and bay leaf

Thé à la camomile
camomile herb tea

Three courses including tea or coffee £17.75

Menu d'Affaires

Each lunchtime there is a businessman's menu available featuring a main course from the trolley

Escargots à la bourguinonne
six snails mingled in garlic
shallots and parsley butter

Filet de volaille à la king
chicken fillets with wild mushrooms
red peppers laced with white wine

Assiette de légumes et pommes de terre

Pudding soufflé au citron
lemon pudding soufflé served warm

Café ou thé et petits fours
coffee or tea with sweetmeats

Two Courses £15.75
Three Courses £17.75

31/5

Menu de Soirée Galante

Designed to complement the dinner dances on Friday and Saturday when the Princes Room features dancing to our resident band, on these evenings each week the chef creates a delicious 6 course menu available until 9.00 p.m. This menu is recommended for complete tables.

FRIDAY 3 AND SATURDAY 4 JUNE 1988

Cocktail de melon Park Lane

Crème de calabrèse Waterloo

Suprème de barbue à la bisque de crevettes froides

Petite salade de champignons crus

Contre-filet de boeuf fleuriste

Assiette de légumes et pommes de terre du jour

Grand marnier aux figues et coulis de framboises

Café ou thé et petits fours

£22.50

Our prices include VAT.
Gratuities are at the discretion of our guests.

10/87

Les Hors d'Oeuvres

Hors d'Oeuvres Variés
Selection of Hors d'Oeuvres from the trolley

Crêpe de Crevettes Mornay
Prawns bound in Cream and Brandy rolled in a pancake covered with Cheese Sauce

Caviar de Beluga
Sturgeons Roe on ice with sieved yolk, white of egg and chopped shallots

Jambon de Parme avec Melon ou avec Pêche
Raw Italian sun-cured ham with Melon or Peach

Avocat aux Crevettes
Avocado Pear with Prawns and Aurore Sauce

Avocat Vinaigrette
Avocado pears served with a vinaigrette sauce

Crevettes au Beurre
Potted Shrimps

Saumon Fumé
Smoked Salmon

Melon Frappé
Chilled Melon

Anguille Fumée Sauce Raifort
Smoked Eel served with Horseradish Sauce

Escargots de Bourgogne au beurre
Whole Snails cooked and served in their shells with garlic butter

Truite Fumée Sauce Raifort
Smoked Trout with Horseradish Sauce

Pâté de Foie Gras de Strasbourg
Goose-liver Pâté

Ecrevisses Grillées Sauce Vert
Grilled Pacific Prawns with a green garlic flavoured sauce

Pâté du Chef
Home made Pâté

Les Potages

Velouté de Tomate
Tomato Soup

Soupe de Tortue au Madère
Turtle Soup with Madeira, served with Cheese Straws

Soupe à l'Oignon Gratinée
Onion Soup with croutons and grated Parmesan Cheese

Germiny en Tasse
A clear beef soup with sorrel, slightly thickened with yolk of egg and cream

Soupe du Jour
Soup of the day

Soupe Froide d'Avocat
Chilled Avocado Soup

Vichysoisse Froide
Chilled Leek and Potato Soup

Les Oeufs et Pâte Alimentaire

Oeuf Brouillés aux Truffes
Scrambled egg with dice of Truffles

Arnold Bennet Omelette
An omelette with flaked Haddock and cream sauce

Omelettes Variés
An omelette of your choice

Spaghetti Bolognese
Spaghetti tossed in butter and served with a bolognese sauce

Les Poissons

Sole de Douvre Grillée
Grilled Dover Sole garnished with fresh lemon and parsley butter

Sole de Douvre Colbert
Dover Sole opened along the back, breadcrumbed, fried and filled with parsley butter

Sole de Douvre au Vin Blanc
Dover Sole poached in White Wine coated with White Wine Sauce

Sole de Douvre Meunière
Dover Sole shallow-fried in butter and lemon juice, garnished with lemon

Sole de Douvre Bonne-Femme
Fillets of Dover Sole cooked in White Wine, Shallots, Mushrooms, finished with Cream

Scampi Frite
Deep-fried Scampi served with Tartare Sauce

Scampi d'Amour
Scampi cooked in butter with Pernod, Caviar and Cream, served with rice

Scampi Maison
Scampi cooked in butter, served with Mushrooms, Asparagus and Bacon

Darne de Saumon Régence
A Darne of Salmon poached in a Court Bouillon served with white wine sauce and goujons of Sole

Darne de Saumon Pôché Sauce Hollandaise
A Darne of Salmon poached in a Court Bouillon, served with Hollandaise Sauce

Truite de Riviere Amandine
River Trout shallow fried in butter and lemon juice, served with Toasted Almonds

Truite de Rivière Clèopatra
River Trout cooked in butter, served with soft roes, Mushrooms and Prawns

Filets de Plie Grenobloise
Fillets of Plaice shallow fried in oil and butter, finished with lemon juice and garnished with capers

Figure 4.27 Ladies or guest menu without prices, 1978
Source: From the author's collection, actual source unknown

utter,
egg,
olive
ns,
ed
illets,
the table,
s,
ndy
ith
cream
e table
a slice
auce
e
pâté
ne Sauce
gg yolk,

Entrecôte Sautée Bordelaise
Scotch sirloin steak cooked in butter and finished with red wine sauce and bone marrow

Filet de Boeuf London House
Fillet of beef with pâté wrapped in puff pastry served with Perigourdine Sauce, carved at the table
For two persons

Filet de Porc Normande
Fillet of Pork with apples, mixed spice, cooked in puff pastry, with sauce demi-glace
For two persons

Les Grillades

Entrecôte Grillée Vert Pré
Grilled Sirloin Steak with tomato, straw potatoes and parsley butter

Châteaubriand Sauce Béarnaise
Chateaubriand steak carved at the table, served with Bearnaise Sauce'
For two persons

Rump Steak Garni
Scotch Rump Steak served with tomato, straw potatoes and parsley butter

Côtelettes d'Agneau Grillées
Lamb cutlet with tomato, straw potatoes and parsley butter

Filet de Boeuf Grillé Maitre d'hôtel
Grilled Scotch Fillet Steak, with parsley butter

Foie de Veau au lard
Grilled local calves liver with bacon

Les Rôtis pour deux personnes

Poulet de Grain Rôti au lard
Roast Spring-chicken with bacon

Caneton Rôti à l'Orange
Roast Duckling with Orange Sauce

Carré d'Agneau Bouquetière
Roast best-end of lamb with a selection of vegetables

Les Legumes

Courgettes Provencales
Sliced baby marrow with Tomato Concasseés

Haricots Vert Frais au Beurre
Fresh French Beans

Broccolis au Beurre
Broccoli spears in butter

Oignons Frits
Deep-fried onion rings

Choux-fleur au Gratin
Cauliflower with Mornay Sauce, sprinkled with grated cheese and glazed

Petit Pois à la Francaise
Peas, cooked in cream with button onions and shredded lettuce

Aubergines Frites
Sliced Egg Plant, deep fried

Pointes d'Asperges
Asparagus Spears

Pommes de Terre

Frites
French Fried Potatoes

Nouvelles
New Potatoes

Sautées
Shallow fried Sliced Potatoes

Croquettes
Duchess potato, breadcrumbed and deep fried

Les Salades

Les Salades de Saison
A variety of different seasonal fresh items to be mixed for the pleasure of the individual palate

Les Entremets

Fruits Frais de Saison Flambés
Fresh seasonal fruits flamed at the table

La Voiture des Entremets
Selection of sweets from the trolley

Crêpes Suzette
Pancakes cooked at the table in butter with an Orange and Lemon sauce flavoured with Grand Marnier and flamed with Brandy

Les Fromages

Variés
Selection of English and Continental Cheeses

Les Canapés

Champignons sur croûte
Sauted mushrooms served on toasted bread

Welsh Rarebit
Cheddar cheese and beer mixture served on toasted bread

Canapé Baron
Sauted mushrooms covered with grilled bacon served on toasted bread

The Farmers Lodge Restaurant

Grapefruit Cocktail	£0·95
Prawn + Tomato Salad	£1·25
Egg Mayonnaise	£0·95
Cream of Celery Soup	£0·85
Fried Whitebait	£1·20

Grilled Hampshire Plaice + Parsley Butter	£6·50
Roast Chicken with Bacon	£6·50
Boiled Leg of Mutton + Caper Sauce	£6·75
Steak and Kidney Pie	£5·50
Grilled Lamb Chops	£5·75
Lentil Shepherds Pie - Vegetarian	£4·75

Glazed Carrots – Broccoli Spears
New boiled potatoes – Roast potatoes,
fried potatoes

Sherry Trifle £0·85 Banana Split £1·25
Chocolate Mousse £0·95 Gooseberry Pie £1·00

Selection of Cheeses £1·00
Coffee – Tea £0·95

Tuesday, September 11th, 1985

Figure 4.28 Handwritten limited choice menu with individual dish prices
Source: From the author's collection, actual source unknown

The two menus shown in Figure 4.29 are examples of limited choice menus (one for lunch and one for dinner), as produced by a five-star hotel restaurant in London in 1969. Here the restaurateur has chosen to give the menu a price instead of the dish.

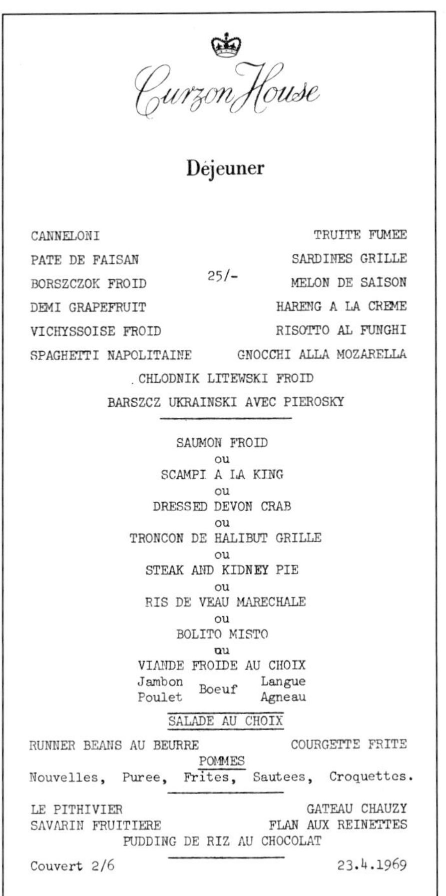

Curzon House

Déjeuner

25/-

CANNELONI — TRUITE FUMEE
PATE DE FAISAN — SARDINES GRILLE
BORSZCZOK FROID — MELON DE SAISON
DEMI GRAPEFRUIT — HARENG A LA CREME
VICHYSSOISE FROID — RISOTTO AL FUNGHI
SPAGHETTI NAPOLITAINE — GNOCCHI ALLA MOZARELLA
CHLODNIK LITEWSKI FROID
BARSZCZ UKRAINSKI AVEC PIEROSKY

SAUMON FROID
ou
SCAMPI A LA KING
ou
DRESSED DEVON CRAB
ou
TRONCON DE HALIBUT GRILLE
ou
STEAK AND KIDNEY PIE
ou
RIS DE VEAU MARECHALE
ou
BOLITO MISTO
ou
VIANDE FROIDE AU CHOIX
Jambon, Poulet, Boeuf, Langue, Agneau

SALADE AU CHOIX

RUNNER BEANS AU BEURRE — COURGETTE FRITE
POMMES
Nouvelles, Puree, Frites, Sautees, Croquettes.

LE PITHIVIER — GATEAU CHAUZY
SAVARIN FRUITIERE — FLAN AUX REINETTES
PUDDING DE RIZ AU CHOCOLAT

Couvert 2/6 — 23.4.1969

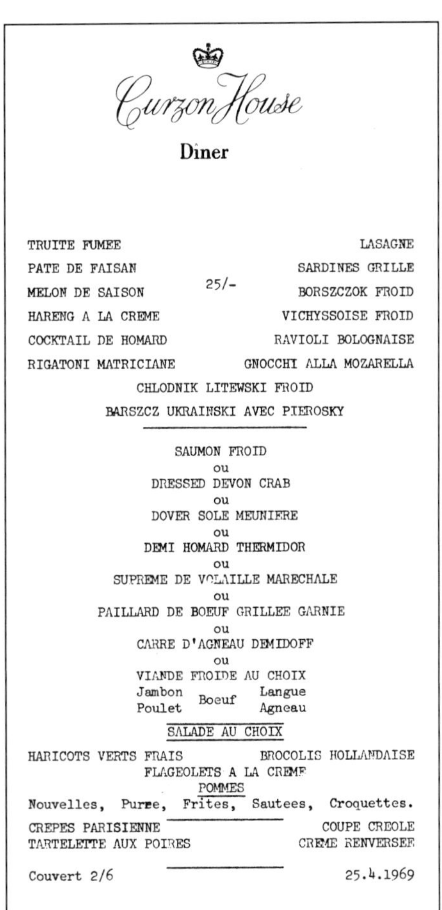

Curzon House

Dîner

25/-

TRUITE FUMEE — LASAGNE
PATE DE FAISAN — SARDINES GRILLE
MELON DE SAISON — BORSZCZOK FROID
HARENG A LA CREME — VICHYSSOISE FROID
COCKTAIL DE HOMARD — RAVIOLI BOLOGNAISE
RIGATONI MATRICIANE — GNOCCHI ALLA MOZARELLA
CHLODNIK LITEWSKI FROID
BARSZCZ UKRAINSKI AVEC PIEROSKY

SAUMON FROID
ou
DRESSED DEVON CRAB
ou
DOVER SOLE MEUNIERE
ou
DEMI HOMARD THERMIDOR
ou
SUPREME DE VOLAILLE MARECHALE
ou
PAILLARD DE BOEUF GRILLEE GARNIE
ou
CARRE D'AGNEAU DEMIDOFF
ou
VIANDE FROIDE AU CHOIX
Jambon, Poulet, Boeuf, Langue, Agneau

SALADE AU CHOIX

HARICOTS VERTS FRAIS — BROCOLIS HOLLANDAISE
FLAGEOLETS A LA CREME
POMMES
Nouvelles, Puree, Frites, Sautees, Croquettes.

CREPES PARISIENNE — COUPE CREOLE
TARTELETTE AUX POIRES — CREME RENVERSEE

Couvert 2/6 — 25.4.1969

Figure 4.29 Printed luncheon and dinner limited choice menus, 1967
Source: From the author's collection, actual source unknown

Changing Trends

Gastronomy is a dynamic subject, for as menus and menu content have changed over time, so has the pragmatic approach to the subject. The changes reflect the times in which we live, encompassing changing dietary attitudes and up-to-date nutritional knowledge, or simply fashion. As an example, no self-respecting restaurant would today present a menu to its guests that did not include at least one dish in each course suitable for the vegetarian.

The greatest change, however, came about in the mid-1960s. During the late 1940s up to the late 1950s, the population of Western Europe indulged in a wave of excessive eating which had never been experienced before or since. In the mid-1960s, doctors' surgeries were filled with people who were grossly overweight and who were ill through overeating. New and better scientific understanding of the composition of foods, subsequent nutritional knowledge and a new emerging wisdom of a better, more balanced and healthy diet, came to the sinners' aid and showed them the errors of their ways.

Governments all over Western Europe began to produce and print leaflets on healthy eating, which were placed in doctors' surgeries, and posted to homes. The media also helped to expose the dangers of overeating and espoused the new wisdom of a healthy diet.

Naturally, the catering industry had to reflect this newly gained knowledge in their cooking methods and the dishes they now placed on their menus.

The general trend of a more healthy and lighter fare on the tables of the restaurants of Europe gained new impetus when some master chefs of France changed the mode of food preparation and presentation for the modern age of gastronomy. As to who was the most important person, this must, in all cases, be an individual choice. I, personally, would choose Michel Guérard.

Michel Guérard

Michel Guérard is considered the most extreme and determined of the master chefs of the new kitchens, when he devised the *cuisine minceur*. This mode of cookery allowed his guests to eat by the best gastronomic excellence and rules, without making the diner fat, or even allowing them to lose weight. Like so many changes in a man's life, these can be of a most personal nature. The story goes that when Michel proposed to his wife, she said that she would be most honoured to be his wife, if he would do her a favour. He asked what the favour was, and she told him that she would be pleased if he would lose a few kilos before the wedding day.

Already a famous chef with a very successful restaurant, he was a little on the round side, and so devised his own slimming diet. The resulting dishes gradually appeared on menus of his restaurant, and *cuisine minceur* was born. The rest is history.

How drastic this new cuisine was is shown by the following basic laws and characteristics:

- ★ Only the freshest and highest quality foods must be used at all times, including herbs and spices.
- ★ No cream, butter or flour to be used at all.
- ★ No sugar must be used in any dishes, only the natural sweetness of vegetables and fruits including some dried may be used, low calorie sweeteners may be used sparingly.
- ★ Use as few eggs as is reasonably possible.
- ★ All sauces should be light and thin, based on good fatless stocks of the highest quality, especially when served with fish and meats.
- ★ All vegetables should be cooked very crisp, in only the smallest amount of water. For this, vegetables should be cut into small even batons, strips, dice or rosettes according to type, with the minimum amount of added salt.
- ★ No spirits must be used in cooking. Only small amounts of white or red wine, according to the type of sauce, may be used in *déglaçage* (brought to the boil), thus reducing the calorie value to virtually nil, but retaining the flavour and perfume of the wine.
- ★ Use more pepper and herbs for flavouring of dishes, less salt.
- ★ All dishes must be cooked *à la minute*, in other words, to order, just before service to the guests, to retain all vitamin content. Let the guest wait for the food, not the food for the guest.
- ★ Meat should have all visible fat removed.
- ★ The meat must then be cooked rare, or at most only medium.
- ★ All *minceur* food should have a concentrated flavour, never watery.
- ★ Fish when cooked should adhere to the bone slightly and should, if poached, always be cooked in fish stock. Grilled fish should be brushed with only the smallest amount of vegetable oils. When fried, only the shallow-fry method may be used, preferably in a non-stick pan, with no or little vegetable oil according to the fish to be cooked.
- ★ Some food and cooking methods are banned, for example, all pastries, potatoes, pastas and deep-frying.
- ★ Wide use of fresh herbs and spices must be encouraged.

- ⋆ Strange, often neglected or out-of-fashion foods, or odd food combinations, should re-appear in the *minceur* kitchen, for example, leg of lamb baked in hay, fillet of lean pork baked in an apple purée, a soup made of a purée of swedes garnished with fresh prawns and flavoured with cumin, carrots baked on a bed of cumin and fresh orange juice.
- ⋆ All soups and some sauces can be bound (thickened) by making purées with the help of liquidisers.
- ⋆ Use non-stick pans, which allow the cooking of many foods in little or no fat or stocks.

For anyone who knows anything about basics of good classical cooking, this is drastic indeed: no *monter au beurre*, no liaison of egg yolks and cream, and no cream at all. Guérard had indeed started a culinary revolution in his now world-famous three-star restaurant in Eugénie les Bains.

For some, however, the revolution was too drastic, and even Guérard had to accept this and so he developed his *cuisine gourmande* and his version of *cuisine nouvelle*. Both are now served side by side in his famous and beautiful restaurant.

There can be no doubt, however, that his '*révolution culinaire moderne*' influenced many other chefs. Roger Vergé's Cuisine of the Sun, Anton Mossiman, Paul Bocuse, the brothers Jean and Pierre Troisgros, Alfred Guerot, Jean LaPorte, and Fernaud Point's *cuisine nouvelle* were all influenced and aided by the ideas of Guérard. In turn, these chefs have influenced chefs all over the world in the acceptance and further maturation of this now well-known, new and modern cuisine, practised by many chefs all over the world.

Cuisine Nouvelle

Cuisine nouvelle or the 'plated art', as it is sometimes referred to, is very much based on the laudable aims of *cuisine minceur*. It serves a healthy meal, while at the same time presenting a meal with considerable visual appeal as well as gastronomic integrity.

It is not as strict in the avoidance of high-calorie foods, such as butter, cream, sugar and flour, but aims to do without them or reduce these where possible. Sweets and pastries are allowed, but with an emphasis on fruit desserts and lightness in general.

The food is served directly on to the plate and not from silver flats and dishes. In some cases, the main course with its accompanying vegetables is beautifully arranged on the plate; in other cases the vegetables are on a separate side plate, next to the main course. The plates used are not just any type of plate, for they are usually especially made, larger by a third than normal-sized dinner plates.

Figure 4.30 Selection of *nouvelle cuisine* dishes, used by the author as a teaching aid
Source: W Bode

The decoration of the china should enhance the arranged foods, and not be too bright or striking, lest it interferes with the colourful dish display. In most cases, the plates are white, but other colours are used including black.

Once the food is arranged on the plate, under high-powered heating lamps, it is covered by a *cloche*, a semi-globe cover, which can be made from silver, china, pewter or even copper. This will help to keep the food hot until it is placed in front of the guests, on an even larger table sub-plate or salver, again made from silver, pewter or copper. All the covers are removed simultaneously to reveal the proffered delicacies of 'the plated art'.

Cuisine nouvelle became a sensation when it first appeared, and became very popular. But in time it also drew its critics. 'Nice but still very hungry when leaving the table', 'too little for too much', or more rudely, 'all arts and no farts' have all been used to describe it.

There can be no doubt that good *cuisine nouvelle* is expensive to produce. It is costly in two ways. First, only the freshest and best of ingredients are used and these naturally command a very high price. Second, modern, time-saving kitchen technology is only sparingly applied to the production of *cuisine nouvelle*. Because of this a large kitchen brigade of highly skilful, artistic and committed professional chefs is employed. These professionals do not come cheap.

Many restaurants jumped on the bandwagon too quickly, without understanding the most basic principles of *cuisine nouvelle*, or indeed having acquired the necessary training. In the process they harmed the reputations of those master chefs and restaurants who served a true *cuisine nouvelle* and the industry generally.

Over the last few years, things have calmed down a little in respect of the controversies of the early *cuisine nouvelle*. Those who know what they are doing are, on the whole, doing very well and have made a considerable contribution to modern eating customs. Those who did not know what they were doing have gone back to preparing food in a more conventional way. All of us, however, have benefited. In Europe, food served is generally more healthy, better cooked and most certainly more attractively presented. On most menus we now find some reference to this fact, when we see dishes marked:

Recommended for those wanting a lighter meal.
Selected for the weight conscious.
Recommended for those who wish to watch their waistline.
Recommended for the slimmer.

The laudable aims of *cuisine nouvelle* may be considered to offer us the 'enlightened choice'. The laudable aims of *cuisine minceur* may be considered 'the remedy, where enlightened choice came to late'. We now have a choice, whether in our homes, in the average restaurant with some of these health-conscious dishes, or in a restaurant specialising in any of the new cuisines. All are now very much part of modern and a wiser gastronomy.

The Origin of Names of Some Famous Dishes and Garnishes, and Historical Culinary Terminology

Aida

An opera composed by Verdi (1813–1901) noted patron of the Maison Dorée in Paris. Dishes created in his honour by Casiir Moisson, President of the first Culinary Academy (turbot, salad, iced bombe).

Agnes Sorel

Celebrated 'dame de beauté' (1422–1450), mistress of Charles VII of France. Dishes created by Taillevent and adapted by Escoffier (qv) (soup, omelette, chicken, veal).

Alice

Countess of Athlone, sister of Edward VII. Dishes created by Escoffier (sole, sweet dishes).

D'Arenberg

Charles Victor, Prince d'Arenberg of Belgium. Dishes created by Albert Chevalier (pear sweet, *consommé*, veal).

Baba

Rich, fermented sponge introduced to France by King Stanislas Leczinski of Poland from whose admiration of the fairy tale, *Ali Baba and the Forty Thieves*, the name is derived. Popularised in Paris by the Polish chef Stochorer at Rue Montgueil. Julien is reputed to have added raisins to the recipe.

Baron Brisse

Writer and gastronome, contemporary and friend of Alexandre Dumas (sole, *noisettes*).

Bearnaise

Named after Bearn, birthplace of Henri IV (qv) (*tournedos* Henri IV, sauce).

Beauvilliers

Famous French restaurateur, one-time chef to Louis XIV (sole).

Belle Hélène

Sister of the Duc d'Orléans, queen of Romania, subject of a famous historical novel by Maquet 1855. Dishes created by Escoffier (pear sweet, *tournedos*, *suprême* of chicken, *paupiette*, salad, eggs).

Béchamel

'The mother of white sauces', created by Louis de Béchamel, Marquis de Nointel, *maître d'hotel* to Louis XIV (1635–88).

Bisque

Shellfish soup created by De La Varenne (1653), author of *Classic Book of Soups*.

Brunoise

Dishes created by Careme after Bruncy, an area in France noted for its spring vegetables (*consommé*, garnish).

Breval

Renowned chef at Maison Prunir in Paris (sole).

Brillat Savarin

Jean Anthelme (1755–1826), famous writer on gastronomy, author of *Le Physiologie du Goût* and other works. Dishes created by Careme (garnish, omelette, salmon, *savarin*).

Cardinal

General religious association inspired by Richelieu (qv) (poached fish, sauce, lobster, cream soup, eggs).

Careme

Marie Antoine (Antonin) Careme (1784–1833), celebrated chef and author of many books on cookery. Creator of many dishes (qv), noted for extravagant decor, one-time chef to Talleyrand (eggs, sole, snipe, partridge).

Celestine

Branch of the Benedictine order (garnish for *consommé*, strips of savoury pancakes).

Charlotte

Derived from the old English word 'charlyt' meaning custard. Modern version adapted by Careme (*Charlotte Russe*, *Parisienne*) and by Lacam (*Charlotte glacé*).

Chauchat

Celebrated chef in Paris (poached sole).

Chaufroid

Known in Ancient Greco-Roman cookery as *Calidus Frigidus*. The modern version is attributed to Chaufroix, chef to Louis XV in 1759 (cold sauce).

Chimay

Clara Ward, Princess of China. Dishes created by Escoffier (stuffed eggs, chicken).

Condé

Louis II, Prince de Condé (1621–86) and Louise Philippe, Prince de Condé (1736–1818), noted French military and noble family. Dishes created by Vincent de la Chapelle with adaptation by Careme (pear sweet, soup, sole, eggs).

Crécy

Area of France noted for the prolific growth of carrots. Scene of the Battle of

Crécy (1364) when Edward III defeated Philippe de Valois (soup, garnish, eggs, sole, *noisettes*, chicken).

Cubat

Pierre, chef to Emperor Alexander of Russia. Dishes believed to be created by Cubat (sole).

Dame Blanche

Comic opera by Boïeldieu from the novel by Sir Walter Scott (*consommé*, clear soup).

Demidoff

Antole Demidoff, husband of Princess Mathilde, daughter of King Jerôme Bonaparte (1813–70). Dishes created by Louis Bignon, chef of the Café Riche and Maison Dorée (chicken, sweetbreads, *consommé*, *entrée*, *poularde*).

Doria

Daughter of Labouchère, married Prince de Rudini. Dishes created by Escoffier (poached fish, *consommé*, cream soup, chicken, always flavoured or garnished with cucumber).

Du Barry

Marie Jeanne Gomard de Vaubernier, Comtesse du Barry (1741–93), favourite of Louis XV. Bouquets of cauliflower represent the powdered wigs of the period. Dishes created by Vincent de la Chapelle (large joints, cream soup, *consommé*, *noisettes*, always contains cauliflower).

Dugleré

Chef at the Café Anglais in Paris, created Poisson Dugleré (*noisettes*).

Duxelles

Created by La Varenne, chef to the Marquis d'Uxelles (sauce, stuffing from mushrooms).

Escoffier, Auguste

(1846–1935) Known as the father of modern cookery, outstanding chef of the twentieth century. Collaborated with Ritz in developing the modern luxury hotel. Author of several books on cookery including the *Guide Culinaire*. He created many dishes which he named after famous women of the theatre (cold fish) and the modern kitchen structure. See page 124.

Feuilletage

Puff pastry, pre-thirteenth century in origin. Well known in the form of Talmouses St. Denis. Immortalised by François Villon (1431–89).

Fricadeau

Created by Jean de Careme, ancestor of Marie Antoine Careme, cook to Pope Leo X (veal).

Garibaldi

Giuseppe Garibaldi (1807–82), Italian patriot with noted French sympathies (biscuits, *consommé*).

Julienne

Jean Julien, French chef, creator of a thin vegetable soup garnished with vegetable strips (*consommé*).

Joinville

François de Joinville, Duc d'Orléans, third son of Louis Philippe, sailor and author (1813–1900) (poached fish, fish sauce, fish soup, omelette).

Judic-Anna

French actress and prima donna (1815–1911). Dishes believed to be created by Escoffier (*entrées*, *consommé*, sole, *noisettes*, sweetbreads, chicken).

Lamballe

Marie Thérèse Louise, Princess de Lamballe (1749–92), devoted friend of Marie Antoinette (cream soup).

Leopold

Prince of Saxe-Coburg Gotha, elected King of the Belgians (1790) (*consommé*, sole, chicken).

Macedoine

Believed to be derived from the small islands of the Macedonian Archipelagos, hence small cuts of vegetables (soup, *entrées*, large joints).

Marengo

Created by chef Dunard to Napoleon I after the battle of Marengo (1799). It is believed that the dish was originally a hasty improvisation from available foodstuffs (chicken *sauté*).

Mayonnaise

Origin uncertain – many possibilities:

1. Invented by Richelieu and changed to mayonnaise to commemorate the capture of General Mamon (Alexander Dumas).
2. Mayonnaise, derived from *manier*, to blend, thus descriptive of the preparation (Crimod de la Reyniere).
3. Derived from Moyeunaise – *Moyeu*, old French for the yolk of an egg.
4. Unnamed before 1589, then mayonnaise in contemptuous memory of the Duc de Mayenne, who insisted on finishing his chicken with cold sauce (mayonnaise) before his defeat by Henry V at the battle of Argues (1589) (Pieree Lacam).
5. From Port Mahon in Minorca, captured by Richelieu. Sauce based on abundance of raw materials needed, that is, eggs, olive oil (*Larousse Biographique*).
6. Associated with Mayenne (Pyreneos, 1610).

Mirepoix

Charles du Mirepoix, Marshal of France (1699–1757) and the name of a French town (diced vegetable flavouring).

Mireille
Poem and comic opera written by Mistral with music by Gounod (potatoes, *consommé*, sole, *noisettes*, chicken).

Melba
Dame Nellie (née Mitchell) (1859–1931). Austrian prima donna and friend of Escoffier who created dishes in her name (iced sweet, toast, *noisettes*).

Mirabeau
Victor Requeti, Marquis of Mirabeau (1754–92), great corpulence, nicknamed 'Le Tonneau', friend of Louis XVI (garnish, *tournedos*, eggs, grilled meats, sole).

Montespan
Françoise Athenais de Rochecchouart, Marquis de Montespan (1641–1707), one-time favourite of Louis XIV (*velouté*, soup, sole).

Montgolfier
Brothers Joseph and Jacques, inventors of the balloon. Name given to light, puffed-up dishes.

Mornay
Philippe de Mornay (1549–1623), writer and voyager, friend of Henri IV of France (sauce).

Navarin
Derived from *navets* (turnips) which form part of the garnish. Note, sea battle in 1827 (*consommé*, mutton).

Orly
Bernard van Orly (1490–1540), noted Flemish painter (fish, chicken).

Parmentier
Antoine Auguste (1737–1817), French agricultural expert and politician, responsible for establishing the potato, hitherto a decorative plant, as a food crop in France. The name has become a synonym of the potato in the kitchen (soup, potato dishes, sole, *noisettes*, chicken). See page 121.

Polignac
Jules Armand, Prince de Polignac (fish, eggs, chicken with creamed mushrooms).

Réforme
Created by Alexis Soyer when chef at the Reform Club (cutlets, *noisettes*, *consommé*, eggs, sole, sweetbreads).

Restaurant
Name derived from *restaurabo* (I will restore). Boulanger inscribed above the door in the Rue de Poulies: '*Venite omnes qui stomacho laboris et ego restaurabo vos*'.

Richelieu
Armand, Jean du Plessig, Cardinal de Richelieu (1585–1642) (large joints, *consommé*, sole, sweetbreads).

Robert

Noted chef to a monastery, celebrated restaurateur (sauce flavoured with mustard white wine shallots).

Romanoff

Russian royal family (1613–1762) (large joints).

Rossini

Giacomo Rossini (1792–1868), Italian operatic composer. Dishes created at the Maison Dorée (*tournedos*, *noisettes*, *consommé*, eggs, omelette, sole, chicken).

Salvator

Salvator Roas (1616–73), Italian painter (omelette, sole).

Solferino

Famous battle between France and Austria (1859), which was followed by the formation of the International Red Cross by H. Dunnant (qv). Potage Solferino, a blend of tomato and potato soup ladled separately into a soup bowl, commemorates the red on white motif of the Red Cross. Garnish of carrot and potato to represent cannon balls (soup, sauce).

Soubise

Prince of Soubise (1715–87), supervised the building of the Hôtel de Soubise, a noted historical residence in Paris. A well-known epicure; use of onions in various forms.

Souvaroff (V)

Alexandre Souvaroff (1729–1800), Russian general noted for his lack of scruples and humanity (pheasant).

Suchet

Louis Gabriel, Duc de Suchet (1722–1826), victor of the battle of Albugera (qv) (sauce, sole).

Sullivan

Sir Arthur Seymour Sullivan (1842–1900), English composer of comic opera, words by W.S. Gilbert. Dishes created by Escoffier at the Savoy (sole).

Savoyard (Savoy)

Name derived from Savoy operas (Gilbert and Sullivan), probable origin of Savoy Hotel (potatoes, soup, eggs, omelette, sole).

Villeroy

François de Neuville, Duc de Villeroy (1644–1730), famous French sailor (sauce, eggs, sole, cutlets, sweetbreads, pigeon, chicken).

Walewska, Marie

(1789–1817), Polish countess, mistress of Napoléon Bonaparte (poached fish).

Xavier

Francisco de Xavier, early Christian missionary (*consommé*, *velouté*).

From this list it can be seen that the terms were codes of preparation which, in the case of, for example, Aida, was applied to turbot, a compound salad, and an ice-cream bombe. Each preparation or code was quite different because of the different basic food, namely fish, salad or ice-cream. Examples of codes of preparation are as follows:

- *Aida* – for fish – fillets poached in white wine, dressed on a bed of leaf spinach, seasoned with salt and paprika, coated with cheese sauce, sprinkled with cheese and baked golden brown.

  In the case of salad (Salad Aida) – a mixture of chicory, tomatoes, sliced artichokes, strips of green pepper, cooked whites of egg, dressed with mustard, flavoured with vinaigrette, sprinkled with chopped hard-boiled yolk of egg.

  For ice-cream (Bombe Aida) – line a bombe mould with strawberries and strawberry ice-cream, fill the centre with vanilla ice-cream generously flavoured with Kirsch.

- *Brunoise* – always denotes finely cut dice of spring vegetables and can be applied to soups, fish, poultry or meats, for example, *Consommé Brunoise*, *Filet de Sole Brunoise*, *Balontine de Volaille Brunoise*, *Roulade de Veau Brunoise*. All would have been cooked and presented with fine dice of spring vegetables in one form or another.

- *Mornay* – always means cheese and so a mornay sauce is a cheese sauce which could be served equally well with fish, fowl or flesh, or even vegetables, for example, *Filet de Plie Mornay*, *Suprême de Volaille Mornay*, *Escalope de Veau Mornay*, *Chou-fleur Mornay*.

Thus, culinary terms or codes denote a special way of cooking and presentation.

The acceptance of these coded culinary terms was very much broadened by their use in the new restaurants, taverns, inns and hotels. These relied less and less on rich clientele, and accepted any paying guest, but retained the terms and names of the old dishes.

Today we find more and more menus written in English, or the national language of the country where the restaurant is found. The menu is still written in French in French restaurants and those restaurants which wish to pass as such, and better restaurants in four- to five-star hotels all over the world.

I have considerable sympathy for the problems of translating the above codes and historical codes for names of dishes. Many are not easily translated into a language, whichever this language may be.

CHAPTER 5

The Gastronomy of the Poor

The development of gastronomy within the framework of the classical menu for the well to do has been dynamic, admirable, artistic and most certainly successful in all spheres of dining. However, there is much more to consider in respect of gastronomy than the framework of the classical menu alone and the food and dishes within it, including the notable contribution of the poor and the peasants.

Always at the least sophisticated end of any society, they were and, in many parts of the world still are, the strong backbone of all available food supply, often to the detriment of their own diet. They were mostly employed in supplying the middle and upper classes, for whom most of them directly worked.

The rations that were left to them were very basic and consisted mostly of plants and cereal food in particular. Only occasionally did meat make a contribution to their own daily meals. Yet in this very baseness of diet of the poor, lies much of the development of what we call gastronomy today.

If necessity is the mother of invention, the poor peasants more than anyone had much need for culinary inventions, of skills and knowledge, which allowed their meagre rations to be turned into acceptable and variable foods and dishes. When you have only potatoes to eat every day, you think of various ways of cooking them, so as to vary their taste and flavour and appearance.

In their ingenuity of providing the one basic and reasonable main meal per day, with some substance, flavour and variety, lies much of the basis of all culinary and most gastronomical advancement. It does not lie in the expensive restaurants, or the skills of the chefs of old or new. Indeed, many of the dishes which chefs have furthered were based on the ideas of the peasants, from whose stock many of them often came. Only very occasionally did they invent their own dishes.

As peasants seldom could afford expensive spices to flavour their food, they used the wild herbs that were so freely available in the fields and pastures in which they worked. In the use of wild herbs lies the basis of most of compositional cookery, which represents a not inconsiderable part of what is good food.

The poor made an important contribution to the evolution of the structure of the classical menu. The one example which illustrates this best is in the making of soups. To all poor the soup epitomises the main meal of the day, consistently popular and, in most situations, easily produced from vegetables, potatoes, barley and pulses. These soups would be made in the manner of *pot au feu* (the pot in or on the fire).

The thinner broth would be consumed first, followed by the thicker part of the stew-soup. This main course was followed by fresh fruit, dried fruits or early stewed fruit, according to season, or even home-made cheese made from the goat, sheep and, later, cow's milk.

Looking back we could say that here we have the original structure of the three course meal, which was to develop into the classical menu of fifteen or so courses.

The third most important contribution to the development of gastronomy under this heading, besides that of the peasants and professionals, must be the contribution of the caring wife and mother in particular, and grandmothers in general, throughout the ages. The effort of feeding a growing and often very large family has at any time made enormous contribution to what gastronomy brings to our table today and every day. When a daughter left home to marry, besides her dowry she was given two other important things to take with her to marriage and the new home. The considerable knowledge of practical cooking skills passed on to her by her grandmother and mother, and, if the family had learned to read and write, a book of family recipes which grandmother and mother had painstakingly copied and added to the one once given to them.

In the evolution of social advancement and change this fact may be obvious for those with an historical understanding, but it is not always given due recognition. More often than not, the wife would most certainly have been aware of the struggle involved in the procuring of the family's daily bread. In turn, this led to a growing respect for food, which has been a marked feature for the poor and all real gastronomers. In the working classes, food had perpetually been associated with hard work done; in the middle classes, food had been closely associated with wealth acquired; in the upper classes, food was the concern and job of others.

This respect and care for food, which is the corner stone of all food preparation, was of real importance to what became gastronomy.

'Cooking is like love, it should be entered in to with abandon or not at all.'(5.1)

That the peasants did; it was often their only pleasure.

5.1 Hon Van, H., 'Proverbs and customs', in *Vogue*, October 1956.

Many professionals involved with the growing, preparation, cooking and presentation of food, will easily claim the same love for food. Indeed, some have every right to this claim, by the care and hard work they give to all matters delightful on our table. It might be a consuming art, or art consumed without trace, but an art it is.

The most important point to be made here is that good gastronomy is not isolated to the limits of the dishes and structure of the classical menu as practised in expensive hotels and restaurants, important though their contribution has been. A good meal or gastronomic experience does not have to be a series of ten, eight, six, or even three courses in a famous restaurant. Nor does it have to cost the earth – money can help, but the right attitude is the relevant factor.

Good gastronomy can be:

a piece of bread,
an apple and
a piece of cheese.

As long as our attitude insists that:

the bread is good and fresh,
the apple is ripe,
the cheese is mature,

and we have the sense or wisdom to know that they are so.

If we can add to this simple meal,
a glass of wine
and find a friend to share it with us,
all the important factors of gastronomy have been satisfied.

The important contribution to our daily bread and gastronomy by the poor, and their very innocence in all matters concerning food, must never be underestimated or forgotten. The author has, in a long life involved with food, also found that they that have the least, the poorest, have the greatest benevolence and willingness to share the little they have with others.

CHAPTER 6

The Marriage of Food and Wine

It is for a very good reason that in previous chapters I have concentrated on man's most basic need and the development of his food, production and service of wine and other drinks. Gastronomy, however, is a triad of people, food and wine, and the time has now come to consider the third component of modern gastronomy, wine, and the happy marriage of food and wine.

As I am not as much an expert on wine as I believe I am to be one on food, my considerations will be limited to the basic rules as to the wedding of food and wine. Modern books on wine and the wider, more open discussions on wine in newspapers, magazines and television will help the reader to a more detailed understanding and appreciation of wine.

It is up to the reader to try different wines, to drink them in small amounts, and to wed them to our food at home. In this way you can make up your own mind as to which wine you like with which food, for at best it is a very personal matter to each of us.

In Chapter 3, the likely invention of wine by the Ancient Egyptians was considered, when the earliest principle of wine-making was applied to dates and other fruits of the Nile Valley. The same chapter also gave credit to the Greeks, who imported the knowledge of the Egyptians' priestly temple vintners to secular Greece, and applied the knowledge of making wine from grapes. Grapes were already a well-established fruit, and no table was considered acceptable which did not have grapes included in the selection of dishes and foods. It is thought that the Greek grape was grown from wines originally found in Caucasia in southern Russia. We know that the diet of the earliest Spartans consisted of a 'black broth' made up of bread, sour wine and salt. Greece was the home of wine in Europe from at least the fifth to the first century BC.

The wine drunk was, of course, very different from the wine we drink today. They were mostly red, heavy, syrupy and sweet wines, and very strong. For this reason they were more often than not diluted with water. As we read Athenaeus and of his Roman compatriots of some hundreds years later, we see that a certain sophistication had been established in respect of wines consumed in the early

Figure 6.1 The glorious grape, the beginning of all wine
Source: The Even Giant Swipe File, The Hart Publishing Inc. 1978

years AD. In their discussions, they did not only consider red and white wines, which were by then well established, but also sweet, medium sweet and dry wines as well as when and with what food dishes they should be drunk. Even certain types of wine, certain wine-growing regions and the age of a given wine came in for much discussion, much as modern wine-drinkers discuss wines today.

Gastronomy has for some time differentiated between two uses of wines: wine which is added to food enhancing the cooking process, and wine which is served with food.

Wine Added to Food

Although the Ancient World was well able to make wine, there were still considerable problems in the storage of wine in the hot climate of the Mediterranean. Because of this, some wine would turn sour and eventually turn into vinegar, a fact which added another culinary flavouring agent to a growing list. The use of vinegar eventually resulted in 'pickling', one of the oldest methods of preservation, and later was used in oil and vinegar in salad dressings.

It is impossible to determine the origin of the practice of adding wine, good or sour, to food when cooking it. It must have been well established during Homer's time for we can read in Homer's *Odyssey* of:

> '. . . *an alcoholic porridge composed of cheese, barley-meal, yellow honey and Praninian wine*'.(6.1)

The Romans, with their genuine dislike of the natural and unadulterated flavour of their foods, used wine on a large scale in all manner of cooking processes and the most unlikely of dishes. The addition of wine to food in the cooking process has remained a custom which has lasted to this day. Most of us have visited a restaurant and experienced or watched the cooking of so-called *flambé* dishes, whereby certain types of food are cooked on a special *guéridon* trolley in the restaurant in front of the guest. In this cooking process, wines and/or spirits are added at the final stage with flames of spirits leaping into the air. What is less dramatically apparent is the fact that wine and possibly some spirits and liqueurs are added to many dishes when they are prepared and cooked behind the scenes. The practice is most widely used in the marinading of meat, poultry and fish, to break down fibres and to add flavour and aroma to the dish. Some very good and classic dishes have been composed in this way, for example, *coq au vin* or *boeuf bourguignon*.

The time required to marinade the meat depends on the age, quality and size of the joint or cut. Marinading for too long can render the meat over-soft, and the wine would become too dominant in flavour, masking the natural flavour of

6.1 Younger, W., *Gods, Men and Wine*, Michael Joseph, London, 1966, p. 3.

the food. Nowadays, the most common meat marinaded is venison, which lacks fat and is often dry. A spicy marinade will greatly improve the appearance and taste of the venison as well as complement its flavour. It may be marinaded in wine for a period of twenty-four to seventy-two hours, whereas the cubes of beef for *boeuf bourguignon* are marinaded for only four to six hours, or possibly overnight, to give this dish its distinct appearance, aroma and flavour. Fish, particularly when it is intended to be deep-fried, will benefit from marinading for an hour or two prior to cooking.

The basic rule is that all dark meats, such as venison and beef, should be marinaded in red wine, and all white meats, such as veal, poultry, lamb and fish, should be marinaded in white wine. Today, when much frozen fish and shellfish is used, a simple marinade of white wine, lemon juice and salt will restore some of the flavour which the fish has lost by 'bleeding' in the defrosting process. When it comes to the quality of wine used for the marinading of flesh, fish or fowl, much comment and advice is available.

> *'When cooking with wine, one must choose wisely and avoid the mediocre.'(6.2)*

I agree that this is most certainly sound advice and vital on special occasions. However, modern wines are so well graded and controlled that most of them are perfectly acceptable for cooking.

Wines to be Served with Food

When the Romans conquered Gaul, they found a higher level of gastronomy there than that which they brought with them; less refined, but far richer in terms of the variety of foods available. Julius Caesar took the vine to France where it flourished, and wine began to replace other drinks. The Gauls already had many cheeses and this was, in effect, the first marriage between food and wine – still a much appreciated combination today. Cookery adapts itself to the raw materials, equipment and fuel available. Thus the French, having received the vine, began to incorporate wine into their eating habits and lives. This, over a period of many centuries, has helped to make France the home of the finest cuisine, and the home of some of the best wines in the world.

Throughout the Middle Ages in Europe, the tradition of good living centred

6.2 Oliver, R., *The French at Table*, Wine and Food Society, London, 1967, p. 127.

around the royal courts and monasteries, whose priests we have to thank for much of the development of wine, spirits and liqueurs we know today. Although wine production and consumption flourished in Italy, France, Spain, Germany and even England, it remained the beverage for the rich, while the poorer people drank beer and ales.

In north-western Europe the diet of the people was based on grain, usually made into beer, breads and pastries of various kinds. It is not surprising, therefore, that some use should have been made of beer in German and Scandinavian cooking, and that it was used occasionally in English cookery from the late tenth century onwards.

It was during the twelfth century that alchemists discovered that it was possible to separate one liquid from another by distillation. It was the preoccupation with the idea of spirits being the soul of life that led to the discovery of spirits. The alchemists believed that they could capture the essences of the earth in the spirits derived from distillation, which were thus reputed to have medicinal and magical powers. Even today an air of mystery surrounds not only the drinking of spirits, but the adding of a few drops to a dish, however small the amount.

The Renaissance saw a gradual decline in the extensive use of spices, and a growing finesse and delicacy in both French and Italian cookery. This evolution was codified by François Pierre de la Varrene. Thick stews and highly-spiced vegetables were replaced by sauces based on meat drippings, combined with vinegar or verjuice.

Between the fifteenth and seventeenth centuries, there was a considerable development in the sophistication of life and tastes, which was reflected in new attitudes to wine and wine drinking all over Europe. This period saw the development of fortified wines – wines with the addition of alcohol – and England became the biggest importer of fortified wines, such as sherries, ports and Madeira, as well as white wines from Germany and red wines from Gascony.

During this time, sherry became established as an aperitif served immediately prior to a meal in England. Port was served at the conclusion of the meal. Whatever the wine imported, it remained an enjoyment for the rich only – the poor continued to drink beer.

The eighteenth century was a period of many contradictions and contrasts. The most prominent contrast was that between extreme elegance and excessive intoxication. Although tea and coffee became increasingly popular, drunkenness became a serious problem. People's capacity for drink at this time appears to have been quite incredible; even Brillat-Savarin considered that a healthy man could live long if he drank two bottles of wine a day! The most popular drinks in Georgian England were port, gin and punch. Negus, too, was widely drunk and consisted of a hot drink made from port wine with the addition of beaten eggs.

A form of cold negus, which could be served either as a beverage or a sweet dessert, was the forerunner of syllabub, eaten today as a sweet. The French acquired a taste for punch, serving it after dinner, accompanied by thin pieces of buttered, salted toast.

A great deal of coarse, heavy port wine was drunk to complement a dish consisting of a base of red meat and game, which required strong wine as an accompaniment. The emergence of France as a nation of gourmets began towards the end of the seventeenth century, and by the reign of Louis XV the gourmet view of eating and drinking was established.

The important difference between the cuisine of England and France was the use of wine in cookery. The English used very little, if any, in their food, and any serious drinking was left until the end of the meal.

In the well-endowed kitchens of the grand seigneurs, many cooking techniques were perfected, and thus the foundation was laid of accessible culinary knowledge upon which great cooks like Careme were able to build their fame. French cookery became an art which, for one to enjoy and appreciate fully, the use of all the senses was required. A new philosophy also grew around French cookery, expounded by the work of Brillat Savarin and others, when it came to the right combination of food and drink.

The age of Careme was one of high refinement, purity and perfection – the *cuisine classique*. Careme was renowned for his pastry, sauces and many other inventions. During the French Revolution, however, there was a small exodus of private cooks from France. Careme and his successors, such as Soyer and Francatelli, came to England and thus began the great conquest by French chefs of the nineteenth century. Early in the nineteenth century, it was the custom of the French to drink ordinary wine neat, immediately after the soup. This was called the *coup d'après*. The fine wines were served between courses or in the latter part of the meal.

The custom of serving the *coup de milieu* also emerged during this period. It was usually a glass of bitter liqueur or spirits served after the roast meat to aid digestion, a practice which was not adopted in England. To the majority of the English, wine usually meant port or sherry, while the French rather naturally took advantage of the wide variety of their home-produced wines.

Escoffier was the great reformer at the end of the nineteenth century. Simplicity was the essence of his cooking and he did away with all the trimmings which failed to enhance the flavour of a dish. Sauces, in which fumets – a reduction of different stocks – were used as a base, complemented the dishes instead of contrasting with or masking the food. This change was reflected in service styles which gradually changed to *service russe*. The courses of a meal began to follow each other in a definite and deliberate procession. Each course consisted of one particular type or group of foods.

By the time of the Edwardians, the system of eating had become quite 'modern', although the amount they ate was still considerable. Their tastes in drinking also appear to have been somewhat eccentric. Claret was frequently drunk with the sweet or dessert, being regarded as the only wine which could follow champagne, which was served with the roast.

Just as meals became ordered in their service by the structure of the classical menu, so the drinking of wines became organised according to country, region, type, age and quality.

Details of the classification of European wines are well covered by experts in many other publications. However, it is worth mentioning here some basic rules which have evolved for the service of wine.

As the service and presentation of food became more categorised and organised in the service *à la russe*, via the classical menu, so the service of wine underwent a similar organisation. Sommeliers classified all the wines available for a meal by:

countries	white
vintage	rosé
regions	champagne
red	fortitifed wines, spirits and liqueurs

and by further identifying the nuances, flavours and tastes of individual wines such as:

new	sweet	very light
young	medium sweet	light
light	medium dry	medium light
medium old	dry	full-bodied
old	very dry	heavy

This classification of wine could more easily combine with the classification of the courses on the classical menu. Subsequently, wines were now served almost like courses of a meal, with a balance from light to medium to heavy to light again.

The number of courses served on a given occasion and the number of wines which were proffered for a given meal were not necessarily the same. Thus a banquet with ten courses may have as few as two to three or as many as eight to ten wines. More importantly, the nuances and flavours of the wines were made to balance the foods and dishes within the meal. As a basic rule, fewer wines were served for lunch than for a dinner or banquet.

Demi Charentais frappé
Half-chilled Charentais melon

Consommé Italienne
Tomato flavoured beef *consommé* with vermicelli

Foie de oie sauté sur le brioche aux cèpes
Sautéd fresh goose liver on *brioche* base with wild mushrooms

Filet de limande grillé aux points d'asperges
Grilled fillet of lemon sole with asparagus tips

Suprême de faisan braisé au sauce abricôts
Haricots verts, carottes Vichy, pommes croquettes
Braised pheasant breast with an apricot sauce served with French beans, carrots, croquet potatoes

Soufflé au zitron
Lemon *soufflé*

Brie, Stilton, raisins bleus, pain riche
Brie, Stilton, blue grapes, rich French bread

Above is reproduced a very nice seven-course gastronomic menu for a party of sixty gentlemen at which I was a guest. If, as in our menu, the first course consists of a portion of ripe, sweet, chilled melon, it does not automatically follow that a ripe, older, sweet wine should be served with the melon. This would be altogether too sweet and sickly a first course. A very dry white wine with the sweet melon would also not give the desired balance, as the contrast here would be too marked, making the sweet melon taste sweeter than it actually is, and the dry wine dryer (almost sour) than it actually is. For this reason, a medium sweet or medium dry wine would be the best choice. As the melon is only the first course, with several other courses and wines to follow, we must also choose a lighter wine. Light in this context being a nuance of wine referring to age, body and alcoholic content.

When several wines are to be served at a meal, a light wine with low alcoholic content should be chosen, so as not to intoxicate our guest before the meal has actually begun. With very few exceptions, light wines are white wines and this now establishes the colour of wine to be served. This is, however, not the only criterion: the texture, colour and flavour of the food should also be taken into account. Each course on our menu should be considered by similar criteria, and we should make our choices from the many wines available and which we consider would complement subsequent courses.

For the second course, the *consommé*, no further wine was served or necessary, as soup, especially a *consommé*, is seldom served with a wine in its own right.

With the third course, the hot *hors-d'oeuvre*, we were served with a small glass of excellent Madeira, which was a surprise to me, as the service of a fortified wine so early in the menu could be considered a little too heavy. But it complemented the pungent flavour of the liver and mixture of wild mushrooms extraordinarily well, and was on reflection a wise, if unusual, choice. That the glass of Madeira was relatively small, and that the guests were all gentlemen, may also have influenced the choice.

The third course was followed by a lightly grilled fillet of lemon sole, topped with a few asparagus spears and brushed with a hint of lemon butter. Subtle, light, fishy but gentle in taste, it cried out for a medium dry or dry white wine, which was duly served to flatter this simple but delicious course.

The red meat main course needed something stronger and older in the way of a wine to enhance all the nuances of this lovely main course, and the 1982 St. Emilion served facilitated this need admirably.

The lemon *soufflé* stood proudly on its own. It needed no wine as it was sharply piquant and refreshing to the palate.

The last course of a ripe Brie and a moist Stilton with a bunch of blue grapes, especially suited perhaps to an all-male gathering, was, in good old British tradition, accompanied by a vintage port – a blissful combination.

The marrying of food and drink must always involve personal preferences. Experimentation is the name of the game: we will not always get it right, and we may surprise ourselves when the choice becomes perfect.

The most basic rules to follow are: start with a lighter wine for the *hors-d'oeuvre*; fish is normally served with dry white wine; the *entrée* is served with a light red wine; the *relevé* with its dark meats and rich sauce and accompaniments is usually served with an older, full-bodied red wine; and the sweet course is served with a white wine again, this time sweet and older, or even champagne if the pocket allows. If cheese is served, a good red wine or, to be very British, a glass of port, should accompany this last course.

Finally we should always consider the guests. For example, for an all-ladies lunch, the choice must be different; for an all-ladies dinner, the choice must be different again. Even the weather should play a part in the selection of wines:

lighter, younger wines would be suitable for a hot summer's day, and older richer wines for the cold winter evening dinner.

What we eat and drink at a pre-ordered banquet has, hopefully, been chosen wisely by our host. But always remember that the choice of food we eat and the wine we drink is always a matter of personal preference.

CHAPTER 7

The Gods, Myth, Magic and Food

'Men do not have to cook and present their food, they do so for symbolic reason, to show that they are human, and not beasts.'(7.1)

Once, early man may have eaten just by instinct, because he was hungry, but as previous chapters have shown, from very early times, man began to associate certain values with his food, a respect for his basic need which went far beyond merely filling his stomach. Eating became an act which was associated, consciously or unconsciously, with deep-rooted sentiments, assumptions, beliefs and customs about the food one ate and the world in which one lived.

This has always been considered true in the more simple societies of the past and present, but nowadays most of us realise that this remains true in modern and more complex societies. For all of us, consciously or unconsciously, eating remains closely linked with all manner of spiritual experiences, historical learning, presented opportunities and social ties.

This chapter considers such sentiments, assumptions, beliefs and customs, and tries to trace their source.

Food From and For the Gods

When man first scoured the earth for his most basic need, he must have questioned many times why it was plentiful at certain times and scarce or not available at all in other seasons. Most certainly when man began to till the soil and make his own contribution to the supply of food, he must have wondered why his efforts, his labours, were successful in one season and less so in the next. As far as he was concerned, he had done everything right, right in the sense that his consideration and efforts had been exactly the same in both the successful

7.1 Leach, E., *Levi-Strauss*, Harper & Row, London, 1970, p. 112.

Figure 7.1 'Sa Majesté est servie!'
Source: Nestlé Pro Gastronomia Foundation, © 1993

and the unsuccessful season. Gradually, man began to associate his success or otherwise with the contribution of something else, or someone else – a higher being or a supernatural power.

Man gradually must have related the usefulness of rain, which came from the heavens above, to the growing of his crop, and when this did not come he raised his head high to the heavens and asked or prayed for it. With this uncertain understanding, he climbed to the top of the nearest hill or mountain to be nearer to the supernatural being who sent the rain, and he made a gift or offering of food to it, hoping that the higher power would look kindly upon his gift and make his next effort more successful in providing a rich harvest.

We may consider an offering the same as a gift, but they are indeed two very different things.

> *'An offering or sacrifice implies unequal status with the supernatural power being the superior in the exchange who may or may not find the offering worthy of his powers. Whereas the giving of a gift will always be between two equals, and will almost always be accepted whether desirable or appropriate.'(7.2)*

This early concern with the supernatural and food is considered to be the basis

7.2 Firth, R., *Food Symbolism in Pre-Industrial Society, Symbols, Public and Private*, Cornell University, Ithaca, New York State, 1973, vol. 3, part 1, pp. 12–34.

of all religious activities. A religious sacrifice, however, will always remain an offering of a restricted kind, implying the surrender of something valuable in favour of a higher being who may or may not accept the offering or do a favour in return. Whereas a gift is always physically accepted and removed, the offering is not, and the whole procedure remains a spiritual act. Whether the offering was acceptable will never be physically apparent, only time will tell whether or not the supernatural being found the offering acceptable, by the granting or refusal of the request made in association with the offering. All early sacrifices consisted of food, and meat was the most highly regarded offering as it was much more difficult to obtain than plant food. Therefore, the sacrifice of a cow, goat, sheep or chicken seems to imply:

> *'. . . you know, I cannot really afford this, but the loss endured will be overcome by the even greater benefit which your great power may bestow on me'.(7.3)*

Food, especially food which was difficult to obtain, remained for a long time the original and most valuable offering to the gods, and was only gradually replaced by other things which became regarded as more valuable. The Romans referred to human sacrifice as the act of barbarians, yet the early Greeks would sacrifice an occasional prisoner to appease the gods. Even the Romans had no hesitation in killing a Christian or two for sacrifice (or was it for spectacle).

As religions became more established, offerings were made in other forms, by giving one's life to God, taking holy orders, or chastising one's body, hoping the pain endured would cleanse the 'soul' and please the higher powers. Fasting during several periods of the year or on special occasions was a common form of sacrifice for many people. Later, one gave money, when this came into common use.

In most cases, however, meat from animals remained the most common offering. When the ritual was over, the flesh was distributed to the faithful. In this way, badly needed meat was added to the often meagre vegetable diet of the general population.

This very economical stance of sacrifice is very much a part of life in many tribes over the world today. The Nuer people of Africa, for example, in their periodical ritual slaughter of animals, assure the pleasure of the gods, as well as the pleasure of all who were present at the offering. (7.4)

7.3 *Ibid.*

7.4 Evans-Pritchard, E.E., *Newer Religion*, Oxford University Press, New York, 1956, p. 112.

The Old Testament makes reference to all manner of sacrifice to the gods. The story of Cain and Abel, Noah and the Patriarchs all contain stories of sacrifice. Indeed, the history of the Israelites in particular has recorded the custom of sacrifice in some detail, not only that of the Passover when they ate unleavened bread and bitter herbs, but also other occasions. The Feast of Weeks (*Shavout*), the Feast of Tabernacles (*Succoth*), the beginning of a new year, sometimes the beginning of a new moon and season, an act of repentance, or fulfilment of a vow, have been reasons or occasion for ritual offering. In the First Book of Kings we are told that Solomon sacrificed 22,000 cattle and 120,000 sheep at the dedication of his temple. If true, it remains one of the grandest sacrifices, or should we say feasts, of all times.

Offerings of all types were still commonplace during the life of Jesus, who, as far as we know, had no objections to this practice. Sacrifices at the Temple of Solomon ceased only when it was destroyed by the Romans in AD 70.(7.5)

In our more modern and complex society we might consider this ancient practice and accompanying attitude immoral or even impertinent. But who among us, even today, can swear that he or she has not, in times of stress or discomfort, tried to communicate with the supernatural with a silent vow: 'Lord (God, Master or whatever), if you do this for me now, if you let this bitter cup pass me by now, I will promise to do something for you later.'

Modern religious practice, however, has switched from concrete food offering to more abstract piety as the object of sacrifice. It is no longer important that our sacrifice is food fit for the gods. Today, when Christians take their basket of fruit or vegetables or freshly-baked bread, or, indeed, a tin of baked beans, and place it at the altar of the church at Harvest Festival, they follow the sacrificial ritual of old, not so much as an act of sacrifice, but as an act of thanking and giving.

Fasting: The Indirect Sacrifice

Fasting has persisted in all major religions as well as in many local cults in one form or another throughout the ages. It expresses a different form of respect or devotion to the supernatural, not by offering the foods to the gods in sacrifice, but by depriving oneself of food by not eating for periods which can last from one day to many weeks. Through fasting one can clear one's body of impurities, atone for sins, protest against treatment, or show an appreciation of hunger suffered by others. No matter what the reason, this somewhat irrational

7.5 Cornfield, G. (ed), *Pictorial Biblical Encyclopaedia*, Macmillan, New York, 1964, pp. 636–46.

behaviour, which can deprive the individual of essential nutrients, has remained common practice for many years. More zealous fasting has sometimes produced the same medical symptoms as are experienced in famines caused by drought or war. Yet, in most cases, fasting is not usually very harmful, because it is limited to certain periods.

The fasting of the Jews at *Yom Kippur* is total, but lasts for only one day. Muslims fast during the entire ninth month of the Islamic calendar (*Ramadan*), but it is limited to the hours between sunrise and sunset. The Roman Catholic Lenten fast should last for the forty weekdays before Easter, but here the fast is normally only in respect of certain foods, for which substitutes are often available.

Fasts in many religions and cults often take place in the 'lean season', that is to say, between the old and reducing harvest when not much grows, and the new expected harvest. In this way, scarce and fast-reducing supplies are spread over time.

Nearly all religions place limitations on fasting. Infants and small children, pregnant women, women who are menstruating, some hard-working manual labourers, fighting soldiers and travellers are often exempted from the fast. When one looks at the eating calendar of the Hindus of India, fasting can appear to be a very complex matter.

> *'Almost any day in the year could be considered a fast day according to caste, sex, age or degree of orthodoxy. A devout Hindu might fast to appease a deity, to obtain a boon, to ward off evils or to honour particular gods. On closer inspection, we find such fasts as were undertaken are usually only partial fasts and such foods as were allowed to be eaten very ably covered the dietary needs of the fasting people.'*(7.6)

The consumption of certain foods and dishes associated with fast or other spiritual occasions has resulted in the gastro-geographical spread of foods into regions where they would not normally have occurred. Thus foods sanctified by religious feast or customs, whether plant or animal, have moved with the pious from place to place, assuring in time a new and more varied supply of foods of all or particular types.

For example, both Christians and Jews placed much sacramental value on wine made from grapes. They cultivated grapes far beyond the Mediterranean and very successfully in many areas of northern Europe, including the Mosel and Rhine valleys and as far north as the British Isles. Later, the monks and priests of Spain, Portugal and France brought the European grape to many parts of the new

---

7.6 Katona-Apt, J., 'Dietary aspects of culturation, meals, feasts and fasts in minority communities of south Asia', in M.L. Arnott (ed), *A Gastronomy: the Anthropology of Food and Food Habits*, The Hague: Mouton, 1975, pp. 297–303.

world. In more recent history, the Jews returning to Palestine, and finding their ancient vineyards uprooted by Muslims who, for religious reasons, are forbidden to drink alcohol, made it one of their first tasks to replant vines on a large scale to meet their spiritual needs.(7.7)

In the same way fruits, particularly the lemon, used for ritual purposes by Jews, have been spread in cultivation all over the Mediterranean regions. Plant-experts cannot agree about the place of origin of the citrus fruit, but it is generally believed that it came from western India. It was possibly cultivated in the Holy Land and was used in Jewish religious rituals from the reign of King Solomon, where it featured at the feast of the Tabernacles. After the Jews rebelled against the Romans in AD 66 and were dispersed into various Roman colonies, they brought the lemon tree and its fruits to new centres of citrus production, such as Algeria, Italy, Spain and Tunisia.(7.8)

Much of the mystery of Christian ritual centres around eating and drinking, and has been a subject of contention. One thinks here of the Last Supper as described in the Gospel according to St Mark, Chapter 14, vv.22–24:

'And as they did eat, Jesus took bread and blessed it and brake it, and gave it to them and said, "Take it, this is my body". And he took the cup and when he had given thanks he gave it to them and they all drank of it. And he said to them, "This is my blood of the New Testament which is shed for many".'

We do not know, of course, whether Jesus's statement was to be taken literally or symbolically, meaning that Jesus's death would be a sacrifice on behalf of all mankind. Paul most certainly made it an issue in his attempt to make Christianity more acceptable to potential converts among the Greeks, Jews, Romans and other pagans. What is true is that many Christians gave thanks at meal-times by breaking bread and by drinking wine from a shared cup. Only much later was this communal eating and drinking made part of the ritual of the Catholic Mass, where those who had been baptised consumed the bread, or wafer or host. The name of which, *Hostio*, derives from Latin and means 'sacrificial victim'.

The Catholic Church's doctrine concerning the Eucharist was firmly established as late as AD 1215, when Pope Innocent III summoned a council at which it was decreed, as an Article of the Faith, that the bread and wine consumed in the Sacrament changed through transubstantiation into the body and blood of Jesus Christ. The only difference now was that the congregation took only the bread or host and the priest alone took both bread and wine. This

7.7 Soper, D., *Geography of Religions*, Prentice-Hall, Englewood Cliff, NJ, 1967, p. 33.

7.8 Isaac, E., 'Influence of religion on the spread of citrous', *Science*, 1959, vol. 129.

was like the ritual of the Jews in their sacrifices when they separated the blood from the body of the animal and let it flow back into the earth – so the blood of Christ was separated from the congregation and given only to the priest and, as in the earliest of sacrifices, the people were allowed only to eat the flesh or body of the sacrifice, not the spirit found in the blood.

The movement of people and their important foods into Europe can be observed more recently in the immigration of West Indians, Indians, Pakistanis and Chinese over the last thirty years, especially into Britain. This movement of people and their native foods and dishes has meant that new wholesale suppliers and special shops and restaurants have become established. These were originally to serve the immigrants, but are now accepted and used by the indigenous population in many cities of Britain. Even the most recent immigrants to these shores, the boat people of Vietnam, have their ritual needs for food:

'Hai and Arik are dressing for the coni (the wedding). The lunar calendar has been consulted for an auspicious date and the wedding feast has been prepared. But Hai and his family will arrive for the ceremony without a gift of tran and can. In Vietnam can is a gift of fruits from the acera palm, and tran, leaves from the climbing pepper plant, both presented by the groom and his family to the bride and her family. To give and accept a gift of tran and can is the recognition of the moral obligation by all parties concerned. Food is used by all cultures in rituals and celebrations, as a symbol to represent something which is conceptual. No matter how rich or how poor the family, tran and can is an essential part of le an hoi (the betrothal ceremony) and le coni (the wedding) and there is none available in Britain.'(7.9)

The reader may be pleased to know that British Airways, when hearing about the problem, found *tran* and *can* by one of their agents and flew them in to Britain so that Hai and Arik were able to get married in the traditional way.

The Forbidden Fruits

Most people on this earth have some rules or taboos concerning food and drink to be avoided, or even forbidden. In some cases such restrictions apply in all

7.9 Carlson, E.P., 'The Food Habits and Nutrition of Refugees Who Have Been Resettled in the UK', Ph.D. Thesis, University of Surrey, 1983.

Figure 7.2 'Il ristretto'
Source: Nestlé Pro Gastronomia Foundation, © 1993

cases and at all times, whereas in other cases abstention is required only during certain periods of time or on set occasions. What is not always clear is how and why these rules came into being. Many opinions have been expressed and some have given reasonable and acceptable explanations, others have never been satisfactorily explained, and some reasons will for ever be lost in the mist of time and have become the bases of myths and magic. Two important Judo-Christian-Muslim rules about the origin of man describe the consequence of eating. Firstly, according to the book of Genesis, we hear that:

> *'Jehovah created Adam on the sixth day and entrusted him with dominion over all the animals and plants and then he created Eve to him as a helpmate.*
> *In this Eden the humans, plants and animals lived in harmony until Eve made Adam break the order against the eating of fruit from a certain tree. With this breaking of this order of eating, Adam and Eve were expelled from Eden and condemned 'to eat their bread in the sweat of thy face.'(7.10)*

The second point to be made is that of flesh:

7.10 *Oxford Annotated Bible*, Oxford, 1965, Genesis, ch. 3, v. 19.

'To cleanse the earth of wickedness, Jehovah unleashed a flood of catastrophic proportions on earth. But along with Noah and his family, a pair of each of the animals which God had created was kept safe from the waters in the ark. When the floods receded, Jehovah allowed the hitherto forbidden sacrifice of animals, thus giving man the right to kill and eat many but not all, with whom they shared the earth.'(7.11)

The story of creation as told in the story of Adam and Eve tells us that all animals possess the spirit of God which resides in its blood. Until Noah returned to the land it was forbidden to eat any animal. The permission given to Noah to sacrifice animals in the name of God made the stipulation that the God-given spirit of the animal must be returned to the earth, by draining all blood from the animal before sacrifice and consumption. This special procedure is still followed to this day in orthodox Kosher slaughter.

The fall from grace through the eating of fruit from the forbidden tree, and the establishment of the relationship between humans and animals, that of predator and prey, is the reason given for the paradox of various taboos against eating normally perfectly good and desirable foods. In the Western world at least, almost all forbidden foods are foods from animals, or certain parts of animals, and only very seldom are these as a result of natural, cultural revulsion, a revulsion which stops Western people eating dogs, cats, rats and worms. Most English people would be revolted at the thought of eating horse flesh, but less than thirty miles across the Channel it is considered, at least by some, to be a delicacy.

In some regions of the world, notably Polynesia from where the word 'taboo' came, it is forbidden to eat some plants, but restrictions on plant foods are few. All fish is forbidden in some parts of Africa; shellfish is forbidden to Jews; duck is unclean in Mongolia, and the eating of carnal flesh would break Muslim religious laws.

In some religions it is often not the case that certain foods are forbidden at all times, but there is a restriction of foods to be eaten at the same time. Some tribes of Eskimo consider that eating a meal of meats from land and sea at the same time is not allowed by the gods. Jews have many restrictions regarding which foods are not permitted, but they find a reasonable diet within the foods which are considered clean. A secondary restriction on the Jews is that meats and foods based on milk products must not be consumed at the same meal.(7.12)

Probably the most widely forbidden flesh is pork, forbidden first in the book of

---

7.11 Pepper, T. and Schrere, C., *The Nimrod Connection, Myth and Science in the Hunting Model*, Academic Press, New York, 1977, pp. 447, 459.

7.12 Simons, F. *Eat Not of this Flesh: Food Avoidance in the Old World*, University of Wisconsin Press, Madison, 1961, p. 1.

Moses and endorsed in the Koran. This restriction applies to Jews and Muslims alike.

It has even been stated that the pig was avoided in the diets of Jews and Muslims because it was obviously a dirty animal, wallowing in dirt, mud and in its own excrement. But the pig will do this only when confined to a small pigsty, and as it has no sweat glands the wallowing is one way of keeping its skin cool by evaporation. A more likely explanation in respect of the Israelites is that they were pastoral nomads and always on the move through the arid plains and hills, an existence to which sheep, goats and cattle had adapted, but pigs had not. Pigs require shade and moisture which prevails in heavily wooded countryside but not in hills and on plains. This ecological consideration might explain that pigs were not normally a part of the Israelites' way of life, and something of an unknown quantity. But this still does not explain why pigs' flesh was not simply ignored, but specifically forbidden.(7.13)

On the Indian sub-continent millions of people go hungry even today, yet sacred cattle, a valuable source of protein essential to humans, roam the villages and towns helping themselves to food so desperately needed by the starving humans. Nearly two hundred million cattle inhabit the Indian sub-continent, a largely vegetarian country at first sight, and the wandering cattle contribute very little in the way of protein to the diet of the people. Yet they compete on an enormous scale for the plant food of the starving millions.

The North American farmer expects to receive approximately 9,000 pints of milk from a good milk cow in a good year. The contribution of an Indian cow is less than 500 pints a year, a very small return of nutrients on a high number of seemingly worthless animals, roaming at will.

The taboo against eating beef in India is often quoted as the supreme example of irrational food prohibition and the ultimate triumph of religion over appetite and reason. Historically, the *Vedas*, the sacred text of Hinduism dating back some 3,000 years or so, does not really bear out the taboo against the eating of beef. The holy text does occasionally object to the eating of meat, but elsewhere the text approves and tells of the slaughter of cattle. It even makes clear that the priestly Brahman caste ate beef and were even taught the correct rules of preparation, carving and portioning when serving it at holy feasts.

Buddhism prohibits the eating of flesh of humans, elephants, horses, lions, tigers, panthers, bears, dogs, hyenas and serpents, but not cattle. Nor was the eating of beef forbidden when King Asok made Buddhism the state religion of India about 2,250 years ago, although he forbad all cruelty to animals and animal sacrifice in particular. Only less than 2,000 years ago did the slaughter of cattle become a religious and civil offence. In 1949, when India became independent,

---

7.13 *Ibid.*

the constitution even included a bill of rights for cattle which is still strictly observed today, and is taken so seriously that the police will round up stray or sick cattle and nurse them back to health in special stables, while many Indian children starve.

Whether religious taboos regarding food are rational or irrational is besides the point here, for if people who follow these religious dietary rules do not flourish, then of course the religion cannot flourish either, which clearly is not the case in India, with a people as devout as ever. One must therefore seek other reasons for the reverence of cattle in India, which satisfies the stomach as well as the soul. About 2,000 years ago an increase in population made India one of the most densely inhabited lands on earth. To feed the increased population, farmers ploughed land which was clearly not suitable for cultivation. This produced an ecological disaster which reduced India to a semi-desert, and only in the last thirty years has this begun to be rectified. At that time religious taboos or sanctions began to serve necessity, they forbad the hungry villagers to kill their cattle and eat them, instead they were to use them for working the land. Even today the ox and male water buffalo are essential to the Indian farmer to plough his fields. Even a farm with less than ten acres needs a pair of these animals and, as India has about 70 million such farms, it follows that 14 million working cattle are needed. A recent survey suggests that far from having too many cattle, India may actually be short of cattle to work the soil.

Expensive tractors and oil to run them are no substitute for reasons of cost alone. Nor can Indian farmers share their animals as European farmers and villagers did, for in India all fields have to be ploughed at the same time to coincide with the monsoon rains.

The Muslim scientist, A.L. Biruni, explained the sanctity of Indian cattle as long ago as the eleventh century as follows:

'We must keep in mind that the cow is an animal which serves man in travelling by carrying his heavy loads, in works of ploughing and sowing and harvesting and threshing, in the household by giving milk and the produce made thereof. Further, man makes use of its dung (as fertilizer and fuel) and in wintertime even its warming breath will help to keep man warm. Therefore it was forbidden to eat cow meat.'(7.14)

Supposedly religious reasons for food taboos will, in some cases, on closer inspection not be for a religious reason at all, but be based on economic or social conditions of the times. The above story of the sacred cows of India makes the point very clearly. Where such prohibitions do exist they can serve both soul

7.14 Harris, M., *Cultural Materialism*, 1979, vol. 1, no. 2, pp. 28–36.

and, indirectly, stomach very well. The much discussed dietary regime of the Hebrew and Mosaic laws in the Old Testament have clearly influenced Muslim and, to some degree, Christian attitudes to food and eating.

The Hebrew laws on food have been considered from all angles and many reasons given and speculations made. In the search for this book I have come across an article by Jean Soler with the title, *The Semiotics of Food in the Bible*. In this article Soler gives two basic reasons for the dietary laws of the Hebrews which have lasted with some variation to this day. The first reason is a religious one and could be called the reason of perfection as seen in the story of creation of the word by the Hebrews of old. Man's food is considered in the first chapter of the first book of the *Torah*.

'Behold I have given you every plant yielding seed, which is upon the face of the earth, and every tree with seeds in its fruit; you shall have them for your food'. (7.15)

According to this, paradise is vegetarian and killing is the only major prohibition of the old Testament. This is a stance still taken by true vegetarians today, but also there is an important consideration in understanding some of the Hebrew dietary laws. For man to eat meat he must first kill the animal from which the meat comes, but as God is both giver and taker of life, to kill an animal who, like man, is created by God and has 'a living soul', would make man, at least in respect of the taking of life, an equal to God. This cannot be.

In this context plants are not considered living things, nor are they considered to possess a soul. Given this fundamental assumption, meat eating constitutes a problem. How then did man find a way to kill and eat the flesh of animals without prompting the wrath of God. According to this hypothesis, the break takes place in the form of the floods of Noah, which are considered the point of reference which coincides with the new dietary regime, allowing man to eat meat.

'Every moving thing that lives shall be for you: as I gave you the green plants, I give you (now) everything.'(7.16)

According to this it is not man who has taken it upon himself to kill and eat meat, God has given him the right to do so. Yet at the same time a new prohibition is added which serves both God and man. God insisted that the

7.15 *Oxford Annotated Bible*, Oxford, 1965, Genesis, ch, 1. v. 29.
7.16 *Ibid.*, ch. 9, v. 9.

'living soul', the 'spirit' of the animal should be given back to God in the act of killing or sacrifice.

'Only you shall not eat the flesh with its life that is its blood'.(7.17)

The mutual prohibition between the eating of plants and flesh places the new distinction between the eating of the flesh and the blood. Once the blood, which is of God, and in which resides the soul or spirit, is given to God and set apart from the flesh, the flesh becomes desacralised and permissible to be eaten.

In this criteria of perfection in the Old Testament, we often find the word 'unclean' or 'blemished'. These two terms are used for secondary taboos in respect of meat which may not be eaten, and can only really be understood in the myth of the plan of creation and perfection as created by God.

Leviticus Chapter 11 and Deuteronomy Chapter 14 are the texts which give some explanation of these important terms. The first speaks of the animals on land and considers them clean if they have a 'hoofed foot'. Normally, hoofed animals are herbivorous since they lack the means of slaying prey. As God initially asked man to live on plants only, but now has given permission to eat the meat separated from the blood, God still insists that we should eat only animals living on plants. Therefore a carnivorous animal becomes unclean because:

'Unto every beast of the earth and to every bird of the air and to everything that has breath of life, I have given green plants for food'.(7.18)

According to this, carnivorous animals are not included in the plan of creation. For should man eat such an animal, one which has killed and eaten of the flesh and blood of another, he would become doubly unclean by his action.

This reason, for cleanliness or otherwise, is also given when considering the birds of the air, and it places the flesh-consuming eagle at the top of the list of forbidden or unclean birds. Only birds which eat plants and seeds should become the food of man. Most Europeans accept this custom when consuming game or fowl, whether they be Jews or Christians. To return to the land animals, the second criterion, that of the 'cloven hoof', eliminates a number of animals such as the horse, ass, and those expressly forbidden in the Old Testament as unclean, the camel, hare, rock-badger – all purely herbivorous creatures. Here the third criterion comes into play. It states that such animals should 'chew the cud'.

One can be sure that ruminants eat grass, in fact they eat it twice, which

---

7.17 *Ibid.*, ch. 9, v. 4.

7.18 *Ibid.*, ch. 1, v. 29–30.

should be sufficient to distinguish true herbivores. Yet it is often difficult to be sure of this when it comes to animals of the wild. Even the Bible makes the mistake in respect of the hare (Leviticus Chapter 11, verse 6 and Deuteronomy Chapter 14, verse 7), where mastication is sometimes mistaken for rumination. Perfect animals as understood in the plan of creation must therefore be living on a vegetarian diet to be clean and suitable as food for man. Moreover they must also be true specimens of the three accepted elements of creation; the firmament, the water and the earth. God created three types of animals for each of these elements:

'Let the waters bring forth swarms of living creatures and let birds fly above the firmament of heavens.'(7.19)

'Let the earth bring forth living creatures, according to their kinds.'(7.20)

Thus it seems that, to be acceptable as food for man, an animal had not only to be herbivorous but had to fit tidily into one of the categories of the three elements of creation, namely earth, air or water, to be perfect and clean. For this reason the only clean creatures of the sea are those with scales and fins for propulsion. Those sea creatures lacking fins or scales – such as the mollusc – and which are propelled only with the sea currents, are unclean. Those creatures which live in the sea but which have legs and can walk – such as crustacea – and which have organs similar to those of land-bound creatures, are unclean, for they are at home in two of the elements created by God – water and land.

When it comes to creatures of the air, we find in Deuteronomy Chapter 4, verse 17, the definition of clean birds as acceptable food for man. Besides the prerequisite that they must be herbivorous, they must also have 'the likeness of any winged bird that flies in the air'. Winged, which fly, and air, are the key words. Thus if a bird has wings but does not fly, like the ostrich for example, it is considered unclean. 'All winged birds that go upon the earth are an abomination to you.'(7.21)

This means that such birds as the swan, pelican and other stilted birds are unclean. Surprisingly no reference is made to their organs (to feet) used on the land as in respect of shellfish, because to introduce this criteria would exclude them all as they have feet upon which they walk on land. Nor is reference made to having organs of two elements, namely wings for flight in the air and feet for mobility on the ground or in trees.

7.19 *Ibid.*, ch. 1, v. 20.

7.20 *Ibid.*, ch. 1, v. 24.

7.21 *Ibid.*, Leviticus, ch. 11, v. 20.

On the other hand all insects are to be regarded as unclean food for man, because they exist between the elements, both flying in the air and walking on the earth.

Again and again in the Old Testament there are statements regarding perfection and classification when it concerns foods acceptable and permissible to man:

> *'Each according to their kind'; 'You shall not breed your cattle with a different kind.'* (7.22)

> *'You shall not plough with an ox and ass together.'* (7.23)

Even in respect of actual cooking we find:

> *'You shall not boil a kid in its mother's milk.'* (7.24)

This refers to one of the basic rules in Jewish cooking which does not allow the mixing of meat and milk products in a meal. This criterion of perfection went so far that any blemishes which an animal may have had made it unacceptable as an offering or sacrifice in the name of God.

> *'You shall not sacrifice to the Lord your God an ox or sheep in which is a blemish, or any defect whatsoever, for it is an abomination to the Lord'.* (7.25)

> *'And when anyone offers sacrifice or peace offering to the Lord, or to fulfil a vow, or a free will offering from the herd or flock: to be acceptable it must be perfect, there shall be no blemish on it. Animals, blind, disabled or mutilated, or having a discharge or little scabs, you shall not offer these to the Lord, nor make of them an offering by fire upon the altar to the Lord.'* (7.26)

This hypothesis of perfection in respect of God's creation is most interesting, revealing and acceptable. Accordingly the dietary regime of the Hebrews, within the myth of creation, was firmly based on a strict classification of God, man, animal and plant, which is strictly defined to a relationship one with another.

7.22 *Ibid.*, Leviticus, ch. 19, v. 19.
7.23 *Ibid.*, Deuteronomy, ch. 22, v. 10.
7.24 *Ibid.*, Exodus, ch. 23, v. 10.
7.25 *Ibid.*, Deuteronomy, ch. 17, v. 1.
7.26 *Ibid.*, Leviticus, ch. 22, v. 21.

The Hebrews conceived the world as an order underlining the creation, and expressed in the Old Testament. Imperfection was an evil, uncleanness is simply a disorder wherever it may occur. Moreover, whatever variation and change has taken place in the course of history, it must have some merit, at least to the orthodox Jews of today, for the dietary regime of the modern Hebrew has not really changed or been shaken in its fundamental structure or beliefs. On closer inspection it is also quite apparent that the Mosaic dietary laws have greatly influenced both Muslim and Christian attitudes to foods and eating. We may consider the avoidance of some foods today, by Christians and others, as based on cultural revulsion, but surprisingly almost all the foods avoided by Christians today, for supposedly cultural reasons, are all to be found high on the list of unclean foods of the Hebrews of old. Jesus may have said:

> *'Not that which goes into the mouth defiles man, but that which comes out of the mouth will defile man.'(7.27)*

The fact remains that to all of us, for whatever reason, some foods remain an abomination.

Another point to be made in respect of this hypothesis refers to the priestly authors of the book of Moses, who placed special emphasis upon dietary laws because food was to be used as a badge, to distinguish and separate people from one another.

> *'I am the Lord thy God who has separated you from the people. You shall therefore make distinction between the clean beasts and the unclean; between the clean birds and the unclean; you shall not make yourself abominable by beast or bird, or anything with which the ground teems which I have set apart as unclean, as I have set you apart'.(7.28)*

This covenant is an individual one which has become the special trait of the Jews. In this way the dietary code of the Hebrews served the same function as that of circumcision, the institution of the Sabbath and the separation of flesh from the blood; the blood being the part that is of God, and the flesh being that of the people. All these cuts were intended as cuts away from social experiences with other people, and to differentiate the Hebrews from other people, tribes and nations. This must have been particularly important when the Hebrews were without a land, on their exodus and looking for their land abounding with milk and honey.

7.27 *Ibid.*, Matthew, ch. 15, v. 11.

7.28 *Ibid.*, Leviticus, ch. 20, v. 24–25.

To keep the Hebrews together, one people, one nation, was, in regard to this hypothesis, one reason for the dietary laws. It seems to have had the desired effect. For when Joseph's brother journeyed to Egypt to buy wheat, he was offered a meal after the long journey by the Egyptians, and said the separation was already observed.

> *'They served him by himself and them by themselves for Egyptians will not break bread with a Hebrew, for that was an abomination for both.'*(7.29)

Clearly the dietary laws, along with other laws and customs, constituted a system of socio-cultural separation to build and assure the fundamental structure of the Hebrew civilisation. The choice of foods, and the importance of cooking and serving them, became particular to man in the same manner as a language. Better still, food, cooking and eating can become a language through which an individual, a group or a class of people, a society, or a nation expresses and differentiates itself.(7.30)(7.31)

7.29 *Ibid.*, Genesis, ch. 43, v. 32.

7.30 Soler, J., *The Semiotics of Food in the Bible: The Annals, Economies, Societies, Civilizations*, vol. 5, 1973, translated by E. Forster, 1973, pp. 943–55.

7.31 Levi-Strauss, C., 'The Culinary Triangle', *Partisan Review*, vol. 33, 1966.

CHAPTER 8

Gastronomy – Technology and the Arts

Gastronomy and Technology

Through the use of technology, man is able to produce more food than ever, better food than ever, and a wider variety of food than ever. And through the food-related sciences, man is better able to understand the inadequacies of some foods and diets, and where necessary he is able to supplement inadequate diets with better foods.

'The health of the modern European is now better than ever; he lives longer and enjoys life more fully than ever before. Medical science has helped, but also a better supply, preparation of food and better nutritional management have been key factors.'(8.1)

Anyone who has a concern for food is aware and appreciative of the contributions which technology has made to modern supply of food. It has not only assured a more stable and better supply of food, but also it has in many ways removed much of the hard work and drudgery from food preparation which was very much a part of the practical gastronomy of old.

Thus it has left the practitioner more time to give thought and attention to the foods themselves and to the creative parts of his or her endeavours. Yet as much as modern gastronomy has benefited from technology, there are at the same time certain dangers which technology can, and has, introduced to modern food. The following examples will help to illustrate these dangers.

The first example concerns the humble dried green pea. Preserved by one of the oldest methods of food preservation – air drying – it has played a considerable part in the European and, in particular, the British diet for hundreds of years. High in protein and fibre and full of natural flavour, the dried

8.1 Miller, J., 'The Body in Question' in *The Listener*, 15 February 1979.

pea has been a favourite for the rich and poor alike. The pea has been eaten in a wide variety of ways, in green pea soup, mushy peas, pease-pudding and pea-fritters. It has formed the base of many an appreciated meal for a poor family, as well as playing its part in higher gastronomy.

The problem with all pulse vegetables, including the green pea, is that they need soaking overnight, as well as two to three hours of cooking time, to make them soft and digestible and to bring out the excellent flavour. The long cooking time did not matter up to the Second World War when the kitchen was the only heated room in the average house – a wood or coal fire was needed almost twenty-four hours a day for cooking, drying clothes, warmth, etc. A pan of green dried peas needing two hours or so of cooking slowly simmering on the back of that fire did not matter.

However, when heating, cooking and other household tasks were carried out using gas or electricity which could be switched on or off when needed, the two to three hours cooking time of the dried peas was not considered time- or cost-effective, and for this reason the green pea lost much of its popularity and place in the average diet.

At about this time, technology came to the good pea's rescue in the form of the pressure-cooker, which allowed it to be cooked in twenty to thirty minutes. The nutritional value and excellent flavour of the pea was saved, and could now be enjoyed again at least by those who could afford a pressure cooker.

Soon chemists took an interest in our little green, or sometimes yellow, pea and its long cooking time. They suggested that dried peas should be soaked in either an alkaline or acid bath before being dried ready for the grocer's shelf. This would break down the compound starch granules of the peas and reduce the cooking time to that in the pressure cooker – twenty to thirty minutes. The process worked well.

There was a danger that prolonged infusion in either an alkaline or acid bath would make the peas lose their lovely green colour and some of their flavour, but if the treatment was controlled well, the result was acceptable. Technology had served our little pea, man and gastronomy well. Or had it?

Chemists continued to experiment with the pea, and by various processes broke it down to a fine powder which could be cooked in ten minutes or so. Sadly, in the process the pea had lost much of its flavour, most of its colour, some of its protein and all of its fibre. The colour needed to be replaced artificially, the flavour by artificial flavouring agents, and our little green pea, devoid of all fibre and much of its valuable protein, reappeared on the grocer's shelf in powdered form to be cooked and eaten in five minutes or less.

Today, technology offers us so-called green pea 'instant' soup, which is based on modified starch and the flavour and colour of pea – it is simply an artificial creation. Both gastronomically and nutritionally speaking, technology has not served our little green pea well, for in the last two examples at least, there is nothing left of the little pea, its protein, colour, flavour or fibre, all of which made it so valuable.

Another example of how modern technology goes awry concerns smoking, again one of the oldest methods of food presentation known to man. Smoking is valuable in as much as it not only preserves food, it also changes the appearance and flavour of food. The initial intention of preserving food by smoking resulted in a new type of food and flavour, which is most certainly gastronomically valuable as it adds variety to basic foods available.

Today, when we have many means to preserve food other than by smoking, we continue, nevertheless, to smoke foods because of the flavour the food gains by being smoked, a flavour to which we have become accustomed and which we nowadays would not wish to be without. Thus smoking has given us two benefits, its obvious long-term benefit of preservation, as well as a new flavour given to familiar food, and the variety this gives to our eating experience.

To see smoked salmon more frequently stored and sold from deep-freeze compartments seems to be double Dutch. Although freezing is one of the oldest methods of food presentation, it does not have the same gastronomic benefit as that of smoking. The only benefit freezing can claim is to assure a more continuous supply of some foods over the various seasons of availability.

Gastronomically speaking, all frozen foods lose by the process of freezing. The loss lies in the defrosting process, which bleeds all foods, particularly fish and meats, of much of their natural flavour and some of their nutrients. At the same time, it imposes limitations on the cooking or presentation methods we may or may not be able to use.

Culinary skills can correct some of this loss by careful treatment, and seasoning, but it can never be wholly corrected. Most of us can tell immediately, merely from the taste of the meat, fish or vegetable we are eating, whether it is fresh or frozen. To see more and more of our food, both raw and cooked, preserved by this method, is gastronomically a step backwards and does not make much sense economically speaking either.

The improved food supply for the average European has largely been achieved by the application of new technology to modern agriculture. Oil-based fertilisers and fungicides and the increased use of energy by machinery and plant have played their part in increasing crop yields. But for some time now considerable doubts have been expressed about the cost-effectiveness of this trend in the long-term. This is especially so when we consider the vast over-production of many basic foods which have to be stored or preserved in some form or other using more energy again to keep it in a fit state to eat.(8.2)

8.2 Anon, 'Speiseproduktion und Energiverbrauch' (Food production and energy use), *Der Stern*, 1981, vol. 43, pp. 80–1.

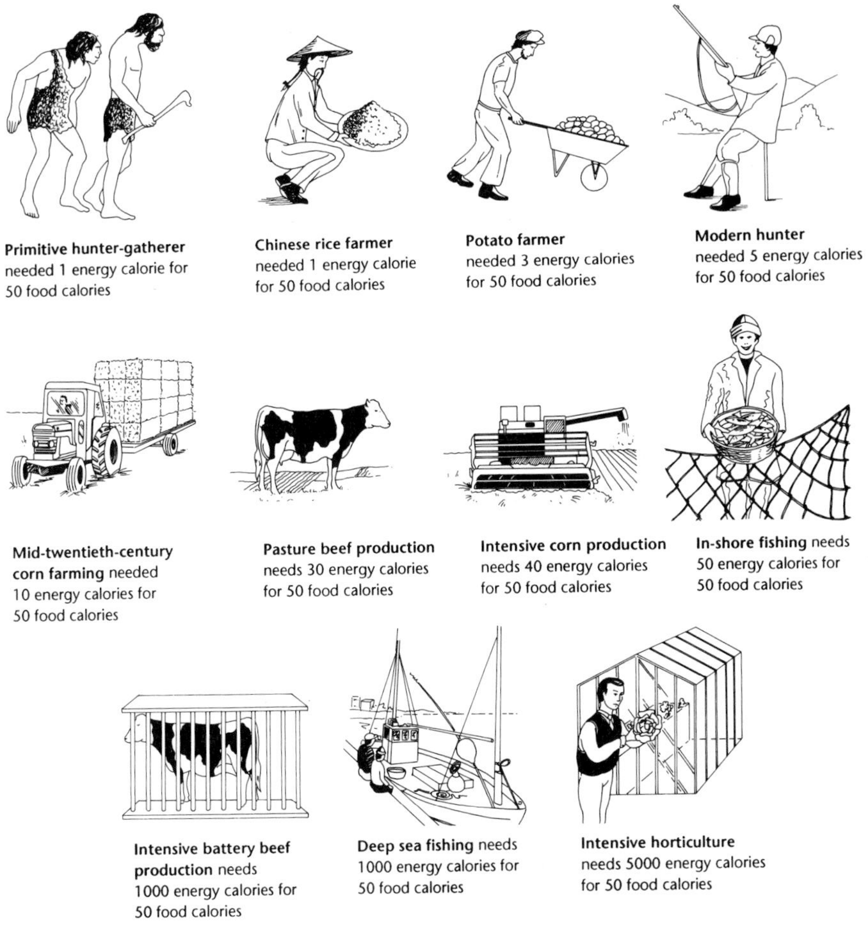

Figure 8.1 The relation of food production and preparation to energy consumption over time, drawn by Monica Polacz and translated by W Bode
Source: By kind permission of the editors of the magazine, *Der Stern*, Hamburg

We now use more energy for the processing and freezing of already energy-expensive foods on a scale equal to or larger than that now used in agriculture. The freezing of food, particularly the freezing of cooked food for convenience, is an excessive use of costly energy. For this process we need an energy input on at least six occasions: planting and harvesting; transport, processing, washing, cutting and blanching; cooking, assembling and packing; freezing; keeping it frozen; and reheating for consumption.

A study has shown that some cook-frozen foods have a food value as low as 30 per cent of its cost of purchase. The cost of production, processing, storage while frozen, and reheating represents 70 per cent of the cost of the food. Only about one-third of the cost can be apportioned to the food value of the package offered; two-thirds represent the production cost, most of it using finite energy.(8.3)

Many more examples could be given, which would show that some aspects of high technology, when applied to modern food preparation and presentation, make less and less sense, both economically and gastronomically. It seems that the more our food is touched by high-powered technology, the more it becomes part of the 'candy-floss' of modern life, and the less it becomes valuable and good food.

This is particularly so when we compare the only other cuisine in the world, the Chinese cuisine, which has, like the French/European cuisine, a world-wide impact, tradition, respect and popularity. The Chinese cuisine, even today in the West, is singularly devoid of all modern technology. Its secret gastronomic weapon has been the simple, wonderful wok. Unchanged for centuries and usually made from simple cast iron, produced with the least of technological know-how and shaped not unlike a coolie's hat, it has conquered the world.

The wok's ingenious shape allows the maximum amount of heat to strike the maximum cooking area, while for moving, stirring and nursing the food, a simple bamboo chopstick or metal spatula is used. The food is cooked most effectively. This, the most basic of Chinese kitchen equipment, is both simple and practical, and has produced some of the finest compositional dishes in the world and – so modern nutritionists tell us – some of the most nutritionally balanced and healthy meals. The food prepared in this simple gastronomic utensil has also conquered the world, in particular, the Western world. From the numbers of Chinese meals sold in this country alone, Chinese food and dishes often seem to be preferred to the food and dishes prepared by modern technology.

Today, the ancient and honourable heritage of the Chinese cuisine supports thousands and thousands of restaurants all over the world, displacing the more high-technology restaurants of the Western world.

In a recent much-publicised discussion, nutritionists tell us of the importance of fibre in our modern Western diet. Here, in particular, food technology has done a disservice to our modern diet by filling the supermarket shelves with more and more over-refined foods.(8.4)

It is of particular concern that food technology has begun to distance man from his food as never before. Although modern man may eat better, he knows less and less about the most basic of foods he eats, basic food preparation and

---

8.3 *Ibid.*

8.4 JACNE Report, 'Diet for a Healthy Heart', Joint Advisory Committee on Nutrition Education, Health Education Council and British Nutritional Foundation, 1985.

food presentation. The process has been a gradual one, but one can now observe a disinterest in food and absence of concern for food, and a lack of respect for and general knowledge about food in a very complex world of food and eating.

Eating has most certainly lost many well-established food and eating customs and etiquettes in a practical, social and aesthetic sense. Ease of availability has bred contempt for what was until quite recently one of man's most basic and important concerns.

Technology has begun to distance man more and more from his food in time and place. With the exception of some meats and fish, as well as some fresh vegetables and fruits, most foods on the modern supermarket shelves today can be between one and twelve months old, varying in age only according to the type of food and/or the process or preservation used. What they may lack in freshness is compensated for by beautiful pictures on the packets or tins, which more often than not bear little resemblance to the actual content. Often the description on packaging owes more to a fertile imagination than fact:

> *'A jam made like grandmother used to make it, would have meant that grandmother needed a doctorate in chemistry rather than the most simple of culinary skill jam making requires.'*(8.5)

Throughout history man has held food in reserve and storage. But the methods of storage and preservation used were among the most natural methods we know, and these were applied to only a few very basic foods. One has only to study the writings of Mrs Beaton to realise that this is so.

Modern food technology will preserve, process, prepare and produce almost anything for convenience sake, for both the home and the catering industry. In so doing, an increasing number of additives are used. To date, the number of additives has grown to somewhere between 2,500 and 3,000.

> *'We eat about three pounds of food per day, half a ton a year or 35 tons in our three score years and ten. With this increase in mostly convenient food, we ate in 1955 1.5 pounds of additives, 2.3 pounds of additives by 1965 or 3.2 pounds by 1974, which today it is estimated has risen to 5.4 pounds per person per year. In the USA it is considered to be about 9 pounds, equivalent to thirty-six aspirin sized tablets every day.'*(8.6)

The Food and Drugs Act 1955 requires that all additives introduced after that date should be tested to see how toxic they are – most additives in use before

8.5 Anon, 'Speiseproduktion und Energiverbrauch' (Food production and energy use), *Der Stern*, 1981, vol. 4, pp. 80–1.
8.6 Thomson, J., 'The use of technical and cosmetic additives in modern food production', *World Medicine*, 1975, vol. 10.

1955 have not been fully tested! One could say that as many as 60 per cent of all additives now in use have not been subject to testing. The tests are usually undertaken on mice, rats, hamsters, rabbits, guinea pigs and monkeys.

'We do not know enough about the metabolic system involved with many of these animals, nor fully how the broken down products are absorbed or excreted. It is still a matter of gathering evidence.

'Tests undertaken via animals do not necessarily apply to humans, when the comparative human animal varies in age, sex, diet and nutritional status, and has a range of genetic peculiarities which significantly affect response to many additives.'(8.7)

It is, of course, perfectly true that many of the additives are basically harmless, especially when they represent extracts or synthetic equivalents of natural foods which we eat quite happily every day. By the same token, the safety of many other additives found in our growing number of processed or manufactured foods, remains in doubt. Even the most respected scientists violently disagree and argue for and against their use, particularly when it comes to the modern additives in the form of artificial colours and flavours added to our food.

'They are a mere cosmetic addition to replace what the process of modern food technology has destroyed. It is with these artificial flavourings and colourings that we find the area of greatest toxicological uncertainty.'(8.8)

Even if we accept the assurance of the scientists and the Ministry of Agriculture, Fisheries and Foods, that only additives which have been proven safe are allowed to be used by manufacturers, what about the accumulative effects of increased and continuous use over many years? We have already seen how the use of all additives has increased from 1.5 pounds in 1955 to 5.4 pounds per person per year in 1974, and no doubt a similar increase will occur over the next years, affecting the growing numbers and amounts of additives in our food. Consuming a meal laced with up to a dozen chemical additions may well be safe; but how safe is it to consume two or three of these meals per day, seven days a week, 365 times per year? No-one really knows. In the meantime:

'Most of the food we consume is doctored, dosed, coloured and convenienced, nearly to the point of non-recognition, and the food industry believes that

---

8.7 *Ibid.*
8.8 *Ibid.*

additives are necessary if they help sales and do not make one noticeably ill.'(8.9)

It is difficult to understand the complex matter of the increased use of additives, but this does not prevent many from being concerned, even frightened, by the obvious and increasing use of additives in our daily diet. Gastronomically, additives make no sense at all. All processed and manufactured convenience foods have a 'sameness' about them which is deplorable, and at best taste of sodium glutamate or big brother, both of which leave an unpleasant aftertaste in the mouth.

Modern food technology has taken away the highlights of a feast, as it has removed the satisfaction of a fast from modern man. Under the umbrella of modern man has begun a dietary existence which leans more and more towards the continuous feast which, because of all the additives, lack of fibre, hidden fats and sugar, and over refinement, has become an ever more doubtful feast.

The strongest concern must be the easy acceptance of all the new processed and manufactured foods by the Western catering industry in general. This was the very industry which, in more than a thousand years of history, had developed, encouraged, perfected and given a lead in a more professional way to all that is best in practical gastronomy. It developed incredible culinary skills and understanding about food; it encouraged an unsurpassed care and respect for food; it perfected the service and presentation of food in the aesthetic sense; and it always took the lead in the custom of eating which, it is feared, is now gradually being eroded and will forever be lost to the changing social and cultural make-up of European life.

It should be reiterated that there is much in modern food technology which is exciting, which is useful and which has removed much of the drudgery from everyday preparation of hundreds of meals per day in thousands upon thousands of restaurants all over Europe. This should have benefited gastronomy with even tastier and better foods, fresher foods, more balanced meals, and higher gastronomic delights. But on the whole the advances made and knowledge gained by modern technology and sciences has not aided and improved today's gastronomy.

More and more of our restaurants are becoming mere outlets for the products of modern food technology. This may be acceptable on certain levels and in certain places, but when one sees some of the most traditional hotels and restaurants becoming mere dormitories for the food manufacturing industry, one cannot help but be sad.

8.9 *Ibid.*

There was a time, not so very long ago, when mankind looked forward to the first strawberry, rhubarb, runner-bean or new potato of the season. Now modern technology provides these all the year round for our consumption. The problem is, though, that they do not taste like strawberries, rhubarb, runner-beans or new potatoes any more. Indeed, are there many of us who do remember what they taste like?

The Modern Restaurant and Technology

Imagine a beautiful sixteenth-century inn full of beams and rich in atmosphere. On entering the restaurant one is confronted with a beautiful room, carefully laid out and suitably furnished. It is the type of British country house restaurant which, until the recent past, was respected by the natives and enthused over by foreigners in particular.

One is met with a friendly smile and taken to the bar with an open log fire. The menu is chalked by hand on to a large blackboard positioned between two sixteenth-century beams, and shows an impressive list of dishes for such a small sixty seater restaurant. It lists a dozen or so starters, pâté, fried mushrooms, a mousse of smoked trout, and several home-made soups.

A selection of fish dishes includes such classics as sole *bonne femme*, haddock fillets in prawn sauce, a whole plaice stuffed with crab meat, and freshly caught Dover sole proffered in various cooking methods.

Entrées to be served are chicken Kiev, *coq au vin*, chicken *de maison*, veal *cordon bleu*, pork chops in apple and cider sauce, *boeuf bourguignon*, prime rib of beef '*au jus*', *tournedos* smothered with a rich bordelaise sauce, and others. Some six potatoes, six vegetables and six salads with more than a dozen different dressings are offered as an accompaniment to the *entrées*. Eight sweets concluded the selection, intended to titillate the palate of the diner. At first sight, the restaurant looks a real find, a gastronomic oasis in a far-away place. However, in this, as in an ever-increasing number of restaurants, nothing is what it seems.

For most of the dishes on offer are, to put it mildly, gastronomic imposters and concoctions which, like the 'home-made soup' or plastic *entrées*, were cooked some 270 miles away and probably as many days previously. They were sealed in vacuumed plastic pouches to be frozen and shipped to this quaint old English inn in boxes of a dozen or so portions, and stored in a freezer until a customer ordered a portion. At such time they are put into the microwave oven or suspended in a pan of boiling water to be heated through.

The notice on the menu board for some dishes stated: 'freshly cooked to order, allow twenty minutes'. This was not a guide to the guest as to how much time was needed by the chef to nurse the dish to perfection, with skill and much care. It was merely the manufacturer's instruction as to how long each item needed to be properly and safely reheated from its frozen state.

Meat, poultry, fish and other dishes which were once cooked fresh and to order, are now cooked in a factory and sold to restaurants whose kitchens consist of not much more than a couple of tables, two or three boiling pans, a microwave oven, and a machine which imprints a charcoal mark on a sole or steak. The mashed potato, looking so dainty in a silver vegetable dish, comes to the restaurant from a 'Taterjet', not unlike the guiding jets on a small space station, to be dispensed as '*pommes purée à la crème*' in precisely measured amounts and neatly shaped directly on to the dish. Of course, the potato is a mixture of dry powder and water, and the *à la crème* bears no relationship at all to any bovine animal which might have helped us to produce cream.

The gravy or sauces almost certainly come from a tin or packet, sometimes even frozen in single-portion pouches, laced with preserving chemicals and made with modified starch instead of flour, which will not break down in the freezing process, and will accept reheating in the microwave oven. The gravy and sauces owe nothing to any natural juices or nutrients or, indeed, flavour of any fish, flesh or fowl with which they are served. In fact, almost anything wet comes out of tins or buckets with the addition of tap water, including such classics as *jus lié*, sauce *hollandaise*, *béchamel* sauce, prawn sauce, sauce *bonne femme*. Not even the *au jus* with the prime rib of beef is spared the indignity of water and chemical powders.

The vegetables served in this restaurant are all frozen, cooked, refreshed and assembled during the morning in small earthenware dishes of one, two or three portions, seasoned and crowned with a knob of butter. They are then stored until the 'busy evening service' when they are reheated in less than 30 seconds to be served as 'a selection of fresh vegetables'. What would be easier than the cooking of fresh vegetables, but you get none of these here.

The only fresh foods to come through the back door of the restaurant are lettuce, cucumbers, tomatoes and watercress. 'The only things we have to buy daily, the rest is delivered on a weekly or monthly basis' is the proud boast of our young manager as he shows us the kitchen and storage facilities of refrigerators and enormous deep-freezers. The salads made from these fresh items are assembled during the day. Some compound salads, such as coleslaw, niçoise and Waldorf, come from gallon jars prepared by a nationally well-known company.

The '*pièce de résistance*' of the establishment is a selection of ten dressings, with which the guest could choose to have his or her salad flavoured and 'highlighted'. All these dressings are easily available, placed on a shelf at eye level for easy reach and application by the 'chef '. The selection of dressings is also supplied by a large company and are 'special' in that they are flavoured with a selection of artificial flavours, with the addition of a chemical which emulsifies the oil and vinegar so that they do not separate again. 'We don't even have to shake the bottle any more when we add the dressing to our salad' is the proud remark of the 'clever' young manager.

Some of the salads are crowned with three or four slices of hard boiled egg, cut from a stick about 12 inches long. This is the product of an American company which assures that the egg stick can be kept in a frozen state forever and, when defrosted, has a shelf life of two to three days in the refrigerator.

'The home-made, warm bread and rolls' served in individual loaves, looking very dainty on small wooden boards with special knives, have nothing to do with any home. They come from a bakery over a hundred miles away and were baked with special chemicals which assured a shelf-life of not less than six months. They will reheat well in any microwave oven and, with their specially additive-blended dough, will make the whole restaurant smell of 'fresh bread' when they are brought to the table.

The trolley holds eight varieties of desserts and cheeses, of which only the Stilton can be considered fresh. The rest of the selection consists of one factory-produced frozen cream gâteau; one frozen fruit gâteau; one frozen cheesecake; a tray of factory-made and artificially-blown meringues filled with frozen raspberries; one lemon mousse made from a packet which can be bought in any supermarket; frozen chocolate profiteroles which were supplied frozen in a plastic pouch (seven per portion); a 'compote of fruits' presented in a beautiful crystal bowl but which has clearly come from a tin; and a 'fresh fruit salad' which was made from a fruit mixture which had also seen the inside of a tin and to which a few pieces of apple, banana and grapes had been added to make it 'fresh'.

As we take our leave of this modern restaurant, we are told that nine similar restaurants have been opened by the company and more were planned when the economic climate improved. One wonders why, on a Friday evening when most restaurants are usually very busy, this one has only a table of three and two tables of two people at 8.30 pm partaking in its gastronomic delights. Are we beginning to see through the charade? I can only hope so.

Throughout the history of food and eating, attempts have been made to falsify or adulterate man's most basic need. In the past flour has been sold which was mixed with chalk; bread has been underweight; meat sold from an animal which died of a disease; milk or beer has been watered down; wine sold which bore no relation to the region from which it was supposed to come or the year in which it was produced; tea and coffee sold after the leaves or grounds had been used; lemon sole has been served as Dover sole; and frozen Canadian salmon has been sold for the price of Scottish fresh salmon. There will always be someone who, for want of professional integrity or concern for the reputation of their establishment, or for 'a fast buck', will try to deceive us. But with the aid of modern technology, exemplified in the working of the above restaurant, opportunities for dishonesty and deceit have never been better. Indeed this now seems part of the training of modern hotel and restaurant managers.

It would be only slightly less deceitful if the management of this type of restaurant stated openly what sort of produce was being offered, and showed the courage of their conviction in having something new and worthwhile to offer and sell. This would enable the members of the public to make up their own minds as to whether they wished to participate in the wonders of modern food technology and, indeed, in their own deception.

The management of this type of restaurant is not that confident, nor could it be that truthful, lest the customers discover that the food is not fresh, not cooked on the premises, and available in tins, packets, bottles, jars and frozen pouches in any supermarket at a fraction of the price charged in the restaurant.

Instead, such establishments identify themselves with an old, established gastronomic tradition not worthy of their product. They sell their wares under long-established and well-respected culinary language and terms which have taken many chefs down the centuries much toil, tears and sweat to devise, create and perfect.

During the last year of the First World War, French and German troops were engaged in one of their many devastating and deadly artillery barrages. During a lull in the exchange of shells, a French officer and his aide approached the German lines under a white flag. The commanding officer gave the order to stop shooting and, with his aide, met the French officer half way between the lines. They talked for what seemed to be a long thirty minutes, then bowed and saluted before they returned to the protection of their positions. Almost at once the French and German officers gave the command to reposition their guns and the battle resumed in a more south-westerly position. The French officer, Emil Cherrier, had approached the German lines to explain to his opposite number that the guns of his battery were not harming his troops much, but were devastating one of the best vineyards in the Marne district, which for more than two hundred years had produced a wine which was much valued in the making of a world-famous champagne.

The villagers had asked if the German officer could be persuaded to train his battery of guns away from the famous vineyard. The French officer was fortunate in finding in the German officer a man who was himself a wine grower and who greatly appreciated the reputation and gastronomic value of the champagne, the vineyard of which should certainly not be destroyed.

Even though they themselves might perish in this bloody and useless war, the famous vineyard should be saved and some good, something of value, should survive the carnage in which they were engaged.

Contrast this marvellous story with the result of applying science and technology in the form of ethylene glycol to Austrian wine in 1983 and 1984, most of which will, for a long time, be unable to grace our tables. Or the food served in our restaurant of technology described earlier. This alone should be reason enough to be wary of at least some aspects of modern technology applied to our food and drink.

Figure 8.2 Early chefs in now famous uniform
Source: The Even Giant Swipe File, The Hart Publishing Inc. 1978

Gastronomy and the Arts

'Art and sciences are both uniquely human actions, outside the range that any animal can do. They derive from the human faculty to look back and visualise the future, to foresee what may happen and to plan and to anticipate.'(8.10)

'Great civilisations or nations write their autobiographies in three manuscripts:
in the book of deeds,
in the book of words,
in the book of arts.
Not one of these books can be really understood unless we read the two others. But of the three the only trustworthy one, is that of the arts.'
(Ruskin John 1819–1900).(8.11)

Paintings and Gastronomy

In the caves of Altamira in Spain, and also in the caves of Lascaux in southern France, cave paintings are found which are estimated to be twenty thousand years old. All over these caves, in the form of these remarkable paintings, we find the hand of prehistoric European man saying:

'This is man. I have been here, this is my mark, my record.' But this pictorial evidence of early European man says much more. His paintings convey not only his presence, but also give us a record of what he thought important enough to tell us about. For his efforts do not record a flower, a loved child, an important elder of the tribe; they record the hunt with spear, the communal and social aspects of the hunt, which alone killed the bull or the deer, and which assured his food, and with it, his life'.(8.12)

Throughout history, the subject of food occurs again and again as one which gives life, pleasure and the joy of sharing, which artists throughout the ages wished to convey and felt worthy of recording. The first illustrations were simple black and white drawings. But as colouring materials were found and their use understood, the paintings incorporated colour, and some representing harvests,

8.10 Bronowski, J., *The Ascent of Man*, 4th edn, Futura, London, 1981, p. 33.
8.11 As quoted by Kenneth Clarke in *Civilisation*, BBC and John Murray, London, 1969, p. 1.
8.12 Bronowski, J., *The Ascent of Man*, 4th edn, Futura, London, 1981, p. 33.

food and eating, became recognised masterpieces of their time.

Some of these drawings or paintings are often simple recordings of what was available. Others, such as those in the caves of Spain and France, represent the hunt, the preparation, the cooking, the dish or the meal. Others represent the sociable sharing of a meal, be it in the fields, around the simple farmhouse table, the rich merchant's table, or the gathering of large tables in the great castles or palaces, hosted by the prince or king. Some represent the dignity of work on the field for food, the thanks to God for a good harvest, or the joy of sharing with others at table.

Others, such as Van Gogh's *The Potato Eaters*, clearly convey social conditions and the hardships of the time. Others again, like the unsurpassable murals and ceiling paintings in the hall of the palace of Augsburg, show the success of the shipping traders and the food they brought to Europe from the four corners of the earth.

Food has been painted on stone, clay, wood, parchment, canvas, paper, walls, ceilings and even floors. Greek vases, pans, pots, bowls and drinking cups were graced with detailed paintings, conveying to us what life was like (at least for some). Down the ages art has reflected a developing appreciation of food and eating, which became gastronomy.

Figure 8.3 Early metal smith and pot maker
Source: The Even Giant Swipe File, The Hart Publishing Inc. 1978

Figure 8.4 Early woodworker
Source: The Even Giant Swipe File, The Hart Publishing Inc. 1978

The Crafts and Gastronomy

Some time in the age of Pompeii, crafts and art combined, resulting in all manner of tableware and kitchenware, from simple yet highly decorated pottery, china to silver and gold, all shaped, formed and fashioned to be both useful and beautiful. This is an interest which has lasted to this day, and which may be seen in the gold plates and cutlery which are used on special occasions in palaces and banqueting halls all over the world. The combination of craft and art is apparent in the selection of highly decorated silver used in large banquets in first-class hotels, or the presentation of the highly valued regimental silver trophies, brought out of the safe on special occasions for formal dinners. Art, craft and food have always been combined at the table and represent a valuable aspect of service for gastronomy.

Figure 8.5 Early fisherman
Source: The Even Giant Swipe File, The Hart Publishing Inc. 1978

The Art of Eating

It has been seen how gastronomy, within the confinement of existing gastro-geography, has developed into the unifying subject it is today. Gastronomy, which was always based on need, has become an art which requires both skilled practitioners as well as skilled appreciators.

Good gastronomic practice or appreciation does not rely on the most expensive of foods, the most elaborate of meals, nor the highest of gastronomic occasions. Good gastronomy is represented in a simple piece of bread, an apple, a piece of cheese – as long as the bread is fresh and crusty, the apple ripe and juicy, and the cheese well matured and full of flavour – to which a glass of good wine would add perfection. If we can then share this simple meal with our family, some friends or even strangers, who with some pleasant conversation share our delight in what we eat, we have the perfect, if simple, gastronomic occasion.

Of course, gastronomy is much more than that, and indeed in many ways has become much more by our invidious and personal interest in food and eating. We may have reason to remember the last, or maybe just one, great gastronomic occasion: a perfect meal at home, with everything just right, in our favourite restaurant, or in the splendour of a large banquet hall, laid out with an array of long tables, glittering with a selection of glasses, one for each wine to be served, the finest of china, the best of silver cutlery, flickering lights on elaborate sculptured candelabra, and the sweet smell of a colourful arrangement of flowers. Add to this the background music of a chamber orchestra, the assembling of more and more guests and the anticipation of what is to come. We glimpse the sequence of courses from the menu, all waiting with their various odours, flavours, colours, textures, tastes and perfect presentation. All of this is paired with good wine to raise our spirits and the occasion, a talk with an old friend, the making of new ones once seated next to you, and hopefully some interesting conversation, and we have a grand gastronomic occasion.

Yet all of this is based on the thoughts and skills which man has developed and given to his most basic need over the last ten thousand years. Women and men laboured hard, cared much and improved considerably their master's food, their children's food and the family's well-being. In so doing, they developed and

Figure 8.6 Early bakers
Source: The Even Giant Swipe File, The Hart Publishing Inc. 1978

perfected all culinary skills and cares which we still apply today. Gradually, at different times and in different places, as various crafts of settled man evolved, establishing the butcher, the baker and the candlestick maker, men gradually found it worthwhile to take an interest in what was hitherto women's work – the preparation and cooking of food. The professional male cook or chef was needed to prepare meals, not just for the few in the family, but on a large scale to satisfy the needs of the people high and low in the towns, castles and châteaux of Europe.

By the motto 'practice makes perfect', these men and women gradually imposed new ideas and new combinations on the same basic foods. They handed down what they had learned, passing on to sons and daughters their knowledge and the culinary skills and arts of the day.

On this the following generation built, improved and perfected. They developed the understanding of the dissection and identification of cuts of flesh, fish and fowl, selecting those which were best suited to given evolving methods of cooking. As the second step in compositional cookery, they had a hand in the development and use of different types of cooking vessels of various materials, shapes and sizes. Being reliant on only some limited basic foods during the seasons of the year, they varied the method of cooking to vary the presentation of staple foods.

Figure 8.7 Bread for sale, the baker's family
Source: The Even Giant Swipe File, The Hart Publishing Inc. 1978

This consideration for variation on a basic theme is one of the artistic features of gastronomy. *Le Répertoire de la Cuisine* lists 47 ways of presenting lobster; 48 ways of presenting salmon; and 283 ways of presenting sole. The *Dictionary of the Kitchen*, edited by Walter Bickle, and one of Europe's most highly regarded reference books on culinary methods and gastronomy, lists 700 *hors-d'oeuvres*; 1,430 soups; 1,183 egg dishes; 2,231 fish dishes; 580 sauces; 4,868 meat dishes, and 1,570 vegetable and pasta dishes.

These dishes are to be enjoyed, hopefully, by *all* our 'senses': the senses of sight, smell, sound, taste, belonging, caring, and living. This is why gastronomy is indeed justifiably called 'the consuming art'.

Gastronomy and Literature

From the day man began to eat his food not just by instinct, but with appreciation, he developed a need to pass on culinary knowledge and skills. At first this came about when a slave passed on his techniques to another slave, when a mother taught her daughter, or a grandmother taught her grand-daughter. When eventually men became interested in all types of food preparation and presentation, the knowledge and skills of the father were passed on to the son, who, until quite recently in European history, took over from the father the knowledge, skills, trade and business. Even in the modern hospitality industry, we can still find butchers and bakers, as well as hotels and restaurants, which have been in existence for many hundreds of years, the knowledge, expertise and proud technical skills being passed on from one generation to another. Indeed, some people believe that this has been the key to their undoubted continuing success. And it has in no small way contributed to the survival of the culinary and gastronomic expertise and customs of Europe throughout the ages.

If practising gastronomy is one way in which gastronomic practices have survived, the second way for survival is through the interest and patronage of the rich and powerful, who had the money, the education and the leisure time to enjoy and encourage it. Education, particularly the ability to write, is important here, for only the rich had the time or the ability to write their many culinary and gastronmic experiences down, comment upon them, and record them for the future. Of course, we find some distortion here, a hiatus between the real knowing and practising gastronomers, often unable to write, and the more appreciating gastronomers who were able to write, but writing more for reasons of appreciation than factual knowledge. This is why so much of early surviving gastronomical writings are more often than not devoid of all technical data, method of preparation, mode of cooking and/or recipes, including weights and measures. Only when it came to presentation did the appreciative writing gastronomers come into their own.

For the culinary historian these somewhat superficial recordings of gastronomic experiences are nevertheless fascinating and tell us much about early man's food, eating, table etiquette and customs, even if they do convey to us some of the excesses and waste at the table of old, which would be unacceptable to the modern gastronome.

With a few exceptions, the period between the recordings of Athenaeus and that of the Renaissance, as far as gastronomic writing is concerned, is very much less blessed with valuable information concerning the subject at hand. The silent centuries, as I have suggested earlier, were for the most part devoid of useful culinary or gastronomic recordings. For these centuries were possibly more concerned with reappraisal and consolidation in what was a whole new and different world.

The next relevant recorded contribution in this field must be that of Erasmus of Rotterdam, who in 1530, with *De Civitate Morum Puerilum*, gave us some of the best considered writing on the prevailing knowledge of food, food preparation, table custom, table manners and basic culinary practices. The Church and its priests all over Europe gave much new impetus to the teachings of new agricultural practices, the storage and preparation of foods, including modern culinary practices. These reached all stratas of society in a revitalising and more relaxed and confident Europe. With the printing press now in more common use, we gradually find more precise culinary knowledge and usable recipes in booklets or books. For example, Sacchi Bartomolomea de Platina's *De Honesta Voluptate*, published in Venice in 1475 and written by the Vatican's librarian, is considered to be the first-ever printed cook book of modern Europe. Many others followed in the various languages of Europe. A typical example of such a book in English is *The Accomplished Gentlewoman's Companion*. This is thought to have been first published in 1684, with the seventeenth edition being published in 1766.

Since that time, many thousands of books have been published on gastronomy, concerning such subjects as food, cookery, household medicine, wine and wine making, famous hotels or restaurants of a given European country, eating customs, table manners, table or general etiquette, and even table talk and after-dinner speeches. All are valuable aspects of gastronomy, but only aspects, not the full spectrum of what today might be considered gastronomy.

Sometime later, as inns and restaurants with accommodation became more widely known and used in Europe, titles with the word 'gastronomy' included were published. They concerned themselves with the management of establishments, and how gastronomy should be approached, considered and managed 'for the benefit of the hosts as well as to give the best of service and culinary delight to the paying guests'.

The following extracts illustrate man's wide interest in 'the consuming art' as found in the writings of some of Europe's famous authors.

François Rabelais (1495–1553)

Rabelais began his adult life as a monk, but later studied medicine and became a doctor. During the Reformation he had a most difficult time because of his liberal views. He began to write books which combined cruel realism and comedy, mixed with scientific knowledge. His most famous book, a novel on a folk tale about a giant called Gargantua (1534) with an insatiable appetite for food, and his Pantagruel (1532) are read all over the world. The latter gives us a long list of foods of Rabelais' times, and the eating customs. We have first mention of the turkey as a new food to roast in Europe, and he makes much of the crane as one of his favourite fowl, not considered suitable at all for the table today. Gargantua used to be a gastronomic term referring to large and long banquets with many courses or drinks, where quantity rather than quality were important.

The small, beautiful town of Chinon in France still has a hotel with that name where a very large omelette *à la Gargantua*, is served today, sufficient for four to six persons. It is often ordered for families. Garganuelle, the mother of Gargantua, has given her name to a special soup, still found in some older cookery books.

Molière (Jean Baptiste Poquelion) (1622–73)

Molière loved his food and wine, and took great pleasure in all that the Paris restaurants of his day had to offer. Later in life, possibly because of some gourmandic excesses of youth, he regretted his overeating, for one of his characters says the now famous lines: 'We should eat to live and not live to eat' (*l'Avare* (*The Miser*), 1669).

This quotation from Molière is not original as it is based on the writing of Socrates, who wrote: 'the bad man lives to eat and the good man eats to live'. In the same play by Molière, we have an interesting conversation between Harpagon and his wasteful chef, Jacques, who is asked to prepare a special meal which Jacques insists should be composed of not less than 'four rich and plentiful soups, a lobster soup, a guinea-fowl soup, a fresh vegetable soup, and one composed from duck and parsnips'. These were to be followed by a *fricassee* of chicken, and a crusty pie filled with wild pigeons, veal sweetbreads and a black pudding served with wild mushrooms. The *pièce de résistance* of the meal, so Jacques suggested, would consist of a large joint of roast veal surrounded by fat poulardes, twelve young doves, six roast pheasants, as well as a dozen each of quails and ortolans cooked to perfection. As the dinner was for less than a dozen guests, one may be sympathetic with Harpagon's utterance that his chef was wasteful and would ruin both his health and economy. Later versions, in French and other languages, omit these culinary details of gastronomic custom of the times. The only thing Harpagon is allowed to utter is that 'the wasteful skills of Jacques and the appetite of his guests will eat him out of home and income'.

Jonathan Swift (1667–1745)

Swift was orphaned at a very early age and had a most difficult childhood, being reliant for his upbringing and support on distant relations which, as he put it mildly, was not the best and did little for his self-esteem. This was most likely the reason for his often bitter, but most certainly strong, satirical writings.

Swift is best known for his book *Gulliver's Travels* (1726), which has delighted children all over the world. This delight, however, is based on a very much shortened version of the book which omits some frightening details concerning the social ills of his day, in particular, his concern for the ills of Ireland. Years after he became well known, Swift suggested, in bitter irony, that the best way to help Ireland's permanent need and hunger was to eat the children of Ireland, the only thing Ireland has in abundance.

'I have been assured by an American friend, that a fresh, well-fed, one-year-old child is the best, most delicate and valuable food man can eat. It can be fried, roasted and boiled, and this being so I have no doubt that a fricassée of a suckling-child or a ragoût would be superb. Children are available all the year round, which cannot be said for most foods in this God-forsaken country, and they are particularly plentiful in March and April when food is very short. This is the case, I have been assured by a French doctor, because the fish in our Summer diet aids conception and that is why so many children are born nine months or so after Lent.'(8.13)

In this most famous book, Swift shows a considerable respect for and, indeed,

8.13 As quoted by Tuneberger, P., *Böckernas Mat* (Food and Artists), Bra–Böcker, Stockholm, 1980, pp. 126–127.

knowledge of food and the culinary arts of his day. His description of Gulliver being fed by three hundred cooks in the land of Lilliput gives a long list of food and dishes and comments upon these, which not only represented the food and dishes which Swift ate, but also showed considerable gastronomic understanding and regard for what is good. Nor does Swift hide his obvious and strongly felt indignation of the social ills and the contrast between rich and poor, and he uses food as a metaphor to expose them: 'The rich enjoy the fruits of the hard working and frightened poor in servitude' represents Gulliver in the land of Lilliput. As his travels continue into the land of the Giants, who, unlike the Lilliputians, are not scared but make Gulliver afraid for his life, it is thought that Swift wished to show the contrasts between both groups – between the 'haves and have nots'.

Samuel Johnson (1709–84)

Dr Johnson loved his food and drink; besides hard work he found nothing more enjoyable than a visit to a good tavern. He was a most welcome visitor to the table of many of his friends, because of his appreciation of a good table and the intelligence and wit of his dinner conversations. Almost daily he visited the now famous Cheshire Cheese tavern not far from his home. Many of Dr Johnson's comments and sayings about food are now very much part of the English language. He clearly looked upon good food and company with great delight, and his not inconsiderable wit is represented in many of his sayings in respect of gastronomy, such as, 'It means not much how people die, it is how they live which is important.' When walking with a friend across one of London's many markets, full of flowers, he was asked which flowers he liked best. 'The cauliflower' was his quick answer.

Clever, maybe, but it says a lot of the man, who coloured English life and language so much during, and even after, his lifetime. Boswell's *Life of Dr Johnson* is a treasure trove of the daily life of Johnson, as it is a book which shows considerable interest in good food and good living.

Honoré de Balzac (1790–1850)

This famous French novelist showed a considerable interest in good food and many of his seventy-five or so novels are strewn with gastronomic references and details, which only a lover of good food could have written. At times, it is true, he seems to be more of a gourmand than a gourmet, when he recollects a dinner in which he ate 100 Ostend oysters, a dozen lamb cutlets and half a duck stuffed with onions and parsnips. These were followed by a sole, a pheasant, and other accompanying side dishes. Even if we allow that people ate more, and worked much harder, and were not so figure conscious as we are today, it must still have been, even for his time, a somewhat excessive feast. He used many of his characters to express his love for and attitude to food. In *La Rabouillence*, his character of Dr Pouquet says: 'A man does well to make himself familiar early in his life, with the study delights and tribulation of culinary chemistry.'

Another character, Madame de Passiers, in *Le Cabinet des Antiques*, expresses that she despises any dinner with more than six participants, for one could not give due attention to either the food on the table or the valuable table-conversation such a dinner required.

In his *The Human Comedy*, Balzac gives a long and most varied list of the best restaurants of his day and the dishes they served. He gives eloquent descriptions of some of the lady cooks he encountered, and the food he enjoyed in the homes of some of his friends. Sophie, the cook of the Count of Popinot, was the subject of much of his culinary praise. Popinot, in *Cousine Pons*, he called a worker of wonders when it came to the delights of her food: 'She prepares the most unforgettable sauce I have ever eaten in my life.' 'Giving praise where it was due was the least a man could do when it came to good food, even if he cannot always pay.'

In *Le Petit Bourgeois* he condemns a dreadful dinner 'consisting of a selection of meat which was not cooked long enough, it seems for the only reason that more portions than is decent could be carved from the insulted joint'. His house at 47 Rue Raynouard, Paris, is now a much visited museum, which shows the original surroundings in which he lived, in which a large and well-equipped kitchen played an important role.

Jean Anthelme Brillat-Savarin (1755–1826)

A French magistrate, politician and gastronome, Brillat-Savarin is probably the most famous writer on gastronomy of modern European times. He started his career as a lawyer at the Court of Belly, became deputy of the National Assembly in 1789, was made a major and commander of the National Guard of Belly in 1793, was banished under the Reign of Terror, fled to Switzerland, and lived for some three years in America. He returned to France in September 1797, and some two years later he became the commissioner with executive powers at the court of the department Seine et Oise and a member of the supreme court.

He published various pamphlets on economy, politics and law, but these works, although valuable at the time, would not have made him famous. What kept his name from oblivion was the publication of his most famous book *La Physiologie du Goût*, which has been translated to every civilised language in the world and is best known in England under the titles *The Pyschology of Taste* and *The Philosopher in the Kitchen.*

Brillat-Savarin worked on his book all his life and published it about a year before his death, never to know what fame and high gastronomic reputation it would bring him.

Considered by some to be somewhat out of date today, the book is still periodically published. It is thought that there is, as yet, no other publication which concerns itself in such detail with the subject of gastronomy. Brillat-Savarin wrote with quiet authority, both as a gastronomic practitioner and as a well-informed and experienced appreciator of gastronomy in the widest sense. He had no doubt about the aesthetic, cultural and social value of a sensible gastronomic life, and although he loved his food, he never became a gourmand. Indeed, it was Brillat-Savarin who said that a good gastronome would leave the table still hungry. He was the first writer who saw the importance of good supply, the best preparation, the choosing of selected wines, the most pleasing presentation at the table, and appreciative friends to share God's gift of food, as the hallmarks of gastronomy. His many quotations regarding food and eating are still the best, and show only too well the care and thought he gave to the subject. In places his writings read almost like a prayer and most certainly show a very high respect for man's most basic need, as well as for the endeavours man has applied to this need to make it an art.

Alexander Dumas (1802–70)

Dumas was, like so many of his time, more of a gourmand than a gastronome. His knowledge of food was vast, and the description of meals consumed, as expressed in his writings, shows a considerable expertise in matters of the table. His record of breakfast at the *Bastion La Rochelle*, the food eaten and referred to in *The Three Musketeers* and the detailed description of a veal roast in *Joseph Balsano*, confirm his most informative gastronomic awareness. When, for a while, his books did not sell so well, he gave his attention to his second love, food, and he wrote his now famous *Le Grand Dictionnaire de la Cuisine*, which was published shortly after his death in 1870. It is not much of a cookery book, but it does give considerable insight into the culinary teachings, attitudes and eating customs of his time. The dictionary gives some information both for the kitchen and the dining table. His recipes are impressive but must be followed with caution, which may be indicative that he was a better appreciator than a practitioner of the gastronomic arts.

Charles Dickens (1812–70)

Dickens was or still is probably the most widely read novelist, storyteller and social critic of his time, and children all over the world today find pleasure in his books. He knew the value of food and used it to tell of the evils of his day. Whether in *A Christmas Carol* (1843), *Oliver Twist* (1837), *Martin Chuzzlewit* (1843) or *The Pickwick Papers* (1836), and any others of his stories, Dickens shows that he had a considerable culinary and gastronomic understanding and regard for man's most basic need. His *Christmas Carol* (1843) shows most touchingly the value of food and a meal shared.

Mr Pickwick's delight in a well-cooked meal is thought to have been very much Dickens' own delight in the gastronomic offering of his day. The spectacle of the controllers of the poorhouse consuming a big, delicious meal, when the boys were fed on gruel, says much for Dickens' social conscience and outrage. Oliver's plea of 'I want some more, Sir, please', is a cry which is understood by every child and every parent in the world.

William Thackeray (1811–67)

In his famous book, *Vanity Fair*, Thackeray shows an excellent culinary knowledge, in particular, the *etiquette sur la table à l'Anglaise*, and he uses this very well to expose some of the prevailing vanity which can become part of gastronomy. He gives us an excellent picture of the gastronomic customs and language of the England of his day.

However, in his very funny book, *The Snobs of England by One of Themselves* (1846), Thackeray is particularly telling when he makes fun of the nouveau-gastronome which, of course, can only be done really well if one has both a good knowledge of food and wine and the prevailing customs associated with their consumption. He expresses very well the different attitudes to food and eating between the sexes, as well as between adults and children. He highlights the very British custom of the separation of sexes after dinner – for the gentlemen to partake of port, to smoke and to talk about business, politics, agriculture and, particularly, horses, while the ladies withdraw to the salon to drink coffee and to discuss their children's illnesses and the problems with the servants.

Thackeray must have clearly observed and smiled at many a gastronomic snob, able to do so only because he himself had a sound knowledge of the gastronomy of the day, as his *Ballade of the Bouillabaise* (1851) shows.

Anton Chekhov (1860–1904)

Although a doctor of medicine, Chekhov made his name as a writer of plays, which are still very much part of the repertoire of any self-respecting European theatre. His plays show again a considerable interest in the delights of the table of his time, as they are most precise when it comes to social and gastronomic etiquette, and the eating customs of Russia. In his novel, *The Lady and the Dog* (1887), luncheon meetings between Dimitrius Gurov and Anna give us the most detailed observation on food, the mode of eating of the time, and the popular wines of the day. Even the *etiquette sur la table* between the lovers is strictly and properly observed, and gives a wealth of useful social as well as gastronomic information for any historian.

In his novel, *The Duel* (1894), the various love stories are intermingled with much culinary and gastronomic details, such as in 'The Happy Inn', where emotions are displayed among the cabbage soups, pigeon, pancakes with sour cream, blinis with caviar, baked river trout, spicy fish stews, and hot tea from hot samovars. The meals of the poorer soldiers and their young ladies, are eaten *al fresco*, and are picturesque with typical Russian fare and wines, during a typical, hot, Russian summer. Chekhov's writings are delightful, both in respect of the food consumed and the occasions experienced. Not surprisingly, then, that the young soldiers call their simple picnic 'our *table d'hôte* under the sky, where God is our host'.

Thomas Mann (1875–1955)

It was the famous German author, Thomas Mann, who said that German literature and German cookery were the best in the world until 1933, when both left Germany and have not yet returned, and may never do so. When a good literary friend replied:

> 'My *dear Thomas, I am very much in agreement with you, that we have much reason to be proud of our literature through the ages, [but] I cannot agree that German cookery is the best in the world.*

With a surprised look on his face, Thomas Mann replied:

'My good friend, I did not mean it all that way, what I meant to say was that no other country in the world has understood it so well, to select and compile a vast variety of dishes as the German chef.

'The French chef is rightly proud of his cuisine, and so is the Italian, but they want only to serve their very own national or regional dishes and very little else. But the German chef offers a list of dishes on his menu, seldom achieved by any other country. He has understood to add to his vast variety of German national and regional dishes, all the best of French, Italian, Russian, Hungarian, Polish and Scandinavian dishes so well that many find it difficult today to know which are true German dishes and which are not'.

Mann came from a very upper-class German family in Hamburg. His most famous novel, the *Buddenbrook* (1901), describes in considerable detail the Saturday night dinners and Sunday lunches. One reads here not of the flamboyant romance of the pleasures of the table, as a French or Italian author would write, but more the puritanical, Protestant table etiquette correctly, and somewhat stiffly, observed. In his class, one knew how to behave at the table. The eldest lady was always served first, then the eldest gentleman at the table, whether family or guest, and so it went on down the line, and when age had been respected, the guest would be given preference of service before family.

As the host carved or served each course, the servant girl would place it in front of the guest with a slight curtsy. Stiff, maybe, but in the description of his meal Mann gives a long list of favourite dishes of the time, reflecting a wide variety of foods, dishes and modes of service as befitting one of the best international families of Northern Europe. Again and again Mann uses food, attitudes to food and dishes, and behaviour at the table as a way to assess the character and most certainly the class of a person, and no-one, not even a guest, would leave the table without having eaten all that was offered. To waste food was disrespectful to the hard work taken to prepare it, as it was disrespectful to God, who had blessed the family with it.

Richard Llewellyn (1907–83)

In his most famous book, *How Green Was My Valley* (1939), Llewellyn gives a most precise and colourful description of food and eating customs in a mining village of Wales earlier this century. He tells of the way the miners walked home on a Saturday, covered in the black coal-dust, with only the eyes showing white, and only the lips and mouth bearing some resemblance to human skin. How, with their pockets full of coins, laughing, joking and singing, they felt rich. They placed their hard-earned money in the big blue apron of their wife or mother, who sat outside the house waiting for them.

> *'Mother had often as many as thirty or forty sovereigns in her pocket, with her husband and sons working, but also to feed during the long, hard week in the mines.'*

With their hearts full of song, they came home to the big, good meal of the week, which, when mother, father and five sons sat down, almost reads like the Last Supper. The grace was said and thanks were given to God for their blessings, for the food, and for Sunday, their day of rest, and the simple worship of God in home and chapel. The whole description of the scene conveys much of what is best in man, in respect of food and eating, as it shows that most important part of gastronomy – man's need, man's respect and man's thanks for his daily bread.

BIBLIOGRAPHY

ANDERSON, R.T.: *Traditional Europe: A Study in Anthropology and History*, Belmont, Ca Wadsworth, 1971.
ARCHAMBOULT, R.D.: *Philosophical Analysis and Education*, Routledge & Kegan Paul, London, 1965.
ARNOTT, M.L. (ed): *A Gastronomy: The Anthropology of Food and Food Habits*, The Hague, Mouton, 1975.
ASHLEY, Sir W.: *The Breed of Our Forefathers*, Clarendon Press, Oxford, 1928.
BACHMANN, W.: *Professional Knowledge, 'The Art of Cookery for the Hotel Restaurant and Catering Trade'*, Walter Bachman, London, 1952.
BAILEY, A.: *The Blessing of Bread*, Paddington Press, New York, 1975.
BAPCOCK GORE, P.: *The American Webster Dictionary*, G. Bell & Sons, London, 1961.
BARTHES, R.: *Towards a Psychosociology of Contemporary Food Consumption*, in Forster and Forster, John Hopkins University Press, Baltimore & London, 1975.
BARRACLOUGH, G. (ed): *Eastern and Western Europe in the Middle Ages*. Thames & Hudson, London, 1970.
BATES, H.W.: *The River Amazon*, Vol. 2, The Naturalist, London, 1863.
BELFORT-BAX, E.: *German Society at the Close of the Middle Ages*, The Social Side of The Reformation, Vol. 1, Swan Sonnenschein Co. London, 1894.
BENNETT, H.-S.: *Life on the English Manor: A Study of Peasant Conditions 1150–1400*, Cambridge University Press, Cambridge, 1937.
BODE, W. and J. LETO: *Classical Food Preparation and Presentation*, Batsford, London, 1984.
BOSWELL, J: *A Life of Johnson*, Oxford University Press, 1970.
BOWDEN, G.H.: *British Gastronomy: The Rise of Great Restaurants*, Chatto & Windus, London, 1975.
BRAYBROOKE, Lord, (ed): *Memoirs of Samuel Pepys 1659–69*, with particular reference to October 1660. H. Colburn, London, 1825.
BRIDBURY, C.R.: *England and the Salt Trade in the Later Middle Ages*, Clarendon Press, Oxford, 1955.
BRILLAT-SAVARIN, J.A.: *The Philosopher in the Kitchen* or *The Psychology of Taste*, translated by Ann Drayton, Penguin Books, 1970.
BRONOWSKI, J.: *The Ascent of Man*, fourth edn, Futura Edition, London, 1981.
BROTHWELL, D. and P.: *Food and Antiquity: A Survey of Diet of Early People*, Thames & Hudson, London, 1969.
BUNYARD, E.A. and L.: *The Epicure's Companion*, Dent, London, 1937.
BURGESS, A. and R. DEAN (eds): *Malnutrition and Food Habits*, Tavistock Publications, London, 1962.
CAMBELL-SMITH, G.: *The Marketing of a Meal Experience: A Fundamental Approach*, University of Surrey Press, 1967.
CAMPBELL, A.G. BERG et al: *Det Glada Sverige (The Happy Sweden): Nature and Culture*, Bonnier, Stockholm, 1942.
CANNON, P.: *Homostasis: A Regulator in Nutritional Needs*, Edited by L.L. Lamgley, Dowdern, Hutchinson & Ross, Stroudsberg, 1973.
CARCOPINO, J.: *The Daily Life in Ancient Rome, the People and the City, at the Height of the Empire*, Yale University Press, Newhaven, 1941.
CARLETTI, P.: *Ragionamenti – 1594–1600* translated as *My Voyage Around the World* by Weinstock, H., Methuen & Co., London, 1965.
CARLSON, E.P.: *The Food Habits and Nutrition of Refugees who have been Resettled in the UK*, University of Surrey, PhD Thesis, 1983.
CHANG, K.C.: *Food in Chinese Culture*, Yale University Press, Newhaven, 1977.
COLES, J.M. and E.S. HIGGS: *The Archaeology of Early Man*, Faber & Faber, London, 1969.
COON, C.S.: *The History of Man: From the First Human to Primitive Culture and Beyond*, Jonathan Cape, London, 1955.
CORNFELD, G.: *Pictorial Biblical Encyclopaedia*, Macmillan, New York, 1964.
CRACKNELL, H.C. and G. NOBIS: *Practical Professional Gastronomy*, Macmillan, London, 1985.
DARBY, W. et al: *Food, the Gift of Osiris*, Academic Press, New York, 1977.

DAUMAS, M.: *Histoire Générale des Techniques*, 3 vols., Paris, 1962–69 Presses Universitaire.
DERRY, T. and A. WILLIAMS: *A Short History of Technology from Earliest Times to 1900*, University Press, Oxford, 1960.
DICHTER, E.: *Handbook of Consumer Motivation: The Psychology of the World of Objects*, McGraw-Hill, New York and London, 1964.
DRAYTON, A.: Translator of Brillat-Savarin's *The Philosopher in the Kitchen*, Penguin Books, London, 1970.
DUBY, G. and R. MANDRON: *A History of French Civilisation*, Weidenfeld and Nicolson, London, 1965.
EDWARDES, M.: *East West Passage – The Travel of Ideas: Arts and Inventions between Asia and the Western World*, Cassell, London, 1971.
EJDESTAM, J.: *Samling Kring Bordet (Congregating Around the Table)*, Raben and Sjögren, Stockholm, 1975.
——: *Gastronomic Kalender (Gastronomic Almanac)*, Bonnier, Stockholm, 1961.
——: *De Fattigas Sverige (The Sweden of the Poor)*, Bonnier, Stockholm, 1969.
ELLIOTT, R.K.: *The Critic and Lover of Art*, in 'Linguistic Analysis and Phenomenology', Brown and Mays (eds), Macmillan, London, 1972.
EMERY, W.B.: *Archaic Egypt*, Penguin, London, 1961.
EVANS-PRIHARD, E.E.: *Newer Religion*, Oxford University Press, Oxford, 1956.
EVELYN, J.: *Diary, May 10th 1637*, as quoted in Tannahill, R., Palladin, London, 1975.
FILBY, F.A.: *A History of Food Adulteration and Analysis*, Allen & Unwin, London, 1934.
FIRTH, R.: *Food Symbolism in Pre-Industrial Society, Symbols, Public and Private*, Cornell University Press, Ithaca, New York State, 1973.
FLANNERY, K.V.: in Ucko and Dimbleby (eds) *The Domestication and Exploitation of Plants and Animals*, Gerald Dunckworth & Co., London, 1969.
FORBES, R.J.: *Studies in Ancient Technology*, E.J. Brill, 6 vols., Leiden, 1955–58.
FORSTER, E. and R. FORSTER: *European Diet from Pre-Industrial to Modern Times*, Harper & Row, New York, 1975.
FORSTER, R. and R. FORSTER: *Food and Drink in History, a Selection from the Annals, Economies, Societies, Civilisations*, Vol. 5, translated by Forster, E. and Ranum, P., John Hopkins University Press, Baltimore & London, 1979.
FREEMAN, M.: *'Sung'* in Chang, Yale University Press, 1977.
GALTON, F.: *The Art of Travel*, London, 1860.
GOODY, J.: *Cookery, Cuisine and Class: A Study in Comparative Sociology*, Cambridge University Press, 1982.
GRANT, A. (ed): *Einhard Eginhard, (The Kings Classics) The Early Years of Charlemagne*, Alexander Moring, London, 1907.
GRAS, N.S.B.: *The Economic and Social History of an English Village*, Harvard University Press, Cambridge, Mass., 1930.
GULICK, C.B.: *Athenaeus, The Deipnosophis*, Vols. 1–7, W. Heinemann, London, 1927.
HAGSDAHL, C.E.: *Kokkonst sone Vetenskap ock Konst, (Cooking as a Science and Art)*, Bonnier, Stockholm, 1879.
HARMON, P.B. (ed): *Cultural and Social Anthropology, Food, the Fundamental Quest*, Second edn, Collection of Essays, Macmillan, London, 1975.
HARRIS, M.: *Cultural Materialism*, Random House, New York, 1979.
HARRISON, A.F.: *Gastronomy*, Horizon, Bognor Regis, 1982.
HARTLEY, D.: *Food in England*, Macdonald, London, 1954.
HECHT, J.J. and P. KEGAN: *The Domestic Servant in Eighteenth Century England*, Routledge & Kegan Paul, London, 1980.
HERING, R.: *Lexicon der Küche (Dictionary of the Kitchen)*, ed. Walter Bickel, Pfannenberg, Giessen, Germany, 1961.
HERODOTES: *The History* 446 BC, translated by Aubrey de Selincourt, Penguin, London, 1954.
HIBBERT, C.: *The Roots of Evil: A Social History of Crime and Punishment*, Penguin, London, 1966.
HOOKE, S.H.: *Middle Eastern Mythology*, Penguin, London, 1963.
HURST, M.E.E.: *A Geography of Economic Behaviour*, Duxbury Press, Massachusetts, 1972.
HYAMS, E.: *Dionysus: A Social History of the Wine Vine*, Thames & Hudson, London, 1965.
JOHNSON, A.H. and M.S. PETERSON: *Encyclopaedia of Food Technology*, Vol. 2, University, Yale University Press, Newhaven, Connecticut, 1974.
JUDKIN, J. and J.C. MCKENZIE (eds): *Changing Food Habits*, MacGibbon & Kee, London, 1964.
KATONA-APTE, J.: *Dietary Aspects of a Culturation: Meals, Feasts and Fasts in Minority Communities of South Asia*, in Arnot, The Hague, Mouton, 1975.

KJELLBERG, S.T.: *Att Dricka Öl (On Drinking Beer)*, Hallsten, Malmö, 1962.
KRAMER, S.N.: *The Sumerians: Their History, Culture and Character*, University Press, Chicago, 1964.
KEYLAND, N.: *Svensk Allmogen Kost (Swedish Everyday Food)*, Bonnier, Stockholm, 1919.
LEACH, E.: *Levi-Strauss*, Harper & Row, London, 1970.
LETO, M.J. and W.K.H. BODE: *The Larder Chef*, W. Heinemann, London, 1969.
LEVANDER, L.: *Mat Ock Miljö (Food and Environment)*, Lund University Press, Sweden, 1940.
LEVY, J-P.: *The Economic Life of the Ancient World*, University Press, Chicago, 1967.
LOWENBERG, M.E., E.N. TODHUNTER et al: *Food and Man*, Second edn, Wiley, New York, 1974.
MALLETT, M.: *The Borgias*, Bodley Head, London, 1969.
MILLER, J.: *The Spice Trade of the Roman Empire, 29 BC to AD 641*, Clarendon Press, Oxford, 1969.
MOLMENTI, P.G.: *Venice, Its Growth to the Fall of the Republic*, translated by H.F. Brown, Vol. 2, John Murray, London, 1906–08.
MORITZ, L.: *Grain, Mills and Flour in Classical Antiquity*, Clarendon Press, Oxford, 1958.
MORRIS, D.: *The Naked Ape*, Corgi Books, London, 1968.
MOTTRAM, V.H.: *Human Nutrition*, Edward Arnold, London, 1948.
MURRAY, J. (ed): *The Oxford Dictionary*, Clarendon Press, Oxford, 1901.
MYER, J.: quoting in *The Oldest Book in the World*, Kegan Paul & Co., London, 1900.
NEEDHAM, J.: *Clerks and Craftsmen in China and the West*, series of lectures, University Press, Cambridge, 1970.
NETTING, R.: *Intensive Agriculture in the Kofyar Hills*, in Harmon, Macmillan, 1975.
NORMAN, B.: *Tales of Tables: A History of Western Cuisines*, Prentice Hall, New York, 1972.
NYLEN, A.M.: *Hemslöjd (Cottage Industries)*, Hapstan Solna, Sweden, 1969.
OLIVER, R.: *The French at Table*, translated by Durrel, Wine and Food Society, London, 1967.
OLSON, A.: *Om Allmogens Kosthall (Everyday Food Needs)*, Lund University Press, Sweden, 1958.
PEPPER, T. and SCHRERE: *The Nimrod Connection, Myth and Science in the Hunting Model*, Academic Press, New York, 1977.
PFAFFMAN, C.: *The Physiological and Behavioural Aspects of Taste*, Illinois University, Chicago Press, 1961.
PICKERSGILL, B.: in Ucko and Dimbleby, *The Domestication and Exploitation of Plants and Animals*, Aldine, Chicago, 1969.
PIGGOT, S.: *Ancient Europe from the Beginning of Agriculture to Classical Antiquity: A Survey*, University Press, Edinburgh, 1965.
PLINY THE ELDER: *Natural History*, translated by H. Rackham, W. Heinemann, London, 1950.
PULLAR, P.: *Consuming Passion*, Sphere Books, London, 1970.
PYKE, M.: *Food and Society*, John Murray, London, 1968.
——: *Man and Food*, John Murray, London, 1970.
——: *Success in Nutrition*, John Murray, London, 1975.
RAGLAND, F.: in Darlington, *The Evolution of Man and Society*, George Allen & Unwin, London, 1969.
RANK, G.: *Svenska Gastabud fran allatide (Swedish Hospitality Through the Ages)*, Bonnier, Stockholm, 1963.
REED, C.A.: in Ucko and Dimbleby, *The Domestication and Exploitation of Plants and Animals*, Aldine, Chicago, 1969.
RENNER, D.A.: *The Origin of Food Habits*, Faber & Faber, London, 1944.
RUFFER, M.A.: *Abnormalities of Ancient Teeth: Studies in Palaeopathology of Egypt*, University Press, Chicago, 1921.
RUSSELL-WOOD, A.J.R.: *Fidagos a Philanthropists*, Macmillan, London, 1968.
SAGGS, H.W.F.: *Everyday Life in Babylonia and Assyria*, B.T. Batsford, London and Putman, New York, 1965.
SALAMAN, R.N.: *The History and Social Influence of the Potato*, University Press, Cambridge, 1949.
SANDBLAD, Z.: *Gamla Seder Och Bruk (Old Habits and Customs)*, Fahlerant, Stockholm, 1888.
SAULNIER,: *La Repertoire de la Cuisine*, Leon Jaeggi & Sons Ltd., London.
SIMONS, F.: *Eat Not of this Flesh: Food Avoidance in the Old World*, University of Wisconsin Press, Madison, 1961.
SINGER, C., with HOLMYARD, HALL and WILLIAMS: *A History of Technology*, 5 vols., Clarendon Press, Oxford, 1954–8.
SMITH, D.B. and A.H. WALTERS: *Introductory Food Science*, Classic Publication, London, 1967.
SOLER, J.: *The Semiotics of Food in the Bible: The Annals, Economies, Societies, Civilisations*, July–August 1973, translated by Forster, E., John Hopkins University Press, Baltimore & London, 1973.
SOPHER, D.: *Geography of Religions*, Englewood Cliff, N.J., Prentice Hall, 1967.
SPAIN, N.: *The Beeton Story*, Ward & Lock & Co., London, 1956.
TANNAHILL, R.: *Food in History*, Palladin, London, 1975.
——: *Flesh and Blood: A History of the Cannibal Complex*, Hamish & Hamilton, London, 1975.
TUNBERGER, P.: *Böckernas Mat (Food and Artists)*, Bra-Böcker, Stockholm, 1980.

UCKO, P.J. and G.W. DIMBLEBY (eds): *The Domestication of Plants and Animals*, series of papers, Aldine, Chicago, 1969.
VAILLANT, G.C.: *The Aztecs of Mexico*, Doubleday, Doran & Co., New York, 1944.
VINCES-VIEVE, J.: *An Economic History of Spain*, University Press, Princetown, 1969.
VRIES, A. de: *Primitive Man and His Food*, Chandler Books & Co., Chicago, 1962.
WARNER, R.: *Antiquitates Culinariae*, R. Blamire, London, 1791.
WATSON, W.: *China Before the Han Dynasty*, Thames & Hudson, London, 1961.
WHITE, A., P. HANDLER and E. SMITH: *Principles of Bio-chemistry*, McGraw-Hill, New York, 1968.
WHITE, L.: *Mediaeval Technology and Social Change*, Clarendon Press, Oxford, 1962.
WHITE, W. and F. COWELL: *The Revolutions of Ancient Rome*, Batsford, London, 1962.
WIEDEMANN, A.: *Das Alte Aegypten (Old Egypt)*, Heidelberg, 1920.
WILSON, E.D., K.H. FISHER and M.E. FUQUA: *Principles of Nutrition*, (third edn), Wiley, New York, 1975.
WINZER, F. (ed): *Eine Kulturgeschichte Europas (A Cultural History of Europe)*, Westerman-Verlag, Braunschweig, 1981.
WYNDHAM, H.R.: *The Atlantic and Slavery*, Oxford University Press, 1935.
YOUNG, H.: *Hunger Drives and Physical Needs* in book of seven articles, London, 1979.
YOUNGER, W.A.: *Gods, Men and Wine*, Michael Joseph, London, 1966.
ZEUNER, F.E.: *A History of Domesticated Animals*, Harper, London, 1963, New York, 1964.

NB Foreign books referred to and quoted have their translated titles in brackets, however, they may not be the actual titles of English translations where these exist.

Articles, special lectures, seminar papers

ANDERSON, N.E. Jnr.: An Early Interpretation of India's Sacred Cattle, *Current Anthropology*, Vol. 18, No. 3, 1975.
ANON: 'Speiseproduktion und Energiverbrauch' (Food production and Energy use), Article in *Der Stern*, Vol. 43, 1981.
BATES, H.W.: 'The River Amazon', *The Naturalist*, Vol. 2, London, 1863.
BATES, M.: 'Man's Food and Sex', *American Scholar*, Vol. 27, 1957.
BODE, W.K.H. and J. THOMSON: 'Gastronomy, Alive and Well?', *Hospitality*, October 1980.
BODE, W.K.H.: Gastronomy, an Art or a Science? Open Lecture to Modern History Society of University of Surrey, May 1981.
——: 'Requiem for a Dried Pea', *Health and Social Services Journal*, January 1978.
——: 'In My View' Results of Practical Microwave Cooking Research, *Hotel and Restaurant Catering*, October 1971.
——: 'Caring about Food', *Hospital Equipment and Supplies*, November 1977.
——: 'Instant Food – Slow Death', *HCIMA Journal*, August 1970.
——: Smörgasbord, *HCIMA Journal*, No. 26, February 1974.
——: 'Gastronomy, Yesterday and Tomorrow', paper given, Council on Hotel, Restaurant and Institutional Education Conference, New Orleans, August 1979.
BRYN, M.J. and M.E. LOVENBERG: 'The Father Influence on Young Children's Food Preferences', *American Journal of Dietetics Association*, Vol. 34, 1958.
CAMBELL, H. and R. BRAIDWOOD: 'An Early Farming Village in Turkey' in *Scientific American*, Vol. CCXXII, 1970.
CAMPBELL, A.: 'Det Svenska brödet' ('The Swedish Bread'), *Svenska Bagari Tidskrift*, Stockholm, 1950.
COMA REPORT: 'Diet and Cardiovascular Disease', DHSS, 1984.
CULLEN, L.M.: 'Irish History without Potatoes', *Past and Present*, Vol. 40, 1968.
CURRIER, R.L.: 'The Hot and Cold Syndrome' and 'Symbolic Balance in Mexican and Spanish American Folk Medicine', *Ethnology*, Vol. 5, 1966.
DINARELLO, C.A. and S.M. WOLFF: 'Fever' in *Human Nature*, 1979.
DOUGLAS, M.: 'Food as an Art Form', *Studio International*, Vol. 188, 1974.
DOUGLAS, M. and M. NICOD: 'Taking the Biscuit: The Structure of British Meals', *New Society*, Vol. 30, 1974.
EBLING, F.: 'Man the Consumer: Attitudes to Food from the Stone Age to the Present', Edith Clark Lecture, University of Surrey, 1984.

FLIEGEL, F.C.: 'Food Habits and National Backgrounds', *College of Agriculture Bulletin*', No. 684, Pennsylvania State University, October 1961.
FIRTH, R.: 'Offering and Sacrifice', *Journal of Anthropological Institute of Great Britain and Ireland*, Vol. 93, Part 1, 1963.
FORSTER, G.M.: Humoral Traces in United States Folk Medium, *Medical Anthropology Newsletter*, Vol. 10, No. 2, 1979.
GARINE de, I.: 'Food is Not Just Something to Eat: The Socio-cultural Aspects of Nutrition', *Ecology of Food and Nutrition*, Vol. 1, 1972.
HARLAN, J.R.: 'A Wild Wheat Harvest in Turkey', *Archaeology*, March 1967.
HARRIS, M.: 'India's Sacred Cow', *Human Nature*, Vol. 1, No. 2, 1978.
HEALD, G.: 'The Great British Eating Habits', Edith Clark Lecture, University of Surrey, 1985.
HIGGS, E. and J. WHITE: 'Autumn Killing', *Antiquity*, No. 37, 1963.
HOFF, J. and J. JARICK: 'Food', from *The Scientific American*, 1973.
HOLE, F. and K. FLANNERY: 'Proceedings of a Pre-Historic Society', *Society*, February 1968.
HON van H.: 'Proverbs and Customs' in *Vogue*, October 1956.
ISAAC, E.: 'Influence of Religion on the Spread of Citrus', *Science*, Vol. 129, 1959.
IVENHOE, F.: in *Nature*, August 1970.
J.A.C.N.E. Report: 'Diet for a Healthy Heart', Report of the Joint Advisory Committee on Nutrition Education, Health Education Council and British Nutritional Foundation, 1985.
JUDKIN, J.: 'Man's Choice of Food', *The Lancet*, 12 May 1956.
KIMBER, G. and R. ATHWAL: 'A Re-Assessment of the Course of Evolution of Wheat', proceedings of the National Academy of Sciences, No. 4, April 1972.
KOTLER, P.: 'The Household Consumer: Behavioural Models', *Journal of Marketing*, Vol. 29, No. 4., October 1965.
LEACH, E.: 'Brain Twisters', *New York Review of Books*, October 1967.
LEHRER, A.: 'Cooking Vocabularies and The Culinary Triangle' (Levi-Strauss), *Anthropological Linguistics*, Vol. 14, 1972.
LEVI-STRAUSS, C.: 'The Culinary Triangle', *Partisan Review*, Vol. 33, 1966.
MILLER, J.: 'The Body in Question', *The Listener*, 15 February 1979.
MOLONEY, C.H.: 'Systematic Valence Coding of Mexican Hot and Cold Food', *Ecology of Food and Nutrition*, Vol. 4, 1975.
N.A.C.N.E. Report, Report of the National Advisory Committee on Nutrition Education, Health Education Council, 1983.
NETTING, R.: 'Hill Farmers of Nigeria', *The Hofyar Hills*, University of Washington, Seattle, 1968.
PERKINS, D.: 'Food and Science' in *Science*, No. 11, 1969.
PILGRIM, F.J.: 'What Foods do People Accept or Reject?', *Journal of American Dietetic Association*, Vol. 34, 1961.
RAGLAN, A.: in *The Sunday Times*, 16 April 1972.
RILEY, M.: 'Declining Hotel Standards and the Skill Trap, *International Journal of Tourism Management*, June 1981.
REMINGTON, R.E.: 'The Social Origins of Food Habits', *The Scientific Monthly*, September 1936.
SOLER, J.: 'The Semiotics of Food in the Bible', *Annals, Economics, Societies, Civilisation*, Vol. 5., translated by E. Forster, July–August 1973.
THOMSON, J.: 'The Use of Technical and Cosmetic Additives in Modern Food Production', *World Medicine*, Vol. 10, 1975.
TUDGE, C.: 'Who Were the First Farmers?', *New Scientist*, 6 September 1979.
——: 'Pleasure of the Flesh', *New Scientist*, 9 May 1974.
WALLEN, E.: 'Sex Difference in Food Aversion', *Applied Psychology*, Vol. 27, 1943.
WALTERSPIEL, K.: 'Essen und Trinken', (To Eat and To Drink) in *Gastronomie*, March 1941.
WENDORF, W., R. SAID and T. CHILD, in *Science*, Vol. CLXIX, September 1970.
WILLEY, G.E.: *Introduction to American Archaeology*, Vol. 1, 1960.
WILSON, A.C. and V.M. SARICK: 'Proceedings of the Academy of Science of the United States', Vol. LX, 1968.
WRIGHT, D.J.M.: in *Nature*, 5 February 1971.
Der Stern, Hamburg, Germany, Vol. 43, 1981.
Other References Consulted: *The Oxford Annotated Bible, New Standard Edition*, 1965.

NB Besides food, my other main interests have been the study of ancient and modern history. Any facts not acknowledged in the above bibliography are simply because I can't always remember the source during a long life of study of food and history. For this, I ask to be forgiven.

Index